# CHAPTERS

1. The Reason Why — 5
2. The Long Road To Revenue — 15
3. We Have A Better Idea — 25
4. The Writing On The Wall — 33
5. Sectorisation 1987 - 1993 — 41
6. Slimming Down — 52
7. Pre-Privatisation 1994 - 1996 — 60
8. The Early EWS Years — 70
9. The Canadians Are Coming — 80
10. Under New Management — 89
11. Life After Death — 99
Tables — 110

*Above:* 56130 arrives at Kennett with 6E23 from Mountsorrel on 2nd April 1985. *Photo: John Hooson*

## Introduction

After a youth spent chasing Class 55s on the ECML, the 56s caught my eye very early. Unlike the Deltics the 56s were introduced during my era so I vividly recall my first sighting at age 11 - 56005 and 56006 on Doncaster Carr fresh from unloading at Harwich in late 1976.

Further sightings at Toton open day in June 79, Tinsley and Wath led me to proudly announce that 56s were my second favourite loco.

By the mid-80s the locos had become commonplace on Tyneside. Having a bedroom window which looked out onto the Newcastle-Sunderland line had its benefits but looking back I'm amazed I got any qualifications at school and polytechnic as my revision notes seemed more to do with 56077 on 32 HEA hoppers than with the first law of thermodynamics.

My interest in the class then turned to the engineering aspects as I began work at Gateshead TMD during 1985. My slight frame made me first choice for those difficult to reach jobs - funnily enough most of them were on 56s.

Time went on and a move to Manchester saw work and family take over as priorities. I found time to join the Class 56 Group soon after it was formed but it took the withdrawal of the class in March 2004 before I became heavily involved in inspecting prospective loco purchases which eventually led to the purchase of 56040 in 2005.

The class were one of the first to have their demise micro-analysed on the internet and Ian Furness's WNXX website is a mine of information which I duly acknowledge as a primary source of information for both Chapter 9 and for research carried out prior to inspecting locos offered on EWS tender lists.

One thing which did strike me during the research for the book was the Grid nickname. I'd never come across this in my time at BR or in my time on the platform ends at Newcastle Central. They were just 56s to us. I believe the name comes from the cast metal grid located under the buffer beam of the aircon-fitted locos to protect the aircon equipment from objects the loco may encounter en route - ballast, sleepers, cows, cars . . . Of course the fact that in later years Gateshead's entire allocation were gridless (56112-56135) may have had something to do with it.

Photographs are as credited but special thanks to Neil Harvey, John Hooson, Gridiron, WNXX site and Roger Elliot for his encyclopedic records of passenger workings

The pictures of the locos in Romania are credited to Antonio Bianco who sadly passed away before he could see his pictures in print.

Finally, for a class which could have very easily been cancelled after the first 60 locos, the class went on to give a service life beyond the accepted 25 year figure. If this book leaves the reader with some idea of the effort required just to keep the locos in traffic then it has served its purpose.

If it also conveys the high esteem with which they were held by many of the train crew who operated them it has ticked another box.

For evidence of the feelings of enthusiasts toward 56s, you only have to look at the crowded trains when 56097, 56040 and 56101 made their debut passenger runs in preservation.

Finally, I'd like to dedicate this book to my Uncle Malcolm who got me interested in railways with Saturday morning visits to his workplace - Gateshead TMD where me and my brother would be taken through Deltics, 40's and 37's. Happy days.

I still judge most of what I do on 56040 by asking myself what he would have thought.

God bless him.

**Keith Bulmer**

## Publisher's Note

On behalf of Visions, I should like to thank David Maxey for 'ghost-writing' this book and turning Keith's impeccable research into such an enjoyable read. David has also added background material where appropriate.

In fact, there was so much material that we were faced with the dilemma of either deleting great chunks or adding extra pages to our usual book size. Needless to say, we chose the latter option.

I should also like to offer my personal thanks to all the photographers who have kindly supplied photos, and especially to Roger Elliott for the detailed information we have included as a table at the back. Thanks also to Paul Furtek for providing little nuggets of information not normally found in reference books.

Everyone involved in the project hopes you enjoy the fascinating story of the Mighty Grids!

**Ken Carr**
**Boreham, Essex**
**October 2009**

# 1. THE REASON WHY

To appreciate fully the strengths and weaknesses of the Class 56 locomotive, it is necessary to consider why the type was called into existence in the first place.

Like all developed countries, Great Britain has a big requirement for energy and, as the economy grows, so this demand increases. Even at times of low economic activity, the demand for energy remains significant and continuity of fuel supply is paramount. It is not the purpose of this book to discuss the Organisation of Petroleum Exporting Countries (OPEC) and its fluctuating oil price in detail, but its very existence is significant in the Class 56 story.

three-day working week and motorists obliged to drive at 50 mph on motorways to conserve precious petrol. It was no surprise, then, when the British government decided to 'cut the cord' as far as possible and reduce the country's reliance on a volatile, imported oil market. Two main areas were identified - a greater use of home-produced coal and the longer-term development of the North Sea oil fields.

As far as greater use of coal was concerned, the government immediately recognised that considerable investment in power stations would be needed and, more relevant to the Class 56 story, improvements to the infrastructure for carrying coal from the

Surprisingly, some improvements had already resulted from Dr Beeching's 1963 report. This infamous document is almost entirely remembered for its swingeing line closures, but it also led to modernisation of the way in which the railways handled freight. The Freightliner and Merry-Go-Round (MGR) concepts, for instance, both sprang from the 1963 report and were developed so successfully that they still exist largely unchanged today.

Before the coming of the MGR train, the scale of the operation was vast. As one example, the three large CEGB power stations along the Aire Valley in Yorkshire

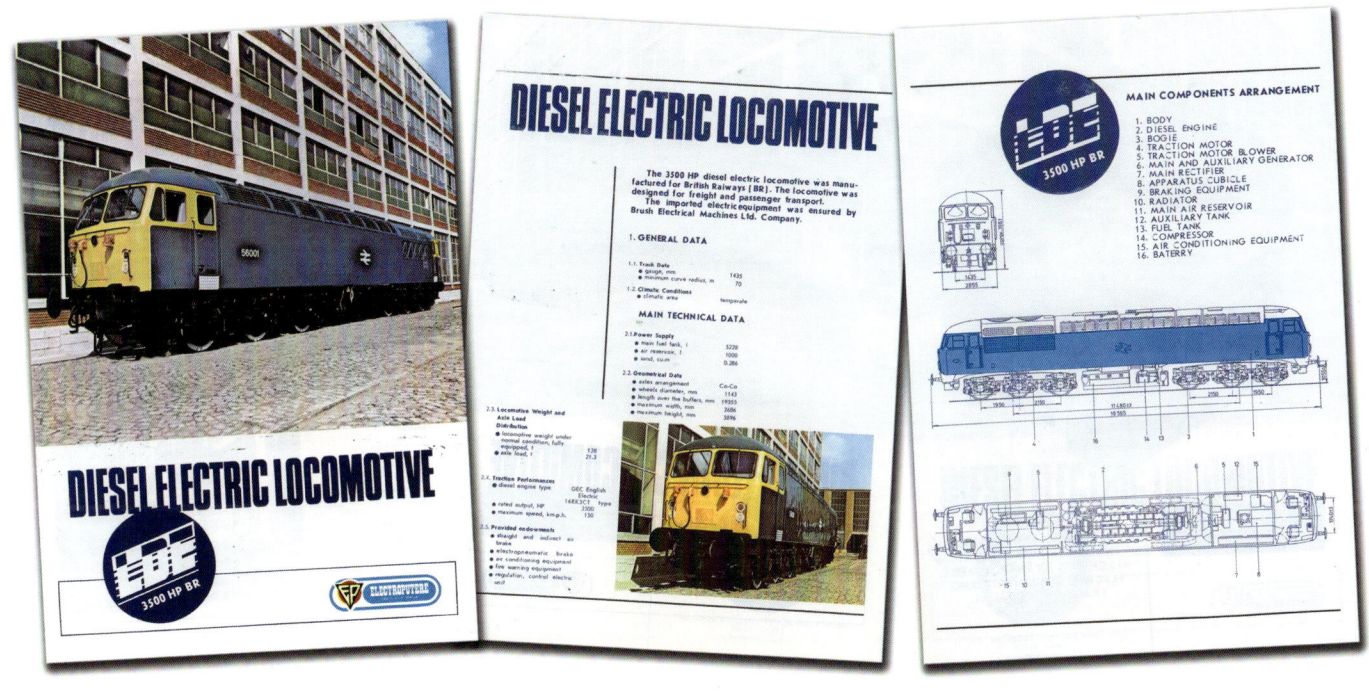

*Above:* Pages from the Electroputere brochure.

Every government has a duty to 'keep the lights on', so it is expected that a strategic plan will exist to ensure this. For many years, the plans of successive governments had recognised Britain's vulnerability because of its dependence on imported oil. In the early 1970s the oil price continued to rise, for two reasons - OPEC's decision to restrict supply and continuing trouble in the Middle East. The situation became especially severe in the winter of 1974, with industry reduced to a

pits of the National Coal Board (NCB) to the power stations of the Central Electricity Generating Board (CEGB). As a result, the British Railways Board (BRB) was instructed to institute a plan for the mass transportation of coal from pit to power station, calling for investment not only in new wagons and locomotives but also permanent way, signalling, maintenance depots and a high-capacity system for loading and unloading trains in quick succession.

were consuming coal from any of more than twenty local collieries. What's more, a typical 2000MW generator, like West Burton, could consume around 34,000 tons a week which, at 16 tons payload and 40-wagon trains, resulted in 2,125 wagon movements in 53 trains every week of the year . . . to service a single power station!

Although effective in shifting the required bulk, the traditional system was grossly inefficient in its use of labour and resources.

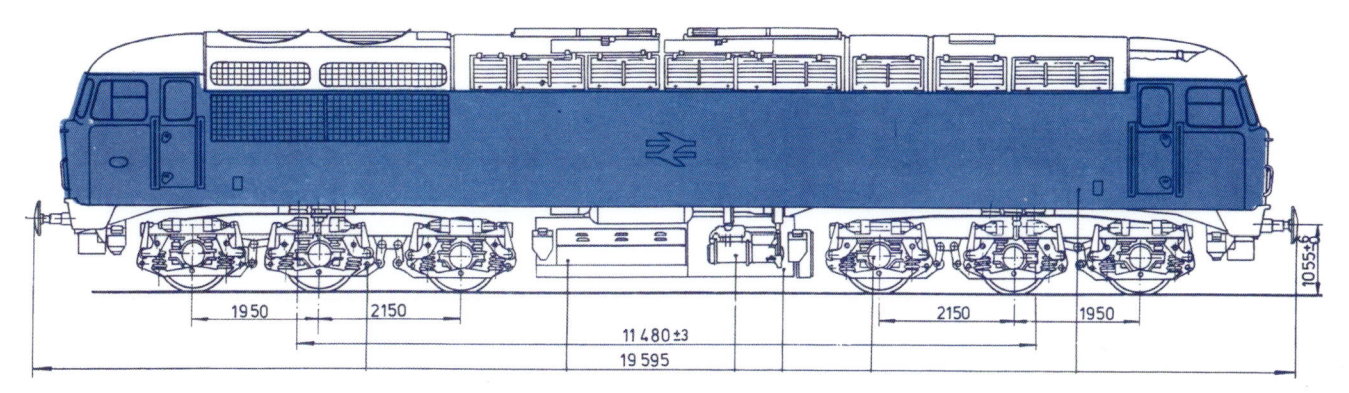

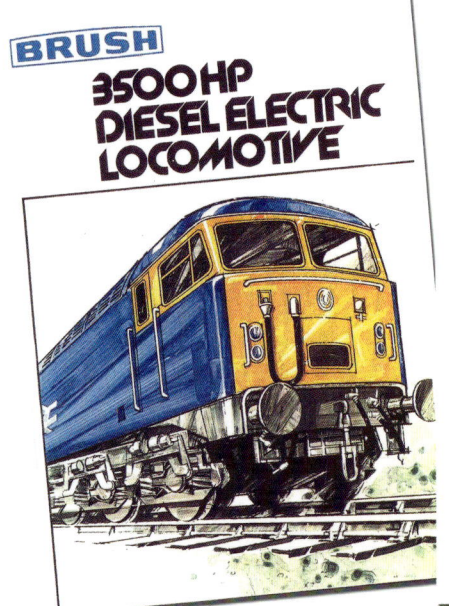

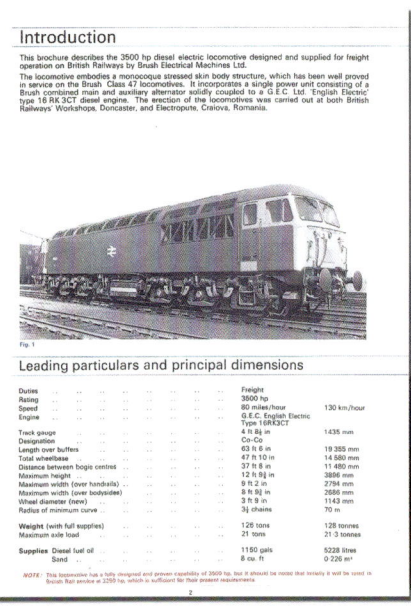

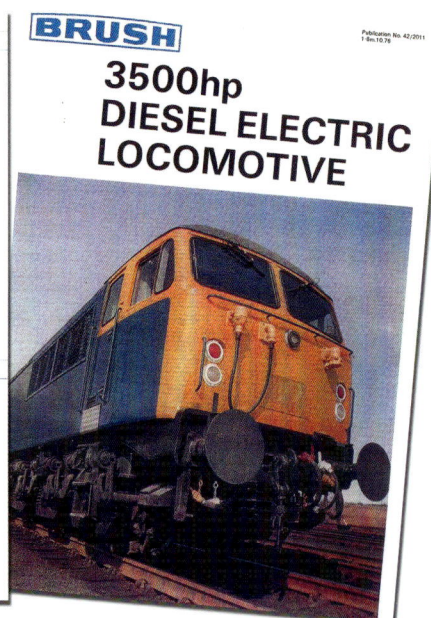

*Above:* Brush also printed up brochures. The first (top left) was produced before any locos had been completed, and was revised (middle & top right) when they were.
*Right:* Drawings from the earlier brochure show the internal layout of components.

As a further example, in the two-week period to 4th March 1972, BR shifted a total of 1.5 million tons of coal in 85,000 wagon loads, representing an average load of 17.6 tons per wagon. Many of these were traditional four-wheelers - a mix of 16-ton mineral wagons and 20-ton bottom-discharging hoppers. Those without the bottom-discharge facility had to be physically tipped to be unloaded (i.e. rotated through 180 degrees), which meant they had to be individually uncoupled from their train. Locomotives had to run round at both ends of their journeys and the individual empty wagons reformed for the return. Manpower levels were high - not only loco crews but also shunting staff and

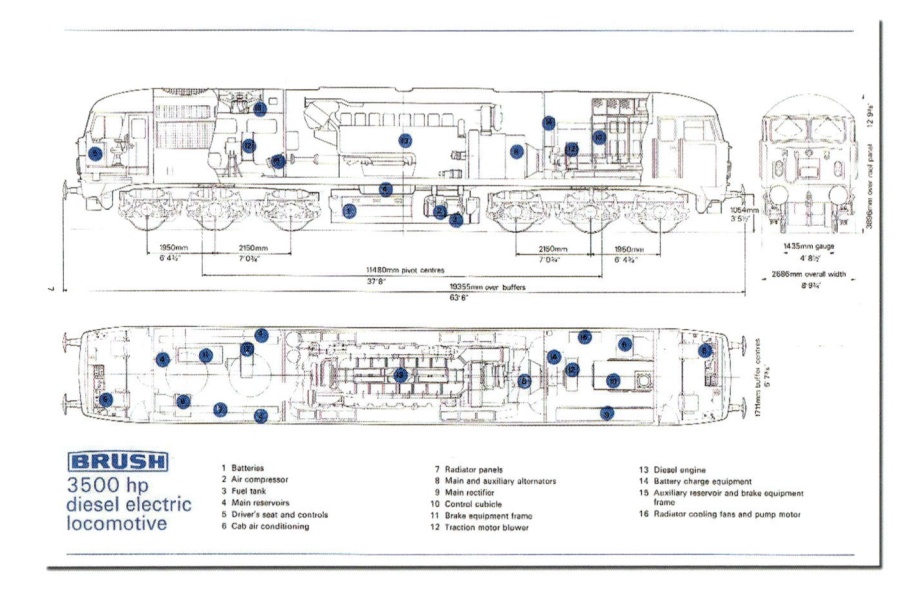

Every aspect of the Doncaster Works build was officially photographed. *Above Left:* The dragbox receives attention on the rectifying jig. *Above Right:* The centre pivot cross-stretcher is on the manipulator before the fitting of the top plates. The relative position of these two parts within the finished frame can be seen in the photo on page 8. Photos: BREL

loading/unloading crews at the two ends. Time was also a factor; the whole procedure often took so long that a loco crew could only make one out-and-back trip in the course of a single shift. So the number of crews deployed, and the number of wagons, was many times more than economically desirable; even so, many empty wagons were left in sidings for long periods between one job and another.

The Merry-Go-Round principle was developed to be a far more efficient replacement and its inventors, Reginald Munns and Jack Stirk, were later honoured for their work by having their names enshrined on a pair of Trainload Coal Sector Class 60s - 092 & 093.

The first MGR wagon prototypes - B350000 and B350001 - appeared in April 1964 from Darlington Works. Apart from the prototypes and 160 wagons built at Ashford, all 10,702 HAA and 460 HDA variants were constructed at BREL Shildon. The wagon itself weighed around 13.5 tons and could carry 32.5 tons of coal, its size and weight governed by the civil engineer's clearance and axle load restrictions.

Once enough wagons were available, tests began at High Marnham, West Burton and Cockenzie power stations. The track layout at both pit and power station generally took the form of a continuous loop on which the train never actually had to stop. Loading and unloading could be carried out as the train moved at slow speed through the terminals. Another benefit of the MGR system was that the incoming driver could be relieved to take his break while another driver took the train through the unloader. New pits and power stations were designed with the MGR concept in mind but, given that the equipment was expensive, older facilities retained the traditional method, especially as many were due for early closure. Hybrids also existed, using a combination of the two. CEGB Blyth Cambois, for instance, was served by MGR trains, but the track layout meant the arriving loco had to run round before drawing the wagons through the unloader. At some pits, wagons were loaded by mechanical diggers, often resulting in damage to the tops of the hoppers. Depending on locomotive, line and terminal restrictions, the typical MGR train would comprise between 28 and 45 wagons. Even today a requirement remains for the original HAA type because of line restriction, such as deliveries to Longannet where HTAs cannot be used because of their axle loading on the Forth Bridge.

The first regular use of MGR trains began in September 1965 at West Burton power station in Nottinghamshire where there was also a circular loop for unloading. Eggborough was next, after which the principle extended to more power stations, and even cement and steel works. Eventually, the technique was applied to the shipment of other raw materials, such as iron ore and limestone.

The already-successful MGR concept enjoyed a rapid expansion as a result of the 1972/3 oil crisis and in the year before Class 56 entered service (1975), the Eastern Region of BR was carrying 60% of its coal traffic in HAA wagons. This domination of rail transport to power stations was demonstrated, negatively, by the severe winter of 1978/79 when widespread freezing of wet coal in MGR wagons seriously threatened generating capacity. In subsequent winters, the inner surfaces of wagons were sprayed with chemicals to alleviate the problem.

*Above:* A general view of the Doncaster fabrication shop. In the foreground, the frames for 56033 are being assembled on the purpose-built jig. To its right are the frames of 56032 and, in the middle distance, 56031 is taking shape. *Photo: BREL*

Before the arrival of Class 56, the mainstay of MGR traffic were Class 20, Class 37 and Class 47 locomotives. In Scotland it was Class 20s and Class 26/0.

As previously mentioned, the MGR system called for loading and unloading at a very low constant speed. This varied between locations and equipment but was generally in the 0.5 mph-2.5mph range. When the MGR trials were being planned, Brush Traction modified a Class 47 with Slow Speed Control (SSC), allowing it to run at a constant 0.5 mph. The first new loco to be built with SSC was D1758 (later Stratford Union Jack celebrity 47164 and now 57305), which was allocated new to Tinsley on 23rd May 1964. Another 200 Class 47s were built with SSC. Some were later integrated into TOPS sub-class 47/0, while all 81 of the freight-dedicated Class 47/3 were SSC-fitted. In fact, 47/3s became the new backbone of the MGR operation until the introduction of Class 56. The 56s pioneered a new form of highly accurate, electronic SSC - a system later fitted to Classes 58, 60, 66 and 67.

By the 1970s, Class 47 had established itself as a very successful mixed traffic type, despite the unavoidable compromises in its design. BR's demands for a loco capable of hauling express passenger trains at 95 mph *and* heavy freight trains at much lower speeds were always incompatible.

The characteristics of Class 47's electrical equipment meant that its continuous rating was measured at 27mph. Continuous rating is the speed at which a locomotive can haul a train for prolonged periods without overloading the main generator and traction motors. In practical terms, this meant that a Class 47 could start a standard load of 36 MGR hoppers, weighing 1,500 tons, and keep it moving on level track. However, if the route involved long gradients and a loco working at full power slowed below the 27mph threshold, there was a real risk that main generator and traction motors would suffer extensive overheating damage. In fact, this happened to more than one 47; as a result, the class's approved trailing load was reduced to 30 HAAs hoppers, giving a typical load of 1,180 tonnes. Obviously this was unpopular with everybody. The loss of six hoppers per train meant that BR had to run one extra for every five to make up the difference. More trains meant timetables had to be amended and, of course, paths found for all the extra movements. It is also interesting to note that

*Above:* An interesting view of the frame turned on its side within the jig. This where the cab will be mounted on the frame. The dragbox is also visible. The centre pivot section is the point where the bogies meet the frame. The ability to rotate the frame through 180 degrees made it much easier for Doncaster's fitters to work on it. *Photo: BREL*

reduction in train length and weight did little to reduce the strain on the 47s' main generators as the recently-introduced rapid-loading bunkers were much more efficient at filling the wagons to capacity (characterised by the coal having been heaped high with a flattened top). This could mean that a 30-wagon train weighed more than its design maximum of 1,180 tonnes, well into the locos' danger zone!

It is worth mentioning here the different demands of various coal consumers. Often, coal from one colliery was found to be ideally suited to a particular customer's process and this might mean the seemingly-wasteful sight of coal coming from afar when there was a colliery within miles of the customer's site. One solution to this problem was the blending or 'sweetening' of coal, which involved taking the output from a 'low'-grade colliery and mixing it with high-grade coal to improve overall composition.

The important factors were calorific value, water content, sulphur content (soot generation) and the physical size of the pieces. Some power stations required pulverised coal as large lumps were unsuitable. On the down side, very fine coal had a tendency to be blown from the tops of wagons - a problem which brought about the introduction of the canopy-fitted MGR hopper.

Given the complexities of supply and demand - the number of coal sources and power stations, the numerous existing constraints such as suitability, bunker capacities, availability of men, locos and wagons - reducing train lengths only

*Above:* Work is progressing well on 56032's frame. Note the plans resting on the dragbox. At this point, the Works staff were still on a massive learning curve; 032 was only the second loco they had tackled. *Photo: BREL*

*Above:* 56031 begins to take shape. This is the view from number 1 end. The monocoque bodyshell is a load-bearing structure, constructed from steel sections covered with a sheet steel skin to provide rigidity. *Photo: BREL*

compounded the problem. Even so, the system set up by BR, the NCB and the CEGB proved to be highly flexible and succeeded in dealing with the complexities and shifting vast tonnages of coal efficiently. A fresh timetable was drawn up each week and adjusted hourly to reflect the varying volumes and destinations demanded by the CEGB, as well as operational issues such as locomotive and crew rostering.

To return to the Class 56, the operating department needed a "more suitable" locomotive for its MGR traffic, a phrase invariably interpreted as "built for the purpose". On some runs, double-heading was employed, most commonly with pairs of Class 20s and Class 37s. The problem with this approach was three-fold: The use of two locos resulted in an increased maintenance requirement. Secondly, fuel consumption was worse than a single unit of equivalent horsepower. Thirdly, run-round facilities at some locations could only accommodate a single loco. In areas of intense MGR operation like the Aire and Trent Valleys, the logistics of keeping trains powered by two 37s *away* from sites with restricted run-round length only added to the complexity of the operation.

When the desire for a "suitable" loco was first expressed, BR's in-house design and manufacturing capacity was already fully-allocated, so the BRB asked British and overseas suppliers to come up with proposals for the new design. Previously, BR policy had favoured mixed traffic locomotives (the Deltics were a notable exception) coupled with an acceptance that double-heading would be used where necessary. The Class 56 concept was a new departure, the first time a main line locomotive would be custom-designed for one type of traffic - the haulage of heavily-loaded but low-speed coal trains. However, like the 47s, the specification was later revised to include the haulage of lighter Freightliner traffic at speeds up to 75 mph, once more imposing compromises on the designers. Ideally, the heavy, slow coal trains needed a loco capable of applying full power at low speed and, more importantly, one with electrical equipment capable of enduring that load continuously at low speed.

Not surprisingly, the eventual specification was rather vague. BR set out what the loco needed to do and made one or two stipulations, or guidelines, but generally left it to the supplier to come up with something suitable. Here are the main points:

i) An initial batch of 60 (with an option for more).
ii) Single-engined, twin-cab unit, with an output in the range 3,000-3,500hp.
iii) Capable of hauling MGR coal and Freightliner container trains.
iv) Maximum axle load of 21 tonnes.
v) Air-braked only.
vi) Driving controls and air brake/safety equipment to conform with current BR practice.

The most important caveat in the specification, however (and probably the greatest influence on the resulting design), was that the locomotives needed to be in traffic very quickly. This meant there was no time to design a completely new locomotive, and the vague specification immediately suggests the development of an existing design or a selective mixture of successful elements from current practice. It could be argued that the long-established and reliable types produced in the USA would have been perfect candidates, but some 20 years were to elapse before that particular penny dropped. Realistically, bidders were only ever going to be from the UK, not least because trying to import locos directly from an overseas supplier was almost certain to provoke an adverse reaction from militant trades unions.

The unions were immensely powerful and influential in the 1970s and this influence had a direct effect on Class 56 throughout its early years. As one example, industrial action in the 1980s had a significant effect on the locomotives' duties; in other words, when they could be used and where - a situation that seems unthinkable today despite threats a decade later to 'black' Canadian-built Class 66s.

Back in 1974, Brush Traction rescued the BRB from its specifications dilemma. The Loughborough company had already drawn up plans for a locomotive it planned to sell to Eastern bloc countries in conjunction with Romanian State Railway's workshops - a link developed as a direct result of the interest shown in *Kestrel* after its sale to the USSR

*Above:* The 16RK3CT engine viewed from the free end. This was a development of English Electric's 16CSVT and featured gear-driven camshafts and two turbo-chargers. Built by Ruston, the engine had a nominal rating of 3,520hp, although it was downrated to 3,250hp for the Class 56. *Photo: BREL*

and later display at a trade fair. So, when the BRB issued its enquiry, the Brush/Romanian consortium was well placed to adapt its design for the British market.

In the absence of an alternative bidder, the Brush proposal was accepted and in September 1974 an order was placed for 60 locomotives. As indicated earlier, they would incorporate a mix of successful elements from existing designs and introduce revolutionary technology demonstrated in the *Hawk* and *Kestrel* projects. Given Brush's long history of locomotive building, and its recent expansion into the field of electrical rotating machinery and electronics, this mix of old and new was not unexpected. Brush obviously wanted to bring some of the newer technologies out of the laboratory and into the market place where the eyes of the world could see its products.

The only problem with the proposal was that Brush was no longer in the locomotive building business! Under normal circumstances, the BRB would have suggested the locomotives were constructed in one of the BREL workshops, but lack of capacity dictated that BREL could only construct 30 of the 60 required.

Enter the Romanian connection. Much of the latest Brush-designed rotating machinery (traction motors and alternators) was already being manufactured in Romania, so a proposal soon emerged for the initial thirty Class 56s to be built at the Electroputere works, but with the project managed by Brush engineering staff. For the second thirty, the stated capacity at BREL Doncaster would be taken up, with other BREL facilities supplying sub-assemblies. For instance, Ashford works would supply fuel tanks, cab doors and rooves, Swindon the radiator housing, air ducting and internal doors, while Eastleigh would construct the cab desks.

Significant logistical challenges presented themselves in building the first thirty in Romania, not least the supply of complete power units from Ruston and electronic control equipment from Brush itself. Conversely, the bogies and wheelsets for all sixty of the planned build were manufactured by ICM Reistia in Romania.

Even a casual glance at Class 56 reveals its Brush heritage and similarity in many respects to Class 47, not least in the adapted monocoque bodyshell - a term indicating that the entire body and roof of the locomotive is a

*Above:* A CP2 bogie awaits the fitting of its floating centre axle. Bogies for the first sixty locos were manufactured in Romania by Reistia and were based on a proven design by Swiss engineering firm SLM. *Photo: BREL*

load-bearing structure, constructed from steel sections to form a frame which is then covered with a sheet steel skin. The importance of the bodysides in maintaining the locomotive's rigidity has been clearly seen on withdrawn locomotives; when the bodysides have been cut away, the frame has noticeably sagged between the bogies.

Although English Electric played no direct part in the construction of Class 56, the engine was a development of an EE series used with great success in Classes 31, 37, 40 & 50. At each successive stage, improvements had been made to the engines' performance and efficiency. For example, the unit used in Class 50 produced 700 hp more than the unit in Class 40. This 16CSVT variant was later improved still further to produce an output of 3,250 hp from the same basic design for use in Class 56. When Class 58 came along, the rating remained the same, but with a greatly reduced size and maintenance requirement as the figure was achieved from only 12 cylinders rather than 16.

Designated 16RK3CT, the Class 56 unit was a 16-cylinder V-form engine, turbocharged and intercooled, with oil-cooled pistons. The updated unit also had gear-driven camshafts, unlike the maintenance-intensive chain drive on earlier engines. Improved technology allowed the four turbochargers on the 16CSVT to be replaced by only two. The new engine was manufactured by Ruston and nominally rated at 3,520hp, although this was down-rated to 3,250hp for rail applications. Departing from English Electric pedigree, the DC traction motors were a development of the TM73-68 MK3 model successfully used under locos of Class 46.

Rather than continue the old practice of using a generator to create traction motor current, the 56 engine was coupled directly to an alternator - a technology in which Brush had considerable experience from its *Hawk* and *Kestrel* work. The main advantage of the alternator is the absence of carbon brushes, so there is no direct contact between moving parts. Instead, the transfer of electrical energy is electro-magnetic. The removal of brushes and brush gear eliminated a significant maintenance requirement compared to the traditional generator fitted to Class 47. Weight-saving was a consideration too; when Brush's *Kestrel* went to Derby for weighing, it tipped the scales at 133 tons instead of the designated 120, so anything that would reduce weight in the new design was worth consideration.

The technology of the day meant that DC traction motors remained the standard for rail applications as they gave much better torque in the lower speed range - essential for a loco which would have to start very heavy coal trains in appalling conditions in colliery sidings where rails were often buried in coal slurry.

As electrical output from an alternator is alternating current (AC) and the traction motors need a direct current (DC) supply, a method of converting from AC to DC was needed. The solution was a piece of equipment known as the silicon rectifier - importantly, another area in which Brush had expertise.

A common problem with DC traction motors is their vulnerability to damage because of a breakdown in the insulation materials used in their construction. This breakdown allows potentially large currents to flow suddenly - an incident known as a flashover. Fortunately, Brush had also pioneered the use of a device known as a short circuiter on the *Hawk* development loco. This component could sense big flows of current and act as an instantaneous cut-out switch before the motors suffered damage.

*Above:* One of the cabs destined for 56031. A number of Class 56 components were built at other BREL works. The cab desks came from Eastleigh, the internal bulkhead doors and roof from Ashford, the cab doors from Swindon. *Photo: BREL*

With suitable control circuitry, the traditional generator can be used as a motor to turn the engine over during starting. This is not possible with an alternator and so an alternative method of starting the engine was needed - two 96v Bosch starter motors with the necessary control equipment. The control circuits ensures both motors are synchronised and that full battery current is only applied when both are engaged.

The bogies built by Reistia (designated CP2 by BR) were based on a proven design by the Swiss railway engineering firm SLM. Notable features were the floating centre axle, necessary to allow negotiation of tight curves in colliery sidings and the non-symmetrical wheel spacing. The centre distance between the outer and centre wheelsets was 200mm (8"), less than between the centre and inner wheelsets. This was to accommodate the very tight arrangement of the axle-hung traction motors.

The bogies were fabricated from steel box section and the substantial cross member between axles 1 and 2 had a machined pocket to accommodate the centre pin location mechanism usually referred to as the traction centre or centre casting. This transmits the traction and braking forces between the loco body and the bogies via resilient pads.

The bearings fitted to the fixed outer wheelset axle journals were spherical roller-bearings manufactured by SKF, while the float on the centre wheelset was achieved with FAG parallel roller-bearings which allowed the axle journal to slide from side to side as the bogie rolled around curved track.

Two traditional cast-iron brake blocks acted on the wheel tread with brake force applied through a pair of bogie-mounted air cylinders. One inner wheel on each bogie had the service brake cylinders combined with a parking brake mechanism. Unlike earlier designs, the driver could apply the handbrake by pressing a button in the cab rather than turning a handwheel to operate a series of chains and linkages.

The brake system itself was a Davies & Metcalfe E70 - an electronic version of the standard BR brake system. It was already in use on the Brush-designed HST power cars. The driver's brake control was much the same as on any other locomotive, but the brain of the system was an electronic unit rather than a complex series of pneumatic valves and controls. The main difference between the two systems was that the E70 used only three wires between the brake

*11*

*Above:* 56031's body has been lowered onto its first set of bogies and the loco stands almost complete. *Photo: Derek Porter Collection*

controller and the electronic controller rather than the complex run of air pipes. The controller had seven positions, each delivering a pre-set brake application.

Control systems on earlier designs of locomotive were mainly hard-wired, making fault finding and repair a lengthy process. The bulk of this equipment comprised relays and mechanical contactors which were often slow to respond to adjustments to the power controller. The electronics used on Class 56 were much quicker to respond and this was most noticeable in the speed of the electronic detection and correction of wheelslip. Much of the electronics in Class 56 had first seen use on Class 50, but the new design had many of its control circuits condensed into circuit boards in replaceable modules fitted in the control cubicle electronic rack. The load regulation of the engine was controlled by a separate module, as were slow speed control, speed sensing, voltage regulation and various power supplies for the control equipment. The system was designed to enable maintenance staff to identify a fault quickly. The modules had indicator LEDs, or test points, to help diagnose which module was defective and, once the problematic module was identified, the loosening of a screw allowed the module to slide out of the rack and be replaced with a good module from the stores. The defective module was sent away to a BREL facility to be repaired and returned for future use. The battery charge system and E70 system also had printed circuit boards as a main element of their control circuits. The speed sensing module can actually be removed and replaced with a special module which allows depot staff to fool the locomotive into thinking it is travelling at speed. This comes in useful when checking the function of speedometers and field diversion systems.

At Doncaster Works the construction process began with the fabrication of five main underframe sections. These were assembled in jigs and welded using semi-automatic equipment. Next the underframe sections were welded together and the bodyside framework added. The sheet metalwork to form both the bodysides and the continuous tray of the sealing plate were then welded in position. The internal bulkheads, which divide the locomotive into five compartments, were then added. The work of the fabrication bays finished with the fitting of fuel tanks and bogie centre pins.

*Above:* A view of the completed 56031's electrical compartment, looking towards the number 2 cab. The application of electronics to Class 56 allowed many of the control circuits to be condensed into circuit boards in replaceable modules. The whole electrical system was designed to help maintenance staff identify faults quickly. *Photo: BREL*

The whole assembly was then relocated to the fitting-out bays where the power unit, electrical equipment, piping, cabling and all other internal equipment were installed. The cabs and roof sections, produced separately by other BREL workshops, were married to the loco at this stage. Dressing and finishing of the bodywork preceded the undercoat and final paint application.

The loco was almost complete at this point and ready to undergo a thorough series of tests to ensure all the components functioned. This included testing the electrical insulation of the alternator and main traction motors as well as the smaller motors fitted to auxiliary equipment like traction motor blowers, compressors, and oil and fuel pumps.

*Above:* A works plate fitted to one of the Romanian-built locomotives. *Photo: Electroputere*

*Left:* In the autumn of 1976, 56013 was displayed at an exhibition in Tbilisi. The loco shares yard space with a Romanian electric locomotive.
*Above:* 56008 on test in Romania in the summer of 1976. *Photos: Antonio Bianco*

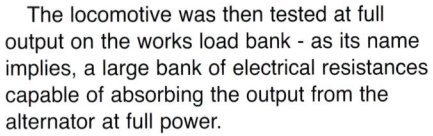

The locomotive was then tested at full output on the works load bank - as its name implies, a large bank of electrical resistances capable of absorbing the output from the alternator at full power.

Assuming the locomotive passed all these tests, it would be released for a main line test run. The nature of these trials varied during the production run as the works became more familiar with the testing required. The high speed trial, for instance, was soon dispensed with, a light engine run to either Tyne Yard or Peterborough taking its place. The final test involved a local MGR duty. Immingham became a regular destination, although other trials sometimes went to Tyne Yard, or even Scarborough on occasion.

To gain service experience of the Ruston 16RK3CT power unit, E70 brake system and electrical and electronic equipment, BR had installed a set of this equipment in an accident-damaged Class 47 loco (47046) and renumbered it 47601 to create the, then, unique sub-class 47/6. The idea was that 47601 would operate on the type of duties Class 56 was designed to operate, allowing BR staff and operating departments to gain useful experience before the first new locos were delivered. Unfortunately, the conversion work took longer than expected and 47601 only entered traffic at Tinsley just before the first of the Romanian build landed at Harwich. As Tinsley would receive the initial allocation, it made perfect sense to base 47601 there, although some 'up-front' experience would obviously be lost by the depot's drivers and fitters because of the 47's late arrival.

As it turned out, this hardly mattered. Problems soon began to manifest themselves after Romaninan-built 56002 was closely examined at Tinsley. The result was that 47601 operated in traffic for some twelve months before the first of the foreign batch was finally commissioned, when 56006 became British Rail's first Type 5 freight loco. The problems with the Romanian locos are dealt with in detail in Chapter 2.

The attitude of the rail unions didn't help. They insisted that crews received a full week's conversion course before they were let loose on the Class 47 test bed. This meant that only a small number of Tinsley crews were trained and that 47601 could only be diagrammed on local duties solely in the hands of Tinsley. Needless to say, this appears to have been ignored on one occasion when a Doncaster man took 47601 to Immingham - a situation that doubtless repeated itself when other Eastern Region drivers received training on Class 56. To all intents and purposes, 47601 *was* a 56 and it operated alongside the regular Tinsley fleet until September 1978. With the Class 58 project looming, the 47 was to become an engineering test bed for a second time.

Eventually, the order for Class 56 rose to 135 locomotives. Unconfirmed stories spoke of a further fifteen, but these appear to have been substituted for the newer Class 58 design which was taking shape as the 56 build came to an end. By this time a third railway workshop was involved after production of the final twenty was transferred to Crewe to free up space at Doncaster for Class 58.

Given that three workshops were involved, it is not surprising that detail differences arose between the various batches. Most of the physical differences were for good engineering or commercial reasons, although some resulted from having to rectify the Romanian locos before they could enter traffic. Other differences were cosmetic rather than physical - simply subtle livery variations.

During the service life of the class, numerous modifications were introduced. Some were reliability experiments, some of which were eventually applied to the whole class, while others came about because of accident damage.

### Construction variations between locos

| Loco No. | Qty | Lot | Built | Livery | Cabs | Cab Desk | Cab Roof Skin | Buffers | Air Con | Bogies & Where Built | Wheelsets | Start Circuit Mount |
|---|---|---|---|---|---|---|---|---|---|---|---|---|
| 56001 - 030 | 30 | 1507 | Romania | BR Blue | Alum. | Alum. | single | Round | fitted | CP2 - Reista | tyred | Floor |
| 56031 - 041 | 11 | 1508 | Doncaster | BR Blue | Alum. | Alum. | single | Oval | fitted | CP2 - Reista | tyred | Floor |
| 56042 | 1 | 1508 | Doncaster | BR Blue | Alum. | Alum. | single | Oval | fitted | CP1 - | monobloc | Floor |
| 56043 | 1 | 1508 | Doncaster | BR Blue | Alum. | Alum. | single | Oval | fitted | CP2 - Reista | tyred | Floor |
| 56044 - 055 | 12 | 1508 | Doncaster | BR Blue | Alum. | Alum. | single | Oval | fitted | CP2 - Reista | tyred | Floor |
| 56056 - 057 | 2 | 1508 | Doncaster | BR Blue | Steel | Alum. | single | Oval | fitted | CP2 - Reista | tyred | Floor |
| 56058 | 1 | 1508 | Doncaster | BR Blue | Steel | Alum. | single | Oval | fitted | CP2 - Derby | monobloc | Floor |
| 56059 - 060 | 2 | 1508 | Doncaster | BR Blue | Steel | Alum. | single | Oval | fitted | CP2 - Reista | tyred | Floor |
| 56061 | 1 | 1509 | Doncaster | BR Blue | Steel | Alum. | single | Oval | fitted | CP2 - Reista | tyred | Floor |
| 56062 - 063 | 2 | 1509 | Doncaster | BR Blue | Steel | Alum. | single | Oval | fitted | CP2 - Derby | monobloc | Floor |
| 56064 - 066 | 3 | 1509 | Doncaster | BR Blue | Steel | GRP** | double | Oval | fitted | CP2 - Derby | monobloc | Floor |
| 56067 | 1 | 1509 | Doncaster | BR Blue | Steel | GRP | double | Oval | engine coolant | CP2 - Derby | monobloc | Floor |
| 56068 - 072 | 5 | 1509 | Doncaster | BR Blue | Steel | GRP | double | Oval | fitted | CP2 - Derby | monobloc | Floor |
| 56073 - 074* | 2 | 1509 | Doncaster | BR Blue | Steel | GRP | double | Oval | fitted | CP2 - Derby | monobloc | Floor |
| 56075 - 083 | 8 | 1509 | Doncaster | BR Blue | Steel | GRP | double | Oval | fitted | CP2 - Derby | monobloc | Floor |
| 56084 - 090 | 7 | 1509 | Doncaster | Large Logo | Steel | GRP | double | Oval | fitted | CP2 - Derby | monobloc | Floor |
| 56091 - 115 | 25 | 1510 | Doncaster | Large Logo | Steel | GRP | double | Oval | modified recirc/heat | CP2 - Crewe | monobloc | Panel |
| 56116 - 134 | 20 | 1510 | Crewe | Large Logo | Steel | GRP | double | Oval | modified recirc/heat | CP2 - Crewe | monobloc | Panel |
| 56135 | 1 | 1510 | Crewe | Railfreight | Steel | GRP | double | Oval | modified recirc/heat | CP2 - Crewe | monobloc | Panel |

*remote control fitted, ** Glass reinforced plastic

# GRIDS 2. THE LONG ROAD TO REVENUE GRIDS

*Above:* 31318 heads through Wrabness on 7th August 1976 with 56001 & 56002 in tow, heading for Tinsley. The two had been transported across Europe by rail to Zeebrugge where they boarded the ferry *MV Cambridge* for the voyage to Harwich Town Quay. They arrived there on 4th August and, after unloading, were shunted along to Harwich Parkestone Quay. *Photo: N.L. Cadge*

By the middle of July 1976, a number of locomotives had been completed at the Electroputere factory and stood ready for testing and shipment. The trials on Romanian State Railways' network involved some passenger working between Craiova and Bucharest as well as coal workings between Turnu Severin and Craiova power station.

With their testing completed, finished locos were usually paired up for the journey across mainland Europe to the Zeebrugge-Harwich ferry, a trip on which they were accompanied by Electroputere staff.

56001 & 002 arrived in Britain on the 4th of August 1976 at Harwich Town Quay, where 001 was unloaded from the *MV Cambridge* ferry at 17.30. After initial checks, the pair were towed to Harwich Parkeston Quay by 08767 and then on to Tinsley by 31318 three days later. On arrival in South Yorkshire, a team of BR engineers set about inspecting the locos. On the 24th September, 56001 took a test train of 26 MGR hoppers from Treeton to Appleby and back, but the loco developed a hot axle box on the return and was still parked at Tinsley a week later with a suspected seized wheelset. Not a good start, and this wasn't the only problem discovered. Before the test run a number of other faults had been identified and logged - essentially items which did not meet the BR CM&EE's standards. A schedule of work was put in place to rectify the problems, but they were many and varied. Some resulted from bad engineering practice and lack of quality control, others were more significant and would stay with the Romanian locos throughout their careers.

The greatest number of deficiencies was found in the bogies, including:

i) Incorrect end float on the centre wheelsets
ii) Insufficient clearances when traversing curved track
iii) Leakage from traction motor gear cases
iv) Excessive clearances on suspension tubes
v) Poorly-manufactured primary dampers and springs
vi) Loose tyres because of a failure to machine to specified tolerances.

Additionally, hand winding of the primary coil springs resulted in inconsistent performance. The coils were able to fully close on occasion, bringing the loco into hard contact with the bump stops on top of the bogie frame. The faulty springs were replaced with machine-wound units from BREL and attention given to the finishing of the bogie

*Above:* A little later in the journey, the trio passes through Ipswich station. At Tinsley, engineers set about inspecting their new locos and rapidly discovered a host of faults. As more were delivered, it became apparent that much rectification work would needed before the imports could put into traffic. *Photo: Graham Hardinge*

15

*Above:* 56003 & 56004 arrived hot on the heels of the first two. The pair wait at Harwich Town Yard on 15th August 1976. Note that the grilles have been covered over during the journey from Romania. *Photo: Graham Hardinge*

welds. These were not considered adequate to prevent fatigue failures in service. (Special inspections of Romanian-built bogies were introduced thereafter to guard against the increased risk of a fracture in the rear transom. These instructions still applied to EWS locos in 2004, not least because all bogies were interchangeable between batches and Romanian-built units could be found under any loco in the fleet except the hybrid 56042!)

Easily-avoidable problems included a lack of protective grease on the bearings and brake rigging, which meant that both items suffered corrosion damage while in transit. Some items such as cab footsteps were loose, simply because nobody had bothered to check that the bolts were tight before the locos left Electroputere.

The seized wheelset during 001's initial test run on September 24th stemmed from the lack of end float. The problem was immediately notified to Reistia which was still manufacturing bogies for the first 60 of the fleet. Locos up to 56008 had already arrived in Britain, while 009 & 010 were en route to Harwich and due on 1st October. This was unfortunate, as Electroputere had managed to achieve a fairly respectable rate of output for its share of the build. The first eight had appeared at a rate of two a fortnight, but the bogie faults had a major impact on the units in production. 56011, for example, was almost complete when the bad news reached Craiova from the BR engineers at Tinsley. The rectification work needed meant that 011 didn't make it to Harwich for another two months, on 30th November. The next two turned up at Zeebrugge on 23rd December, after which the backlog magically cleared. The next two sailed on 3rd January 1977, closely followed by another pair on the 6th and three more by the 15th, bringing total arrivals in Britain to twenty.

By now, the manufacturing process at Reistia had been adjusted to ensure that bogies were machined and assembled correctly, but that still left ten locos in Britain with serious defects. BR could have sent the whole lot back to Romania but it was more practical, and cost-effective, to carry out the rectification work here. The cost was charged to Brush, who no doubt passed the invoice on to Electroputere and, ultimately, Reistia.

56001-010 were despatched to Stratford for their bogies to be removed. The bogie frames went to a Brush-owned company in the West Midlands for attention to the poor weld quality and clearance problems. The wheelsets went to BREL Doncaster where the end float was set correctly and tyres and bearings attended to.

Considering all this, it is perhaps poignant that the class ended its days in general service in much the way it began, with many bogie swops taking place between locos to keep the surviving fleet in traffic.

Although the Romanian-built bogies were a major cause for concern, inspections soon revealed other problems areas on the locomotive bodies. The major issue everyone associates with the Romanian locos is the poor method of cable management - running electrical cables through normal pipe instead of specific cable trunking or conduit. To make matters worse, the edges of the pipes were not dressed to cover sharp edges so, in no time at all, abrasive metal would rub through the cable insulation and cause a fault.

The fabricated framework for the blower motors was so flimsy that it had a tendency to break apart, while the brake frames were inadequately welded to the floor and liable to break loose on occasions.

A much more visible problem was Electroputere's failure to pre-tension the bodysides before welding the sheet steel skin into position, resulting in a rippled effect. A number of semi-matt paint finishes were tried out on the finished locos to try and reduce the visual impact of the ripples, but they remained noticeable especially in certain lighting conditions.

BR laid all of these problems at the door of Brush, and its choice of sub-contractor, even though the faults were rectified at various BREL workshops and BR depots. Information was fed back to Brush on a regular basis so that British engineering wisdom could be passed on to the Romanian factories. The advice was clearly taken on board; during the course of the build, commissioning time in Britain came down from more than seven months to little more than two when the final locos arrived.

However, although manufacturing problems were efficiently dealt with, the solutions to other shortcomings in the design were not so clear-cut. For example, adapting the pattern of Class 47 underframe sections for the Type 5 loco may have contributed to the unwelcome tendency of the cab floors to vibrate when the power unit was running at around 600 rpm. This problem refused to go away and at one point desperate BR engineers even contemplated modifying the engine's control system so that it wouldn't run in the critical speed range! When the cabs weren't vibrating, they were prone to draughts, not only because of poor fitting of components but also the basic design.

When the ride quality was measured by the Research Department, it was found to be only just within the acceptable limits in both the vertical and horizontal planes. The ride was generally described as poor, especially when the loco 'bottomed' on the fixed stops. The remedial work on springs and bogie clearances appears to have brought some improvement but, to this day, the Class 56 has a ride quality all its own. Some describe it as soft; the loco seems to loll about and any unsecured pipes or screw couplings make contact with the body, creating the characteristic clang associated with riding on a 56 footplate. Locos up to 56090 were fitted with an air-conditioning unit at each cab end with a metal grid to protect the unit from damage. On these locos, unsecured air pipes could make contact with the grid when the loco ran over pointwork or uneven track at speed, adding to the clanging in the cab.

Of course, pressure to get the new locos accepted and into traffic was building day by day, and the last thing BR needed after solving all the technical problems was to have the unions and train crews 'black' the locos because the driving cabs were unfit for purpose. Given that the cab was the driver's 'office', he had a right to a comfortable environment in which to do his work . . . or so the argument ran. Curiously, the same argument resurfaced more than twenty years later when the first of the Class 66s entered service . . . .

As the rectifications progressed, some members of the class were allowed out on test trains so that BR engineers could evaluate the success of the work. 56002 was noted at Featherstone on 25th November 1976 and 56006 retraced the steps of 001 when it took a 26-wagon rake of hoppers from Treeton sidings to Blea Moor. Two days later the same loco worked a full rake of 36 MGR hoppers over the Pennines between Healey Mills Yard and Marsden, on the eastern approach to Standege Tunnel. This trial was in anticipation of the re-routing of Fiddler's Ferry-bound coal trains from the soon-to-close Woodhead route.

Rectification of Romanian workmanship was being carried out at Tinsley Depot and it proved a lengthy process (an average of six months for the early examples, which speeded up to three months for the last ten or so - see table). As a result, Tinsley was soon full of 56s queuing up for cosmetic surgery. To make some room, 56014 & 015 were towed to Barrow Hill on the 8th of January 1977, and were soon followed by 016 & 017 - not for the work to be done but on a kind of secondary waiting list. Subsequent arrivals from the docks were sent straight to Darnall carriage sidings, close to Tinsley, for storage.

Following rectification, 56006 became the first of the class to be released to traffic at Tinsley on 25th February 1977, unofficially entering the history books as BR's first Type 5 freight loco - a distinction which has failed to earn it a place in the National Collection.

Locos deemed fit enough to risk a trial run from Tinsley were provided with a train of flats loaded with rails from the sidings at nearby Broughton Lane. 56001 was noted passing Holbeck, Leeds, on 17th February 1977; the same loco had a similar load on 22nd February as the 09.10 Broughton Lane-Peterborough working. Presumably, these tests were a success as 56001 entered traffic soon afterwards, on 28th February, along with 002, 003 & 004. 56008 appeared on the 09.10 to Peterborough on February 24th, but wasn't released to traffic for another six weeks, on 13th April.

Reports from the time indicate an operational fleet of ten - 56001-008, 014 & 015. They could mainly be found operating around Shirebrook and Lincoln in March 1977, but appearances at High Marnham were becoming increasingly regular. In the coming months the Tinsley fleet settled down and was often used turn and turn about with 47601 on MGR duties operated by the depot.

By the time the rectification work finally reached an end, the first Doncaster-built locos were nearing completion, creating an interesting overlap. When 56001/002 landed in Britain, the early Doncaster locos were only just beginning to come together. Even so, 56031 entered service in May 1977, by which date only fourteen of the twenty-six Romanian locos delivered had been passed fit for traffic - 56001-56008, 012, 014, 015, 017, 019, 020 . . . and 022, which began earning revenue on the same day as 56031 - 24th May 1977.

Although 56004 hauled the first passenger train on 22nd June 1977 - rescuing the 1020 Penzance -Leeds at Wincobank, just south of Leeds - the first opportunity for enthusiasts to travel on a pre-arranged working behind a Type 5 came on 24th July 1977 when 56008 worked the 'Melton Mowbray Pieman' railtour from Barnsley to Melton Mowbray. The train was organised by British Rail's Sheffield office and its shrewd selection of motive power probably ensured that Class 56 enthusiasts outnumbered the pork pie fanciers on board!

Deliveries from Electroputere continued in pairs, such as on 27th July 1977 when a Class 37 was noted hauling 56027 & 028 westwards at Manningtree. One or two made the trip alone, such as 56008 on 15th September 1976 and 56011 on the following 30th November. The accompanying table shows the arrival dates for all thirty imports.

In an exemplary display of neatness, BR decreed that Toton should receive all thirty of Doncaster's output, in the same way that Tinsley had been lumbered with the Romanian thirty. By late-August 1977, 56031-4 had arrived at the Nottinghamshire depot and they were soon put to work on the Fletton (Peterborough) flyash trains from Ratcliffe and Drakelow power stations near Burton-on-Trent. Understandably, demand was high for these new locos (not least because they worked) but, as before, traincrew and maintenance staff needed to familiarise themselves first. 56032 went to Saltley for two weeks in early August 1977, with 033 replacing it for the rest of the month. Ironbridge and Kingsbury were regular destinations for Saltley crew-training trips.

It didn't take the authorities long to realise the AC output of the 56's alternator was a useful mobile electricity supply and on 5th September 1977 56019 was despatched from Barrow Hill to Heaton T&RSD where it supplied electricity during a power workers dispute. The loco went back to Barrow Hill after ten days of stationary alternation. In the same month 56008 went to Sheffield Midland and 56029 to Bradford Hammerton Street on further emergency work as the industrial action continued.

The class breached the Birmingham area for the first time that October, although it was a Tinsley loco, 56029, rather than the expected Toton machine which worked into Three Spires colliery near Coventry with an Ironbridge power station MGR.

October 1977 also threw up 56005, awaiting attention at Stratford. This one had been released to traffic on the previous 14th March after the bogie repairs, one of the earliest to be dealt with, so its reappearance at Stratford may have been for further rectification following lessons learned on other locos.

Just over two months old, and not subject to intensive re-engineering, 56034 appeared at Coalville on 27th October for crew training. The rest of Toton's existing allocation could be found that day at Westhouses, Burton-on-Trent and Bescot, working trains to Ratcliffe, Ironbridge, Rugeley and Didcot. Their sphere of operaton had extended to the Immingham and Scunthorpe areas by December.

1978 began with 56004 banking 'Peak' 44009 from Barnsley to Dodworth with the 'Class 44 Farewell' railtour on 21st January. In the same way that Class 66 was later blamed for the demise of the 56, one wonders what Class 44 fans thought about the new traction type shoving them up Dodworth bank. Perhaps unprintable.

Soon after the second charter outing for the class, 56033 appeared on a Doddeston to Crewe Basford Hall high-speed test run, while 56038 went to the Western Region for crew training - a move which eventually resulted in 035 working into Didcot power station for the first time on 7th April. In fact, the class was breaking new ground daily. Bristol became 'new track' when 56043 brought home a dead 50047. 043 remained on the Western and turned up at Reading depot in May for crew

*Above:* Harwich Town Yard provides free parking to 56027, 028 & 029 on 26th July 1977. 56011-030 were delayed because of BR's insistence on rectifications before shipment. *Photo: Graham Hardinge*

**Delivery & introduction of the 30 Romanian-built Class 56s. Batch number 1507.**

| Loco No | Works No | Zeebrugge handover | Released to Traffic |
|---|---|---|---|
| 56001 | 750 | 04/08/76 | 28/02/77 |
| 56002 | 751 | 04/08/76 | 28/02/77 |
| 56003 | 752 | 13/08/76 | 28/02/77 |
| 56004 | 753 | 13/08/76 | 28/02/77 |
| 56005 | 754 | 09/09/76 | 14/03/77 |
| 56006 | 755 | 08/09/76 | 25/02/77 |
| 56007 | 756 | 08/09/76 | 13/04/77 |
| 56008 | 757 | 15/09/76 | 13/04/77 |
| 56009 | 758 | 01/10/76 | 27/05/77 |
| 56010 | 759 | 01/10/76 | 28/07/77 |
| 56011 | 760 | 30/11/76 | 29/06/77 |
| 56012 | 761 | 23/12/76 | 18/04/77 |
| 56013 | 762 | 23/12/76 | 01/08/77 |
| 56014 | 763 | 03/01/77 | 28/03/77 |
| 56015 | 764 | 03/01/77 | 21/03/77 |
| 56016 | 765 | 06/01/77 | 27/05/77 |
| 56017 | 766 | 06/01/77 | 13/05/77 |
| 56018 | 767 | 14/01/77 | 23/08/77 |
| 56019 | 768 | 14/01/77 | 13/05/77 |
| 56020 | 769 | 15/01/77 | 20/05/77 |
| 56021 | 770 | 09/03/77 | 17/06/77 |
| 56022 | 771 | 16/03/77 | 24/05/77 |
| 56023 | 772 | 30/03/77 | 11/07/77 |
| 56024 | 773 | 30/03/77 | 15/06/77 |
| 56025 | 774 | 18/04/77 | 05/07/77 |
| 56026 | 775 | 18/04/77 | 15/07/77 |
| 56027 | 776 | 07/07/77 | 19/09/77 |
| 56028 | 777 | 07/07/77 | 14/09/77 |
| 56029 | 778 | 07/07/77 | 12/09/77 |
| 56030 | 779 | 19/07/77 | 21/10/77 |

*Above:* 56053 hauls empty flyash vehicles through Peterborough while en route to Fletton, 30th August 1979. The locomotive was only eight months old when this photo was taken. It had been accepted into traffic on 29th December 1978. *Photo: Paul Bettany*

training and maintenance familiarisation in advance of the class's diagramming on the Didcot CEGB jobs.

A single day at Stanton Gate on 3rd May revealed 56039, 043, 013 & 005 in succession on MGR trains. A week later, 022 was in the area on similar work.

As mentioned earlier, the Class 58 project was in the offing by now. While 47601 was being re-engineered as 47901, the new design of bogies intended for Doncaster's next build - the CP1 - were installed as test units under 56042 from new. As the loco's frames had to be specially reconfigured and machined to accept the CP1s, 042 was always going to be a one-off. Its selection for these trials consigned it to a life as a non-standard loco and its specialist nature ensured that maintenance was nearly always carried out at Toton. Unlike the rest of the class, which could exchange bogies and wheelsets *ad infinitum* if defects occurred, 042 had only the one set - a situation which made it prone to long periods out of traffic while parts were repaired rather than exchanged. Not surprisingly, a lack of spares brought about its withdrawal in 1990 - the first of the class to go and after only eleven years in traffic. Despite being refered to as "class 58 bogies" the units under 56042 were not interchangable with the later CP3a and CP3b types fitted to the 58's.

56042 was always considered something of a rarity by enthusiasts, but after its evaluation period by the Derby research department it was used day-to-day like any other 56. Records show it travelled as far as Gateshead, Warrington and Kent on occasions, although the umbilical cord tieing it to Toton meant it couldn't wander at will - especially when Class 58 spares and maintenance expertise were concentrated at Toton after 'genuine' 58s entered traffic.

The neatness of the allocation plan began to fray a little at the beginning of October 1978. By then, Doncaster had delivered locos up to 56048 (18 of the planned 30), but four of the early allocation - 031-034 - were transferred to Tinsley on the first of the month to allow the Yorkshire depot to cover duties from its satellite depots. Four continued to operate from Tinsley itself, ten were out-based at Shirebrook, three at Wath and two at Doncaster. 34 locos allocated to Tinsley to cover 19 duties may seem a little excessive, but a significant number were still required at various depots for crew training, not to mention maintenance downtime.

If the commissioning of 56006 was the first landmark event in the Class 56 story, and the non-standard 56042 the second, then the third must surely be the emergence from Stratford of 56036 in Large Logo livery in August 1978. Considered revolutionary at the time, this

*Above:* A brand-new 56042 stands in Doncaster Works yard on 5th March 1978 while two fitters inspect the loco's experimental CP1 bogies. The frames of 042 needed to be specially configured to allow the fitment of CP1s. The loco's entry into service was delayed until May 1979 whilst tests were carried out. *Photo: Pauline McKenna*

GRIDS

*Above:* 56047 descends the Acton incline while heading for the Hayes Tarmac terminal with a train from Cliffe Vale on 24th July 1979. At this time, Class 56s were still a rare sight at the London end of the Western Region. *Photo: Paul Furtek*

scheme was to become the standard on the later build from 56084-134 as well as a handful of the existing fleet.

Following the delivery of 56048, Toton received the next 24 locomotives from Doncaster, giving it, briefly, the number range 56035-56072. However, it would lose 56033, 035-038, 040, 041, 043, 044, 045 & 046 to Cardiff Canton by the middle of 1979, although 56036 would return to Toton less than a month after transferring to the Western Region.

On 22nd November 1978, 56052 arrived at Tyne Yard with an MGR rake. This was reported in the railway press as a Ferrybridge to Blyth working, although the time of arrival, 12.45, and the fact that 56052 wasn't released to traffic until 6th December indicate this was the loco's loaded test run before release from Doncaster.

With only 56052-056 added to operating stock between November 1978 and March 1979, workings settled down and news of locos breaking new ground began to tail off. It was therefore exciting news for north-west rail fans when 56022 unexpectedly appeared at Stanlow refinery near Ellesmere Port on 9th March 1979, presumably deputising for something during a layover at Warrington. However, this was a false dawn; several years passed before 56s became a regular sight at Stanlow on oil trains.

56040 provided the first noteworthy event of 1979 when it became the resident maintenance training loco at Cricklewood in May. 56049 followed on 16th June for driver training work and was often used on the Brent-Stewartby refuse train. By July 56050 had taken over the refuse duties but it also worked the Toton–Northfleet coal train on 1st August - the first time a 56 had rolled its wheels over Southern Region track. Seventeen days later, 56040 became the second.

56053 put down another marker for the future on May 14th with the class's first appearance on a duty which would become familiar territory - dragging an electric loco and its train (the 13.30 Birmingham New Street-Euston) over a non-electrified route with a Sunday diversion between Birmingham and Nuneaton.

Formation of the month was a 45-wagon MGR rake which 56035 hauled into Didcot on the last day of May. Ultimately this trial was deemed unsuccessful, not because of any shortcoming in the loco's ability to haul the train but because of problems with the power station's unloading equipment.

*Above:* 56069 had only been in traffic for four days when this shot was taken outside Cricklewood depot on 16th December 1979. *Photo: Paul Furtek*

*Above:* The initial problems with the Romanian locos weren't helped by a number of them becoming involved in accidents. 56026, captured here at Guide Bridge, ran into trouble in December 1977 and went to Stratford DRS for repairs. It re-emerged five months later. *Photo: Paul Furtek*

Toton held an open day on 9th June at which the undoubted stars were the remaining Class 44s. 56036 flew the flag for Type 5 freight power in its experimental Large Logo. One railway journalist described the new livery as "garish" and hoped BR would see sense!

A few days later the government announced a 7% reduction in fuel supplies to BR as the predicted oil crisis, which originally brought about the need for the Class 56, began to have an effect on everyday life. This resulted in BR running 10% fewer trains, and although no services were cut completely, their frequency was reduced. The lack of protest from BR led cynics to suggest that poor availability of motive power generally would have resulted in the same 10% reduction in services anyway!

One of the first reported sightings at the London end of the Western Region occurred on 25th June when 56053 appeared on the Cliffe Vale-Hayes Tarmac company train. The following month 56059 was out-based at Wellingborough for crew training, involving a regular light engine trip to Leicester to assist the 08.30 Cliffe Hill-Hayes & Harlington stone train to Wellingborough. Occasionally the train loco, a Class 47, would be removed and the 56 allowed to run through to West London and back.

Another passenger turn, still something of a rarity, took place on 1st August when 56038 rescued 47423 at Wichnor Junction north of Tamworth on a NE-SW express. The 56 was commandeered from an MGR train and worked to a spot next to Saltley stabling point, from where 47482 appeared to take the train forward.

The WR received the paper allocation of 56035 & 036 on 1st July. The next day 036 appeared physically at Canton depot for crew familiarisation. Twenty-four hours later, 035 ran from Toton to Margam for similar duties. Margam was obviously keen to make the most of its new arrival; later the same day the loco was spotted leaving Patchway Tunnel with a loaded MGR train and returning with the empties. On 4th July, 035 passed Severn Tunnel Junction with a loaded steel train, by which time Margam sidings had accumulated 56035, 038, 041 & 043. Cardiff obviously wanted a longer look at its new loco type; 56036 was still at Canton on the 7th.

56035 was on the Port Talbot-Velindre trip on July 24th. The next day both crew trainers had their multiple working equipment tested as they were readied for a trial working - the 08.10 Port Talbot-Llanwern iron ore. This was much publicised as Britain's heaviest train - 27 PTA tipplers weighing in at 2,740 tonnes - and pairs of 56s formally took over this duty on August 6th. 035 & 036 performed on the 7th, 035 & 038 on the 9th, while 041 & 043 tried their hand later that month. These challenging trains had previously been in the hands of triple-headed Class 37s. No increase in trailing loads was possible as train length was governed by run-round facilities; so, like the Didcot trial, nothing to do with loco shortcomings. Eventually the run-round loops were extended, allowing 56037 & 041 to work 30 PTAs (a massive 3,304 tonnes) on 29th September. This run was wholly successful and all the ore trains were increased to 30 wagons from October.

By way of comparison, three 37s could manage 27 of the 100-tonne tipplers and breast Stormy Bank summit at 8 mph. With 30 in tow, a pair of 56s managed 12 mph at the top of the bank. The extra power available and the civil engineering work at both terminals:

i) reduced the number of locos required
ii) increased train payloads,
iii) improved overall train performance, causing less delay to other traffic.

As an added bonus, the swear boxes at Margam and Canton were down-sized as crews no longer faced the frustration of persuading three Class 37s to work in multiple.

Class 56 continued to break new ground, either through circumstance or intent, for the rest of 1979. In August, for example, the West Coast Main Line suffered disruption when the 13.29 Manchester-Birmingham derailed at Bushbury Junction on the 13th. The following 13.22 Lime Street-Plymouth had to be dragged back to Stafford by 56052; the same loco had already worked the 07.47 Penzance-Liverpool from New Street to Stafford via Cannock to avoid the derailment site.

Later that month on the 18th 56040, with a Class 47 coupled inside, ran through to Kent with a 43 wagon train from Welbeck to Northfleet, although a shortage of 56-trained crews prevented Type 5s from taking over this working fully until October. This service was a prime target for 56 conversion as it was

**GRIDS**

generally hauled by a Class 45/47 combination requiring two crews.

The traditional August shutdown of South Wales steel works temporarily diverted the local 56 allocation onto other work, notably moving finished steel between Margam, Trostre and Velindre. They also appeared on oil trains out of BP Llandarcy, running to Aberthaw, Llanwern and Ebbw Vale. Against the run of play, 56041 set off along the Welsh Marches line on August 20th and reached at least as far as Hereford.

Meanwhile, the conversion to Class 56 continued in the north. 56031 arrived at Knottingley in September for driver training, followed by 56002 in November. However, the lack of a national agreement with the rail unions for single-manning the new locos meant they were unable to take over from Knottingley's single-manned 47/3s until May 1980.

Having become an LMR loco again after its short trip to South Wales, 56036 happened to be in the Wolverhampton area on November the 4th when the 13.40 Euston-Shrewsbury, strengthened to load 14, rolled in for its usual loco change from electric to diesel traction for the onward run. Despite the lack of train supply power, the 56 took the train all the way to Shrewsbury but probably returned light engine.

By November, the class was becoming a common sight on coal workings through Clapham Junction. 56056 appeared on the 15th November, with 56048 following nine days later. On November 21st 56067 emerged from works and set off on its loaded test run - the Doncaster Decoy-Immingham MGR. Presumably all went well as the loco was released to traffic - along with 066, 068 & 069 - on December 11th.

November's most notable working, however, featured 56064 on a passenger train following a double Class 47 failure. Barely two months old, 064 took over the 08.35 ex-Birmingham New Street at Fenny Compton from 47330. The 47 had been commandeered from a southbound freight at Leamington when the original train engine, 47001, failed. The second failure at Fenny Compton, and the substitution of the 56, produced a 91-minute deficit on the clock when 064 rolled into Paddington with the train and both 47s in tow!

56065 arrived light engine at Motherwell on December 17th for the start of trials on the Hunterston to Ravenscraig iron ore trains, but not before another little drama. When overhead line problems on the northern section of the WCML stranded the 09.35 Euston-Inverness, the northbound 56 galloped to the rescue. Reports differ as to where it worked the train from, and where to, with some speculating that it ran via Newcastle. As for the Ravenscraig trials, they were judged unsuccessful and Scottish iron ore workings remained in the capable hands of pairs of Motherwell 37s.

Despite the success of the pairs on the heavy Margam-Llanwern iron ore workings, the Western Region seemed more than willing to use the new locos on lighter and faster freight services than their design spec decreed. In December 1979, a 56 occasionally turned out for the 19.10 Pengam-Stratford liner, while the 19.45 Pengam-Coatbridge often reached Crewe, where the 56 waited for the return working.

The LMR also used 56s on liners sometimes, but only nocturnal spotters would have been around to see Toton's 069 on the 01.01 Nottingham-Ripple Lane on 21st December.

1979 rounded off with 56s at Shrewsbury for crew training, primarily for workings to and from the Shotton steel works sidings at Dee Marsh. Crews were already trained for the section to Crewe via Hereford and Whitchurch, so the short run to Shotton via Wrexham was needed to enable through running. 064 was still engaged in training at Shrewsbury the following February.

56069 kicked off another fascinating year by rescuing 50008 and the 11.22 Liverpool-Paddington on January 18th 1980. The 50 had failed near Leamington Spa, again.

New track offered itself in February when High Marnam power station became cut off from the east at Pyewipe Junction after a freight train derailment at Clifton-on-Trent. Trains for High Marnham had to take a longer route via Retford and Worksop to gain access.

Another round of Nuneaton drags in March threw up 56066 on a single trip on the 9th, followed by 059 in similar fashion the following Sunday. Further passenger mileage from 066 arose, unplanned, on April 10th after 50014, fresh from overhaul at Doncaster, took over the 09.50 Edinburgh-Plymouth from a Deltic at York. The 50 encountered problems around Washwood Heath and had to be towed the short distance to New Street by 066. Imagine that - Deltic, Class 50 *and* 56 haulage of the same timetabled service in the space of a hundred miles! What would we pay for something similar today?

The transition in the north showed itself at Knottingley's open day in May. The old order didn't have long to go but the depot displayed 47301, 302, 304, 308, 371, 372, 373, 374 & 376 at the event, alongside 56021 and an almost-new 56074.

Other new locos continued to appear at regular intervals. 56076 was noted at Beckingham on 16th April, heading towards Gainsborough on a running-in turn with 36 HAAs in tow. Both 56077 & 078 emerged from Doncaster a month later.

Healey Mills became the focus of attention as April ran into May. 56025 arrived on April 27th for the start of crew training in advance of wholesale transfers at the start of the new timetable. The result was the depot losing fifteen 47/0s and 47/3s on May 10th, transferred to Tinsley, Immingham and Stratford

*Above:* A remote control experiment was tried out on 56073 & 074. They also had a flashing light fitted to the cab roof. 074 nears completion in early 1980 at Doncaster and will soon receive a new coat of paint. *Photo: Derek Porter.*

*Above:* After 56036's experimental Large Logo livery was unveiled in June 1979 at a Toton Open Day, it was decided that all future new Class 56s would receive the revised scheme. Despite its all-conquering nature, rail blue only appeared on three classes of locomotive from new - Classes 50, 56 and 87. The first of the 'production' Large Logo locos, 56084, waits in Doncaster Works reception sidings on 24th October 1980. It was not accepted into traffic until 26th November 1980 (allocated to Tinsley) and had only worked for eighteen hours when it was involved in a collision and had to be sent back to Doncaster for repairs. Photo: Paul Bettany

and replaced by fifteen 56s, predominately for Knottingley-based MGRs. The locos came from Tinsley's allocation - 56021-56032 and 56034, 073 & 074 - but eyebrows were probably raised only three days into the new regime when 56023 and one of its first MGRs was towed through Featherstone by 40169! Despite its recent re-allocation to HM, 56074 was at the Derby research centre on May 11th, allegedly for tests on its remote control equipment.

Also of note in this period, 56061 worked two Nuneaton round-trip drags on May 11th, while 067 spent three days parked at Hither Green depot on the Southern Region from the 15th to the 17th.

077 achieved instant attention on May 25th when it hauled the APT-P set in the Rocket 150 cavalcade. The loco had worked into the Rainhill area from York three days earlier, towing 92220 *Evening Star*, 'Schools' Class *Cheltenham* and 790 *Hardwicke*. Later in its career 077 had a small plate fixed on the bodyside, commemorating its part in the Rainhill celebrations.

Of far more relevance that weekend to those with little interest in the past was the appearance of the hybrid 56042 on a passenger train - the 11.35 Lime Street-Poole which the loco worked from Reading to New Street.

Meanwhile, back on the North Wales border, 56033 worked the first train into Dee Marsh sidings on 13th June 1980 in preparation for a new flow to transfer a stockpile of iron ore from Shotton to the South Wales plants. Shotton no longer made steel and had become a coating plant, a change of use which created a great deal of work for Class 56 in the ensuing years - primarily the daily transfer of hot rolled coil from Llanwern to Shotton for processing. This 'heavy metal' operation ran for the reminder of Class 56's career - 1,700 tons of hot sheet straight from the rolling mills of Llanwern, which still had to be warm when it reached Deeside, hence a need for speed. Trains were regularly worked over the Welsh Marches route by single 56s and it was often possible to feel the heat from the trailing load as it rushed through station platforms!

The import terminal at Bidston on the Wirral had also become redundant as far as iron ore was concerned, but found further use unloading Australian coal bound for Fiddler's Ferry power station near Widnes. This change of sourcing reduced the number of long-distance flows from the Yorkshire coalfield to Fiddler's Ferry from fifteen to only six return paths each day.

In another South Wales development, 56035 went to Ebbw Junction for crew training before the class took over a new flow of imported coal from Newport and Cardiff docks to Didcot. Staff at Swindon were also trained and the train loco would often be piloted through the Severn Tunnel by a second 56.

By the middle of 1980 Cardiff's allocation of ten locos (033, 035, 037, 038, 040, 041, 043 & 044-046) had nine regular duties. In order of priority:

i) 16.10 Danycraig-Stratford Freightliner and 02.10 return
ii) 07.00 Llanwern-Dee Marsh steel and 14.28 return
iii) Five daily trips to Didcot power station, requiring three locos
iv) Port Talbot-Llanwern iron ore, requiring two pairs.

To provide enough locos for all these turns, nine out of the ten had to be in traffic but, given their availability at the time, it was quite usual for one of the iron ore trains to revert to 3 x 37 traction.

The second phase of Class 56 milestone number three involved two locos - first in September 1980 083's release to traffic as the last new locomotive out-shopped in standard BR blue; and second, 084 entering service on 26th October, the first to be out-shopped in the Large Logo era proper.

The planned closure of the Woodhead line reared its head again in November 1980 when 56032 worked an MGR trial at Marsden as part of the alternative route evaluation for Yorkshire-Fiddler's Ferry trains - an operational constraint first investigated some two years earlier.

By the end of 1980 Cardiff had lost four of its 56 allocation, with 036 heading back to Toton in July and 033, 045 & 046 transferring to Tinsley on December 29th. The remaining seven - 035, 037, 038, 040, 041, 043 & 044 - continued to cover the Port Talbot-Llanwern iron ore circuit, the Danycraig-Stratford Freightliner and the Coatbridge liner.

*Above:* On 28th September 1980, 56014 was involved in an accident at Worksop. Damage to the loco resulted from a collision with the leading brake van. LIke the rest, this one also went to Doncaster for repairs, eventually returning to traffic in March 1982. Photo: Andy Pix

Conversion to Type 5 power continued as 1981 began. By February, 56054, 065 & 070 were stabled at Stoke Cockshute sidings in advance of their introduction in the Stoke area. At around the same time, 024 appeared at Thornaby for crew familiarisation.

By April, 56018 had clocked up enough hours to warrant a classified overhaul at Doncaster. The plan had been for works attention every four years but, given that 018 entered traffic in August 1977, this was some four months sooner than envisaged.

56013 & 50002 enjoyed a different day out on 10th March when they performed compression tests on the buffers of PGA hoppers. A rake of 60 was propelled into Merehead quarry to check that their buffers had enough strength to withstand the proposed increase in train length.

56083 made a surprise appearance on Teeside in the middle of May, working a number of coal, chemical and steel trains. On the 19th, for instance, it was noted passing Stockton with chemical tanks in tow.

In May and June 1981, the previously infrequent appearance of Class 56 on the Nuneaton drags become an established practice. The regular closure of the main line between Rugby and Birmingham called for diesel haulage of electric services over the non-electrified diversion between Nuneaton and Birmingham. Saltley generally provided the locos, and although ETH 47s were the preferred choice of the operations department, anything could turn up once all of those had been allocated. Class 56s were usually in abundance at the weekends so they became frequent performers. The 14th June 'Nuneaton diesel gala' produced 40060, 40162, 47080, 47200, 47262 & 56054. Sadly, the Type 5 disgraced itself by failing at Daw Mill.

On May 31st four more locos were transferred from Tinsley to Healey Mills - 56087, 088, 089 & 090. After only eight days, they went back to Tinsley - possibly the shortest depot allocation in the history of main line diesel traction. For the sake of historical context, this happened in the week that Finsbury Park lost its surviving Deltics. 55007, 009, 015 & 018 transferred to York, where they would see out their days on King's Cross-York semi-fasts.

The first naming of a Class 56 took place on 2nd June 1981. 56038 became *Western Mail* (a local newspaper) in a ceremony at Cardiff Central station and then worked the 12.10 Cardiff-Portsmouth as far as Bristol. 56071 & 078 were unlikely visitors to Stewarts Lane on the Southern Region later that month - visiting rather than re-allocating there. The second Class 56 naming occurred on 23rd July when 037 received the name of *Richard Trevithick*, but not before it was spotted, with covered nameplates, hauling a replica of the *Penydaren* loco through Cardiff. The naming took place later at Merthyr.

The north-east became the centre of attention in September, with Gateshead soon to become the latest depot to receive a Type 5 allocation. 009 was running around Tyneside and Wearside that month, followed by the appearance of 56093, which had recently been outshopped in large logo blue livery, on a Butterwell to Blyth power station training run. 027 arrived at Gateshead itself for staff familiarisation in October.

Most of the coal trains in the north-east at this time were either 20-ton HTV or HEA

*Above:* By the summer of 1980, up to five trains from Cardiff/Newport Docks were running to Didcot power station with imported coal. 56001 returns to South Wales with the empties at Shrivenham. Photo: Martin Loader

*Above:* The 1980 Rocket 150 event was a chance to show off Britain's newest locomotive (at the time) - 56077. This one had only been in traffic for five days when it was used to tow steam exhibits from York to Bold Colliery on 22nd May before taking part in the cavalcade three days later . . . hauling an APT set! Photo: John Powell

23

*Above:* There are numerous pictures of Class 56s working MGR coal trains from the Midlands *to* Didcot power station in the 1980s, but few taken at their destination. On 12th June 1983, 56064 draws slowly forward into the unloading building before dropping its load through the slatted floor. Each loco moved through at a steady 0.5 mph, as the wagon doors were tripped by the blue actuators on the right. *Photo: Martin Loader*

*Above:* In late 1980, the Stoke-on-Trent area received Toton Class 56s as replacements for Class 47/3s on the MGR trains out of Trentham colliery. Here, the first to arrive, 56057, stands in Cockshute yard during crew training on 25th November 1980. Unfortunately, servicing problems led to the withdrawal of the class from these services in 1981 and 47/3s took over again. *Photo: Paul Bettany*

hoppers working power station circuits. Before the 56s came, the HEAs were often hauled by pairs of 37s and, occasionally, by a Class 47. The HAA hoppers came later. Until then, it was not uncommon to see a mixture of 56s on modern HEA hoppers and vacuum-braked 37s on HTV rakes with a brake van.

Further evidence that Leamington Spa was a good place for haulage bashers to 'deckchair' (i.e pick a station and sit and wait until a loco failure produced a 56) came on 30th October when 004 rescued 47508 on the 11.50 Paddington-New Street. The 56 worked the train forward to Birmingham.

On 22nd November 1981, Gateshead received its initial allocation of 56075 & 076. They were reinforced by 077 & 078 in December and by 079, 080 & 081 on the third day of the new year.

Thus began a long association with Class 56 which lasted until their final withdrawal in 2004. Although some depots in the area closed, others rose in importance and it is now impossible to think of the type in the north-east without remembering Gateshead, Thornaby, Blyth Cambois, Sunderland South Dock and Tyne Yard.

# 3. WE HAVE A BETTER IDEA

*Above: 56029 enters Healey Mills yard with a loaded MGR working probably bound for Fiddler's Ferry power station. Photo: Steve Titheridge*

In the early 1980s the withdrawal of many older classes such as the 25s, 40s and 46s, combined with the reduction in the vacuum-braked wagon fleet, allowed the air-brake only Class 56s to widen their scope of operation still further. While many of the older wagon types were making their way to Shildon and Ashford for breaking, others made redundant by changing traffic patterns were cascaded to improve existing services. For example, PTA bogie hoppers sidelined because of cuts in the Scottish steel industry transferred to Foster Yeoman workings.

Industrial unrest, a major factor in the demise of the Callaghan government in 1979, continued. Ironically, the resulting election of a Conservative government under Margaret Thatcher gave the unions even greater cause for complaint, but the major confrontation of the miners strike was still two years away when 1982 dawned. Rail unions' anger at this time centred on the proposals for flexible rostering; this festering dispute resulted in 34 days lost to strikes, with stock standing idle at many locations.

1982 is probably best remembered, though, for the Falklands War and the visit to Britain of Pope John Paul II. On the railway front, although not quite in the same league, 40122 was reinstated to traffic and the first of the next generation of Type 5 motive power emerged from Doncaster. 58001-58006 were under construction during the year, and 58001 was rolled out for the press by the end of it.

The Selby diversion was nearing completion in 1982 - a long-overdue improvement which would not only speed up East Coast passenger services but also allow British Coal to continue removing millions of tonnes of Yorkshire sub-strata from beneath the old route between Doncaster and York. Class 56s based at Knottingley were almost

*Above: 56035 Taff Merthyr and 56038 Western Mail rumble through Cardiff with one of the Llanwern iron ore trains on 14th March 1983. 038 had been the first class member named in June 1981. 56s had replaced triple-headed 37s on these trains in 1979. These 30 wagon loads weighed up to 3,304 tonnes! Photo: Adrian Tibble*

entirely responsible for the movement of coal extracted from the Selby field.

The poor standard of the imported build had already prompted BR to place its add-on order for a further fifty-five locomotives with its own workshops - a bald statement of fact masking a pertinent question: Why order so many extra locos of an essentially out-moded design when the Class 58 was in prospect? The comparative ease of maintenance between the two types - the cramped and time-hungry interior of the Brush loco and the deliberately modular construction of the BREL Type 5 - makes the question doubly pertinent, but British Rail's philosophy of the early 1980s (if we can dignify it with the word) is lost in the mists of time. Whatever the thinking, Doncaster was nearing the end of its second construction batch (number 1510, covering locos 56091-115) as 1982 began. With the space required to begin the Class 58 build, production of the final twenty switched to Crewe (batch no. 1510; 56116-135). The one firm fact that does emerge is BR's original intention to build 150 locos of Class 56, but sanity prevailed when it was realised how much cheaper the in-house design would be to produce. The accountants simply made a paper adjustment of the allocated funds. So, for 56136-150 read 58001-015!

Back in the real world, the first three frames for the Crewe build - 56116/117/118 - were noted on 21st February 1982, but another year would pass before the first one was ready for delivery, creating an overlap with the last of the Doncaster construction.

BR continued with its new-found enthusiasm for naming locomotives, sometimes adopting a traditional approach - commemorating people and places with credible railway links - but also establishing a new and, some think, dubious practice of naming engines after its customers. In the case of British Coal and the CEGB, collieries and power stations were commemorated. Following the first three Class 56 namings in 1981 (*Western Mail*, *Richard Trevithick* and *Taff Merthyr*), 56040 was named *Oystermouth* at Swansea on 25th March 1982. In the middle of June, 56074 became the first Eastern Region loco to receive a name when its *Kellingley Colliery* plates were unveiled at 'The Big K', as it was known locally.

Enthusiasm for names then waned for more than a year, at least on Class 56, and 56031 had to wait until September 1983 before acquiring the *Merehead* plates commemorating Foster Yeoman's Somerset quarry. Before the ceremony, 031 worked into the quarry in multiple with 032, towing a pair of Mark 2 coaches for invited guests. The locos left with a massive train of 43 PTA tipplers, weighing in at 4,400 tonnes. As on previous occasions, the half-mile train was split at Acton, with the portions going forward behind each loco.

To round off this brief naming review, other examples included 56124 - named *Blue Circle Cement* on 24th October 1983 - and 56135, which became *Port of Tyne Authority* at Newcastle Central five days later.

Rewinding to 1982, the class took up further duties on the Western Region on 27th February. 56013 & 091 arrived at Westbury for trials before their introduction on the local heavy stone traffic which had increased significantly because of a boom in road and general construction. The locos arrived from Tinsley on loan, and their choice was interesting as equipment and layout differed between the batches. 013, for example, was from Romanian Batch 1507, while 091 was the first of Doncaster batch 1510. Apart from 56001, no other locos from batch 1507 were allocated to the Western Region during the BR period.

The middle Doncaster batch (1509, comprising 56061-090) was eventually represented on the WR by 061, 065 & 068 which arrived in 1985, followed by 072, 074 & 075 in 1988. No members of the final batch - 091-135 -were ever allocated to WR depots under BR (for batch differences, refer to the table on page 14).

56013 & 091 were typically trialled on Westbury-Acton workings. In time, class members were allocated to Bristol Bath Road but out-based at Westbury, the hub of the stone operation.

By mid-April, the class was becoming commonplace in the area. 56047 was noted at Westbury shed on 17th April, although Modern Railways magazine reported a month later that Westbury was next in line for Class

*Above:* Naming of Class 56s was never prolific. The Western Region started the ball rolling with three in 1981. Two years later, 56031 became *Merehead*, only the sixth of its class to named. Here, 031 approaches Circourt Bridge, Denchworth, with 6V11 10.03 Wolverton to Stoke Gifford ARC stone empties. Photo: Martin Loader

*Above:* 56019 hauls an empty MGR from Didcot power station through Wolvercote on 8th September 1982. This loco was used as a stand-by power generator at Heaton carriage sidings in Newcastle for four months from May 1977 following a power workers dispute. *Photo: Martin Loader*

58s once Toton had received its full allocation. In the event, the Western Region wisely kept to one Type 5 variant, gradually reinforcing the Westbury strength with more 56s. 037 arrived in August and was noted on trips to Merehead, 046 transferred from Healey Mills on 5th September and four more followed in October - 039 from Tinsley, 043 & 044 from Cardiff and 045 from Healey Mills. 036 and 034 joined the growing Bath Road fleet from Tinsley by the end of 1982. The official allocation was often supplemented by visitors; for example, 067 (TO) and 041 (CF) were stabled at Bath Road on 26th September.

The workings were varied. 56052 worked the newly-introduced Frome-Hayes Tarmac train on 9th October, and the shape of things to come was demonstrated on the night of December the 6th when 036 & 043 worked in multiple on a nocturnal test train of 66 Foster Yeoman 51-tonne PGA hoppers. Weighing in at 3,366 tonnes, the train ran from Merehead to Southall where it was split in time-honoured fashion. The two locos worked the portions separately to Brentford and Acton. Like the Port Talbot iron ore trials, it was proved that longer, heavier trains could be worked by the class, but implementation was often governed by the ability of the receiving terminals to handle increased length.

Significant Class 56 event number four was already under way at the start of 1983. The last of the Doncaster locos, 56115, transferred into BR stock on 30th January, eight months after its frames were laid. Earlier in the month, 56116 had reached the grey primer stage at Crewe. The loco undertook two test runs in February and went 'on the books' on 13th March - some *thirteen* months after frame-cutting.

Bristol received more 56s from Tinsley in the new year. 56033 arrived in January and 047 transferred from Toton in March. 031 joined them from Healey Mills by the middle of April. Crew training resumed in advance of new workings. 034, for instance, was noted in the Bristol area on a training run on 15th March, hauling 12 HAA hoppers.

As expected, Class 56 took over all Foster Yeoman workings from the start of the new timetable in May, with some, like the Merehead-Purfleet diagrams, calling for double-heading. Over the years, these trains had been worked by all manner of traction, but pairs of 37s had become established before the Class 56 conversion. The new (or not so new by now) Type 5s followed a list of types that had included Class 47s, WR

*Above:* Construction of the final twenty Class 56s was switched from Doncaster to Crewe in 1982 to allow Doncaster to concentrate on building Class 58. 56118 takes shape on 6th February 1983. *Photo: Paul Bettany*

*Above:* On 2nd July 1983, 56124 stands in the Crewe paint shop. Another eight weeks elapsed before the loco set off on its test run to Shrewsbury. Teething problems prevented it from entering service until 25th September. *Photo: Jerry Glover*

diesel-hydraulics and Class 50s. Working side-by-side with the 56s was the Class 58 development loco 47901. After initial allocation to Cardiff in November 1979, 901 transferred to Bristol in October 1982 and became a common site at Westbury on stone workings or at Bath Road under repair.

Needless to say, a few problems arose. On 18th July, 56031 failed on the 09.30 Wolverton-Stoke Gifford stone and was rescued by 37159 & 208 which had been lined up for the following 11.25 departure. The 09.30 eventually left after a 2-hour delay and the 11.25 was cancelled. On the same day, 56044 stalled at Woofferton on the 4S81 Pengam-Coatbridge liner and 37267 came to the rescue.

Often, it was 56s doing the rescuing, such as the 28th of July when 033 rushed to the aid of a stricken 50050 on the 07.40 Penzance-Liverpool. The 50 had caught fire and the 56 was requisitioned from a stone train at Tytherington. It is thought it worked through to Birmingham and returned 'home' with the 10.47 1V90 Glasgow-Plymouth as far as Bristol.

Only two days later, 56053 worked the 08.25 Manchester Piccadilly-Cardiff between Birmingham and Cardiff Central. Reports suggest the loco also worked the return leg, but this is unconfirmed. Similarly, it is reported that 040 worked into Paddington on 19th August with a failed loco and its train, but no other details are recorded.

As well as 56s rescuing passenger trains which failed en route, the occasional shortage of Class 47s and 50s brought about their diagramming to scheduled services from start to finish. By the same token, the lack of a replacement loco at a train's destination often resulted in 56s completing the planned diagram by working two or three consecutive services. In the former category, 032 worked 1B35 18.21 Paddington-Bristol Temple Meads throughout on 21st October.

The passenger rescue workings of the WR fleet sometimes proved elusive, but 56 fans could always resort to organised railtours originating in the area or passing through it. WR operating authorities made an extra effort to satisfy them on 20th August when the advertised 47901 was unavailable for the 'South Wales Venturer' charter, and produced this irresistible line-up:

| | |
|---|---|
| 50040 | London Bridge-Westbury |
| 56036 | Westbury-Cardiff |
| 37198 | Merthyr branch both ways |
| 56045 | Cardiff-Barry-Margam |
| 56052 | Margam-Llanelli-Cardiff |
| 50040 | Cardiff-London |

Eventually, Class 56 could turn up on almost anything but, despite several valiant attempts over the years, 1990 would come around on the calendar before one rolled across the Saltash bridge into Cornwall. Until then, Plymouth was about as far as they got. As one example, 56048 reached Laira on 4th September 1983, hauling an HST set for repair from Bristol St. Philip's Marsh. But the most common reason for 56 sightings at Exeter or Plymouth was the haulage of failed locomotives to Laira for attention, usually Class 50s.

The strengthening of the Bath Road fleet continued into 1984. 56048 & 049 arrived from Cardiff in mid-February, and the Great Western main line corridor to the south-east began to see more and more 56s on aggregates traffic. On 10th February, for instance, 043 & 050 appeared on a Westbury-Purfleet stone train, followed by 045 & 046 four days later. Tinsley's 094 provided a bit of variety on the 17th, partnering the more familiar 050. And so the whole operation settled down into routine, with individual locos often working the same train all week before a maintenance changeover at the weekend. As expected, WR examples dominated:

| | |
|---|---|
| w/c 11/5 | - 56048 & 049 |
| w/c 18/5 | - 56044 & 049 |
| w/c 25/5 | - 56046 & 050 |
| w/c 1/6 | - 56046 & 034 |

At least the spotters were happier than the haulage bashers. Tight control of the WR fleet meant that the whole lot could be ticked off in short order, and a weekend visit to Westbury, Bristol and Cardiff revealed the majority. However, this wasn't always the case; the odd one managed to slip away, like Cardiff's 56038 which went for an MGR haulage holiday in the Toton and Leicester area in May 1984.

*Above:* 56107 receives attention inside the shed at Thornaby on 19th June 1983. At this time the loco was based at Tinsley. *Photo: Jerry Glover*

*Above:* The first Class 56 to visit the North Wales coast. 56085 heads a trial run of flyash from Fiddler's Ferry to Llandudno at Llandulas on 29th September 1982. The flyash was used in the construction of the A55 trunk road. *Photo: John Powell*

Expansion of the aggregates traffic took 56054 onto the Southern Region in June 1984 for crew training runs between Eastleigh and Ardingley. Although a Toton loco at the time, 054 transferred to Cardiff the following September along with 051, 053, 055 & 056. This release of LMR locos was made possible by Toton's receipt of new build Class 58s - up to 58015 by the end of September 1984.

The flyash workings from Fiddler's Ferry power station near Widnes started in April 1983, following a two-week trial in September of the previous year involving 56085 and 56042. Flyash is a waste product from power stations and the Fiddler's output had been earmarked for construction of the new A55 road along the North Wales coast. This flow brought 56s into the areas on a regular basis, usually working to Llandudno from Widnes. 56067 appeared first, on 21st April, although the 2nd of August produced the unusual sight of 057 & 064 working together on the train. Normality returned with the appearance of a single 56087.

Apart from the flyash workings, Class 56 visits to the North Wales area have been infrequent, although when Crewe took over production of the final twenty locomotives, some were tested along the coast straight from works with a rake of stock or vans. It would seem that locos up to 56124, at least, worked a trial to Shrewsbury. 117 was noted there on 18th February and 124 on 26th August. By the time the final half-dozen were out-shopped from Crewe, the Holyhead service had become the standard method for trialling ex-works units. 56131, 133, 134 & 135 were all recorded on that working - the 1D43 09.20 Euston-Holyhead - piloting the rostered Class 47. Locos usually ran all the way to Holyhead and, if there were no problems, all the way back to Crewe, with the 47 only providing services power to the stock.

Fast-forwarding a whole decade, when the new freight companies began overhauling their newly-acquired Type 5s between 1993 and 1995, Crewe used a rake of Res vans as a test train with a Res 47 tucked inside as insurance. Other than the test runs, North Wales enjoyed a Loadhaul-liveried 56 on the 6D52 0706 Holyhead-Humber coke train in the mid-1990s, while EWS diagrammed one to the Mostyn Docks-Immingham steel train in 2001 . . . which more-or-less provides a full summary of Class 56 workings along the coast . . .

. . . except for the much-travelled 56042's appearance on the A55 flyash train, followed by its involvement in Research Department bogie rotational testing on the Blaenau branch in the spring of 1983. Further testing by the BR engineers took place in April 1984 on the same branch, this time to carry out deflection tests on the timber viaduct at Afon Llugny. If only they had asked for 56073 & 074, the undoubtedly nervous driver could have watched the test from dry land, using the remote control fitted experimentally to both these locos.

Returning to 1983, the May timetable created many re-allocations as usual, with all Healey Mills 56s transferring to Tinsley or Bristol. For the Tinsley batch, it was only a paper transfer as they continued to be out-based at Knottingley for the Aire Valley MGR trains. Healey Mills received Class 31s from

*Above:* This is why it's called flyash, and why it's usually carried in covered wagons. 56068 heads through Prestatyn en route to Llandudno on 15th August 1983. *Photo: John Powell*

29

*Above:* Life's a drag. 56071 after arrival at Birmingham New Street on 24th July 1983 with the 10.00 Euston-Wolverhampton which it had dragged from Nuneaton. The Class 86 took the train forward by electron power. *Photo: M Headley*

*Above:* A typical scene at Doncaster in the 1980s. 56008 heads through the centre road with an MGR working on 16th May 1983. *Photo: Adrian Tibble*

*Above:* 56072 runs light through Nuneaton on a snowy 16th February 1983. *Photo: Adrian Tibble*

Tinsley to replace the Type 5s (hardly a like-for-like swop) and also lost some if its Class 40 allocation to the LMR at Longsight.

In a further reorganisation, Birmingham area loco maintenance, previously carried out at Tyseley and Saltley, transferred to Bescot on 1st August with heavier repairs going to Crewe or Longsight. The changeover took several weeks to implement; by the 20th, Tyseley still had 40063 under repair for derailment damage, 56096 needing wheelset work, and also 56067. On the same day, Saltley's repair & maintenance collection included 20150, 45013, 46046, 47362 and 56039.

Class 56 continued to work Nuneaton drags in haphazard fashion on Sundays in 1983. Proof that anything could happen was demonstrated on March 28th when 56101 worked the 10.00 Wolverhampton-Euston from New Street, but encountered problems at Nuneaton and couldn't return to Birmingham. Its next diagrammed duty, the 13.00 ex-Wolverhampton, was worked by 25269!

Despite the occasional mishap, these workings remained a regular feature of Sunday travel in the West Midlands until 1992, when essential repairs to Arley tunnel necessitated a diversion via Stafford. Intercity, which had to hire in the dragging locos to keep its trains running, found this routing worked much better. Hire charges were eliminated as the trains' regular AC traction could run round at Stafford and proceed via the Trent Valley to Euston.

Despite the influx of Australian coal through the Bidston terminal, Class 56 continued to shift the product of the Yorkshire and Nottinghamshire coalfields to Fiddler's Ferry, producing a regular flow of MGRs through Stockport and Stalybridge. With the line via Woodhead now closed, the earlier test runs to evaluate the Type 5s' capability over the more challenging Diggle route immediately proved their worth. Locomotives used on this work were often Tinsley allocations from the later batches, although most of the thirty Romanians appeared over the years.

The sight and sound of Class 56 dicing with Diggle was comparatively short-lived. When faster Class 158 units were introduced to passenger services, there were fewer daytime paths for heavy freights, and so they ran via Todmorden instead.

Coal traffic from Nottinghamshire also found its way to Garston via Stockport, where 56015 was noted on 26th August 1983.

As well as the coal trains, the odd 56 could also appear on a passenger turn in the north-west. The 29th October, for instance, threw up 56003 assisting 47433 on a Nottingham-Glasgow service. The start point for the rescue is unknown, but the 56 certainly worked the train between Manchester Victoria and Preston.

Crossing from west to east, the 31st of July produced the first reported sighting of a 56 on the Yorkshire coast when F&W's 'White Rose Rambler' railtour arrived from Doncaster at Scarborough behind 56122. The charter had started from Plymouth with 50008 in charge as far as Bristol, from where 56033 worked forward to Toton and gave way to a pair of 20s. The same locos worked the return legs, apart from a Class 50 substitution on the final Bristol-Plymouth section.

Back at the day-to-day, efficiency improvements to the MGR system continued

**GRIDS**

to be implemented some twenty years after its introduction. One such investment was the Oxley chord, a new section of line allowing direct access between the Staffordshire collieries and Ironbridge power station, rather than a time-consuming run-round en route. 56060 was spotted working the 11.01 Ironbridge-Silverdale empties over the new chord on 9th September 1983, but 47/3s continued to appear alongside the newer power, confirming they were still a useful component in the MGR operation.

The hybrid 56042 was allocated to the Derby research department during 1983 and often ventured out with a test coach in tow to monitor its bogie performance. One such test occurred on 2nd July when the loco worked an MGR rake between Leicester and Loughborough. A month later the 7O85 Toton-Northfleet MGR provided a similar facility.

56036 made the news on 12th August when fourteen of its empty ARC wagons derailed near the Bletchley flyover. The loco was untouched by the incident, but the breakdown crane was summoned to re-rail the wagons, providing 25300 with some extra work.

By the end of 1983, delivery of new locos from Crewe had reached 56128, with 56129 complete and frames laid up to 56135 - a considerable speeding-up of the programme compared to the works' early performance.

But, as construction of Class 56 neared its conclusion, dark clouds were beginning to gather on the horizon.

1984 was the year of living dangerously. Although it is not the function of this book to be a social or political tract, it must be acknowledged that the miners strike of 1984 had far-reaching consequences for traditional labour relations in Britain, with some calling it the last great battle in the class war. Others might argue that the class most affected was the 56, but that is taking a slightly narrow view of such a momentous year.

It is true that the locos' workload was greatly reduced during the early months of the strike, and that the major programme of pit closures, the root cause of the dispute, went ahead in the ensuing years. Britain's demand for power remained, though, and actually rose during the 1980s boom. The answer was to increase tonnages of cheap imported coal, which still needed moving from docks to power station. So, it is a little misleading to suggest that Class 56 had its reason to exist undermined by the 1984 dispute.

Obviously expecting major trouble when the pit closure plan was announced, the government had developed a scheme to bring less-efficient stand-by power stations back into front-line service, including oil-fired and nuclear stations. It had also settled an earlier dispute with the miners to allow time for coal stocks to be reinforced at the coal-fired stations. Beginning the strike in early spring, when demand for power rapidly declines, also played into the government's hands. Even so, once the stockpiles were used up, the ability to shift oil and imported coal into the stations would become critical.

With this in mind, it is rumoured that Mrs Thatcher personally intervened to improve a proposed pay offer to the rail workers to ensure they had no reason to take secondary action in support of another dispute. Similarly, action by dock workers and steel unions in conjunction with rail staff could have dealt a

*Above: 56132 nears completion at Crewe on 28th April 1984. Photo: Paul Robertson*

mortal blow to the government but, despite secondary action in some areas, the dockers and steel workers did not deliver the blanket support the miners wanted. The result was that, by one means or another, power stations continued to supply current to the grid.

[By way of historical background, the Conservative government was supremely confident about taking on the might of the trades unions after winning a landslide majority in the 1983 General Election.]

The strike began on March 12th and had an immediate impact on rail freight movements. Within six days, all production had stopped in the South Wales pits, with barely any coal movement taking place by rail. Despite the pay bargaining manoeuvre, rail staff did take secondary action in some areas, with coal movements 'blacked' at certain depots. Trains were either cancelled or worked over different routes by more compliant crews.

In July, rail union leaders Jimmy Knapp and Ray Buckton issued a statement proudly claiming that only ten coal trains were running each day rather than the scheduled 356. Whether this is true is equally questionable, but the industrial action had certainly stopped a great many freight locos. With so many standing spare at depots, Class 56s and the newer 58s were diverted onto flows they had never worked before. On Teeside, for example, 56s were deployed on steel trains. In the Midlands, Class 58 began to appear on the Toton-Ashburys Speedlink services - a gross waste of power as the load often comprised only a couple of VGA wagons or a single bolster weighing considerably less than the locomotive. All around the country, occasional activity took place against the backdrop of 56s standing in yards on rakes of empty MGR hoppers, while depots looked distinctly overcrowded on weekdays. On one

*Above: Two weeks later, 13th May, 56132 had reached the paint shop. The following week it went out on test and, after a bit of final tinkering, was delivered to Gateshead on 10th June. Photo: Paul Bettany*

*Above:* With the number of daily coal trains much reduced in July 1984, the miners strike was having an impact on Class 56. Those that weren't left idling in depots could be found on all manner of non-coal-related workings, such as this - 56042 shifting an oil train past Healey Mills. *Photo: Steve Titheridge*

day in May, four stood idle at Healey Mills - 078, 096, 106 & 112 - while a similar survey at Barrow Hill in July revealed 122, 102 & 015.

LMR and ER locos side-lined by the dispute often joined the WR allocation for brief periods. Between November 1984 and June 1985, all the WR-allocated 56s worked the Westbury-Purfleet service, but the following list is interesting because of the significant number of Toton- and Tinsley-allocated locos joining them on this service: 56001, 56016, 56031-56041, 56043-56050, 56052-56059, 56067, 56068, 56075, 56082, 56084-56087, 56090, 56117.

Although the South Wales steelworks needed large volumes of coal, the WR fleet was not directly affected by the strike. Steel traffic continued normally, with 56s powering a number of the Port Talbot-Llanwern iron ore trains. Stone services, too, ran as scheduled, although 'foreign' locos made occasional appearances, such as 56049 & 071 on the ARC bogie tipplers into Merehead on 12th October 1984.

With so many 56s standing spare in the coalfields, it is not surprising that the odd one ventured much further away. On 1st June 1984, Tinsley's 56094 was reported as the first of the class to appear at Eastfield, after it had towed 47004 from Gateshead. The loco returned light engine immediately, lest it became stranded in Glasgow where no crews had the traction knowledge to move it.

After almost a year's duration, the bitter dispute came to an end on 9th March 1985. Although a degree of normality returned, the landscape had changed forever. Even in the early months, serious concern had arisen about the long-term future of the coal industry and of certain pits in particular. Some had become unusable after such a long period without essential maintenance and water pumping, and would never be worked again. By abandoning these older pits and preventing maintenance staff from doing their work, it could be argued that the miners union played into the government's hands - one reason why only the so-called super pits survived in the long-term. In fact, the number of closures turned out to be far greater than the government's original plan had proposed, partly because the cheap imports had gained such momentum.

This change in the pattern of operation, and the longer distances from port to generator, re-drew the map as far as the railways were concerned and forced a major rethink on how coal was to be moved in the future.

*Above:* On 24th November 1984, 58017 & 56086 stood idle at Toton as the strike ground on. The 58 was only a month old and already struggling to find work. *Photo: Paul Bettany*

# 4. THE WRITING ON THE WALL

*Above: 56034 & 048 pass Hungerford Common with the Purfleet-Merehead stone empties on 3rd September 1984, just before Foster Yeoman's announcement that it was investing in General Motors Class 59s to replace pairs of Grids on these workings. Photo: Martin Loader*

If the headline events of 1984 had cast a question mark over the long-term future of Class 56, another development in the same year was to have a far more significant effect on the British-built Type 5 freight locomotive, although some fifteen years would elapse before the full impact was felt.

As the year drew to a close, the Foster Yeoman company ordered four Class 59 locos from the American General Motors for its stone workings out of Merehead Quarry, with delivery due in December 1985. For some time, Yeomans had been unhappy about the reliability of the Class 56s BR provided to work its trains, but its solutions to the problem proved increasingly contentious. At first it proposed that a dedicated fleet of 56s be established, with maintenance carried out by its own staff to improve both availability and reliability. Mindful of its militant unions, the BR Board politely declined, or refused point blank, depending on which contemporary account is to be believed. This was slightly curious when the best Type 5 availability figures at the time came from smaller depots with a dedicated allocation. Knottingley and Blyth on the Eastern Region, for instance, consistently achieved a high figure, as did Toton with its 58s. These locos, of course, were maintained by BR staff, not the private sector - undoubtedly a factor in the BRB's thinking. A cynic, of course, might suspect that Board members, having seen the physical pitched battles of the miners strike on their televisions, had recoiled at the prospect of similar scenes on the railway.

Yeomans refused to be deflected from its cause and opted for the American route - a double slap in the face for BR. Not only would the 56s be displaced from the stone traffic, but the company's own staff would maintain the imported locos. Given the militancy of the rail unions, these proposals may seem like prodding a tiger with a hot poker, but they also reveal the depth of Yeomans' frustration with the unloved Class 56.

Fast-forwarding a year or so, repeated reliability problems with the class eventually prompted BR to consider consolidating all 56 repairs at one depot - a centre of excellence like Toton. With the fleet spread around five depots - Toton, Tinsley, Bristol, Cardiff and Gateshead - the standard of maintenance was patchy. Average miles per casualty were no better than 6,000 against a target of 15,000 and, throughout its life, the class never achieved much better than 79-82% availability. Figures varied regionally, depending on the local CM&EE's aspirational target.

Despite the problems, the 56 was still the best BR could offer at the start of 1985 and still more were transferred to the Western Region to cope with the increasing demands of the construction industry. Like the A55 project in North Wales, the class was to play a big part in transporting materials for the construction of the M25 London orbital motorway.

In January, 56057 moved from Toton to Bath Road while Tinsley's 56001 was earmarked for Bristol, having received a number of modifications aimed at improving its reliability. 001 worked south via the 6C06 Immingham-Severn Tunnel Junction freight on 19th April, exchanging places with 56043 which went back to Tinsley.

By the middle of May, 56061, 065 & 068 had also joined the Bristol collection, although such a solid WR allocation didn't stop foreign 56s appearing on the Region. 56014, for example, appeared at Bath on 23rd February with a westbound oil train.

Despite the arrival of the 'improved' 56001, regular reports of failures continued to appear in the railway press and did nothing to improve the locomotives' reputation.

In another significant development, Bristol Bath Road began carrying out 'F' exams on the WR 56 allocation in 1985. 051 & 056 were identified as the first for the treatment, which also included a repaint into Railfreight Grey livery. Landore had earlier carried out major exams on 56047, 048 & 049, but they were out-shopped in large logo blue, similar to 56036.

Typical duties to and from the west included oil, coal, steel and liner trains, as well as the aggregates traffic between Westbury and Purfleet. Notable sightings of the time included 56036 providing rear-end assistance to 56053, which had unusually set off unaided with one of the heavy Port Talbot-Llanwern

*Above:* Toton's 56072 passes St. Albans with an MGR on 4th July 1985. *Photo: Paul Robertson*

iron ore trains on 16th May and failed to restart at Gaer Junction Newport. A month later, the 4S81 Pengam-Coatbridge liner was powered by both 56036 & 034. In complete contrast the same day, 56054 & 061 worked through Newport under power with a single box van and 3 SPA plate carriers.

Double-heading was becoming commonplace, perhaps in an effort to reduce the impact of a failure, although some trains actually required the use of two locos. In addition, many of the heavy freights were piloted through the Severn Tunnel - a regular task for a 56, producing pairs on workings such as the Didcot-bound MGRs. Occasionally, a Class 37 pilot would produce a not-so-common pairing. As examples, 37214 & 56040 appeared on 12th September, followed by 37162 & 56051 the next day.

In the same way that LMR locos worked onto the WR, so the process worked in reverse. As one example, the diagrammed Toton loco was replaced on 22nd June by Canton's 56049 on the Hayes-Cliffe Vale Tarmac empties.

The Westbury-Purfleet stone trains continued to be worked by Cardiff's allocation, although strangers from the Midlands appeared regularly in the early months of 1985 until their coal workings restarted at the end of the miners strike. Between November 1984 and June 1985, the following were noted on the stone: 56016, 058, 059, 067, 075, 082, 084, 085, 086, 087, 090 & 117.

August the 19th's Purfleet working was handled by 56048 (BR) and 56052 (CF). Manned by a Southall crew, it was one of the very few trains passing through the Ripple Lane area that day as the local guards were on strike.

Failures-wise, the locos continued to suffer. 56043, completely crippled, was noted at Severn Tunnel Junction in September awaiting a tow to Doncaster in the consist of the 09.45 STJ-Bescot freight. The loco entered the works on 5th October for an Intermediate overhaul. In the same week 56048 caught fire, 56018 failed at Chandlers Ford with the Ardingley stone train and 56037 came to a halt at Theale with engine trouble.

Despite these problems, WR pairs rostered to the Purfleet workings continued to work with some consistency, although a Midlands interloper occasionally appeared on these trains. Giving the lie to any assertion that coal workings had returned to their pre-strike pattern, Westbury depot held the following collection of Tinsley and Toton locos on November 19th: 56033, 034, 035, 040, 043, 051, 055, 057, 062, 066, 075, 082 & 108. A further visit on 28th December revealed 56075, 119 & 120 alongside WR-allocated 56056 & 068.

Considering the long delays experienced during the introduction of Class 56, it must have come as a pleasant surprise to someone when the four Foster Yeoman Class 59 locos touched down on the 24th of January 1986, only one month late. What's more, they worked almost straight out of the box. And so began a period of change on the railway, during which the Class 56 would be both involved but also seriously affected.

Understandably, Foster Yeoman was keen to find out just how much its new American locos could handle, but the Somerset company wasn't the only one looking across the Atlantic. Reports of the period suggest that BR itself was moving closer to giving out tenders to US suppliers than at any time since the 1955 modernisation plan. The greatest enthusiasm for US-built locos was coming from the freight sector, largely because of disenchantment with the new Class 58. BR's supposedly definitive heavy freight loco was suffering problems, primarily turbocharger surging and chronic wheelslip which had

*Above:* 56074 awaits its next turn at Peterborough on 14th January 1985. The first of the Eastern Region's locos to be named, its *Kellingley Colliery* nameplates were unveiled on 14th June 1982. *Photo: Adrian Tibble*

forced operators to reduce trailing loads. Reports of US availability figures in the 90-95% range must have made the Brits green with envy, especially as most BR fleets were giving no more than 70-80%.

There was more than a passing interest, then, when Yeomans set up a test on Savernake bank on the Berks & Hants line on 9th February 1986. The main line was closed to normal traffic for the three hours of the trial, which began with 56055 & 031 hauling 59002 and 43 PTA hoppers from Westbury to Woodborough. There, the British locos were detached, leaving the American import to tackle the bank with the 4,386 tonnes trailing load of the hoppers. The plan was to re-attach the 56s to provide an additional 250 tonnes of weight if the 59 successfully managed to shift the first load. It didn't. The loco developed an earth fault and had to be rescued. So it was that 055 & 031 heaved 4,386 tonnes up Savernake (plus their own weight and that of the dead 59) to the trial's terminating point at Theale. Curiously, there were no reports in the railway press afterwards about how well *they* had performed.

Once egg had been wiped off faces, a repeat was organised soon after, with 59001 as train engine, 59004 in reserve, and 56033 & 049 as additional weight . . . or assisting engines if required. This triall went well and the rest, as they say, is history.

Following the successful trial, indecent haste best describes the replacement of Class 56 with American power on the stone workings. Their involvement ceased on Friday the 14th of February 1986 when 56035 & 047 hauled Yeoman product away from Westbury for the last time. On the following Monday, 59004 appeared on the daily Purfleet and for most of the week. Thereafter, other GM locos worked the turn solidly for a fortnight until 56052 & 055 made an unexpected reappearance on the 25th.

Despite the regularity, a single daily turn for three working locos meant they weren't clocking up significant hours - barely 81 each after the first fortnight. The exception, 002, had clocked up only 16; it was still awaiting replacement cables after suffering the earth fault during the first Savernake trial.

A whole month passed before the first reported Class 59 failure in normal traffic - 001 on the Purfleet job of 13th March 1986. As there was no Class 56 to hand, 47128 had to rescue the train, but the new locos' unblemished record during their first month of operation must have concentrated minds within BR management.

On an equally positive note, Class 56's performance wasn't all doom and gloom at this time. Some locos achieved long spells of reliable performance and the nature of the diagrams often produced the same loco on the same train day after day. 56033, for example, worked the Westbury-Ardingley duty for four consecutive days from the 20th March, 56001 worked the Coatbridge liner for a whole week as April rolled into May, and 56034 performed impeccably for five consecutive days on the Westbury-Ardingley ARC train at the start of the new month . . . possibly spurred on by the thought of being abandoned in Chichester Yard for four days like 56060. This one had failed on the Ardingley train on 7th February and had been dumped to await an indeterminate retrieval.

*Above:* 56004 was seriously damaged in a head-on collision with a pair of Class 31s on 30th July 1982. Initially the loco was stored at Immingham, but later moved to Doncaster where repairs were finally authorised in early 1984. The loco, complete with new cab, stands outside the Test House in May 1984. *Photo: Derek Porter*

As well as the high-profile double-headers they retained, WR 56s also worked on a number of oil flows such as 56053 on the 6A16 Robertson-Theale Murco tanks on 1st May 1986. It wasn't all plain sailing, though, and the Type continued its mission to seek out and spread any permanent way that wasn't in tip-top condition. 56040, for example, did the civil engineers a favour by highlighting a weak spot at Theale oil terminal on 11th April. Its derailment highlighted the variety of motive power in everyday use - 33043 recovered the cement tanks and the breakdown train was brought to site by a pair of 31s.

As if the spectre of American imports wasn't bad enough, the class also suffered threats from within the BR ranks. On 17th December, 37902 successfully worked the 6M33 Llanwern-Dee Marsh steel train unaided, a development which would ensure 56s became less common over the steeply-graded Welsh Marches route. The previous day's working had been entrusted to 37694 & 695 and it was this variant which became the normal traction on these trains, although 56s continued to appear on occasions.

Although the Western Region was an understandable focus of attention in the mid-1980s, there was plenty of Class 56 activity elsewhere. On the Eastern Region, locos continued to be allocated to Tinsley and Gateshead, from where they worked a variety of flows in addition to the mandatory MGRs.

A trip along the East Coast Main Line usually revealed examples at almost every location beyond Peterborough, where the class could be seen on the Fletton flyash trains. Doncaster was obviously a good spot, not just in the works yard or stabled at Carr Loco, but also working MGRs through the area.

*Above:* After eight years in traffic, 56038 underwent its second major overhaul at Crewe. Here, the work has reached the half-way stage on 15th June 1986. *Photo: Paul Bettany*

*Above:* 56062 approaches Oxford on 22nd April 1986 with 7V65 11.56 Desford Colliery-Didcot power station MGR working. At this time, the majority of coal trains to Didcot (there were often as many as fifteen a day) were in the hands of Class 58s, so a 56 was both a rarity and a bonus. *Photo: Martin Loader*
*Below:* 56007 looks immaculate after a recent repaint as it approaches Holgate, York, on 24th July 1986. *Photo: Neil Harvey*

GRIDS

*Above:* 56132 heads through Marsden with 6E20 Glazebrook to Haverton Hill tanks on 9th August 1986. *Photo: John Hooson*

York Yard North was another likely location. Toton and Gateshead locos exchanged places there on MGR traffic heading for the Aire Valley power stations. Even further north, Tyne Yard always contained a few, but they were usually hidden behind the concrete flyover - a legacy from the days when Tyne also had the hump.

East Coast rescues arose occasionally too. On 14th June 1985, for instance, 56009 took over 4E77 Coatbridge-Tilbury at Newark after the failure of 47305. The train eventually continued on its way an impressive 722 minutes late. Similarly, 56s also ventured into East Anglia on rescue missions. On November 12th 56012 arrived at the Norwich Trowse terminal with a stone train in tow. Barely a month later, 56117 appeared at Stratford with the 4C64 liner from Follingsby after working the train from Doncaster following the failure of 47482.

As for feeder services on the East Coast, the Stanlow-originating Shell Mex trains to Jarrow and Leeds were regularly entrusted to Class 56 and were also likely to produce 'rare' LMR and WR locos on Tyneside. On 20th May 1986, 56035 worked into Leeds Oil Terminal with 6E25 from Stanlow and returned with 7M82 empties, while 56038 produced for three consecutive days in September 1986 and reappeared on 15th October. Sadly, these workings were not without their dramas either. On 4th August 1986, for example, 56103 came to a halt three times while making the climb over the Pennines with 6E18 Stanlow-Leeds, which must have thrilled the operating department no end. Two months later, the same climb caught out 56008 on 6M54 Leeds-Stanlow. 56073, working MGR empties from Fiddler's Ferry to Healey Mills, abandoned its wagons and took the tanks forward - an interesting demonstration of traffic priorities. Less dramatic, 56088 made it to Skipton from Stanlow with a bitumen working, the first recorded sighting of a 56 there.

To emphasise the numerical spread of the batches, a survey of South Yorkshire depots on a weekend in June 1986 revealed the following:

| | |
|---|---|
| Worksop | 56013/108/109/111/118 |
| Shirebrook | 56011/023/024/027/094/095/097/099/101/106/107/110/112/115/128/135 |
| Tinsley | 56005/009/025/028/077/086/091/096/103/105 |
| Healey Mills | 56042/120 |
| Knottingley | 56002/003/004/018/020/021/022/026/073/074/081/092/098/100/102/116/117/121/122 |
| Doncaster | 56008/014/016/019/029/127 |
| Frodingham | 56119 |

At the same time, Doncaster works held: 56012 for unclassified power unit repairs, 56060 & 063 for Intermediate overhaul, and 56058/051/131 for collision repair. In the same month the following also visited Doncaster for unclassified attention, such as a bogie change or a load bank test: 56075/015/095/107/017/035/037.

On another weekend in June, a survey ranging from the London Midland depots to the north-east revealed 85 locos concentrated at only thirteen locations:

| | |
|---|---|
| Toton | 56063/069/082/088 |
| Worksop | 56016/024/094/113 |
| Bescot | 56080 |
| Saltley | 56058 |
| Shirebrook | 56004/026/074/075/079/093/096/106/108/112/117/123/124/126 |
| Barrow Hill | 56018/19/30 |
| Tinsley | 56010/013/015/022/027/099/101/107/129 |
| Healey Mills | 56073/077/098/120/122 |
| Carr Loco | 56005/008/091/109/125 |
| Gateshead | 56111/116/130 |
| Blyth | 56021/056/134/135 |
| Sunderland | 56078/095/119/128/133 |
| Thornaby | 56007/076/081/103 |
| Doncaster Wks | 56017/028/064/066/071/087/089 |

Of the notable workings in the north-east and on the East Coast generally, 56006's visit to Gateshead was mildly surprising in April 1985. How it arrived there, no-one knows, but the next day local operators put the 'pioneer' to work on a rake of HEA hoppers from Wearmouth colliery to Blyth Cambois power station.

Slightly more eyebrow-raising was 56134's rescue of a failed DMU - the 10.43 Carlisle-Newcastle at Wylam the following October. The same month, the lack of any available 56 resulted in a slightly under-powered 25323 having to struggle northwards with a Stanlow-Jarrow oil train, while a southbound Tyne-York coal train resorted to the unusual pairing of

37

25288 & 56115. A month later, BR Type 2s again became the motive power of choice when 25175 & 25201 replaced a failed 56105 on York-Tees coal empties.

1986's East Coast notables included 56077 making a test run to Scarborough on 28th March after repairs at Doncaster and the appearance of 56023 on the 14.45 Leeds-King's Cross from Doncaster to London on 9th May. Once released at the terminus, the loco was immediately attached to the 18.50 Harrogate service and this time made it all the way to Leeds, if not Harrogate! Two weeks later, 56098 surprised spotters at Doncaster when it hauled the correctly-formed HST set northwards, including power cars 43101 & 117, on what was rumoured to be the 11.30 King's Cross-Dundee service. To round off the passenger dabbling that year, 56076 removed a failed 47529 from 1S77 King's Cross-Edinburgh on 24th September to allow 47586 to take the train forward.

This was merely light relief, though, from the daily grind of shifting freight. The pattern of loco operation had begun to change during 1985. Knottingley, for instance, was seeing far more 'foreign' 56s from Toton, a precursor to major changes in November involving the re-allocation of some thirty locos. Twelve moved from Tinsley to Toton (029/030/071-076/084-088), eight from Gateshead to Tinsley (56076-56083) and ten from Tinsley back to Gateshead (56113-56122). The latter resulted in the transfer of the *Blyth Power* nameplates from 56076 to 56134. The logic behind these transfers seems to have been the hope that grouping of similar build batches at the same depots would bring benefits in terms of quality of maintenance.

North of the border, the 56 continued to be a rare beast, although the frequency of sightings did increase during 1986. 56130, for example, arrived at Millerhill on 17th March with 6S56 Blyth-Fort William; a fortnight later, 56133 worked south from Millerhill with a polybulk service.

In the autumn there was a flurry of 56 activity on a Tuesdays and Thursdays-only coal working to Oxwellmains cement works near Dunbar. The trains worked in from the south during the night and awaited the passage of the 07.35 Edinburgh-King's Cross HST before returning with empties. Six 56s worked these turns in the space of two months:

| | |
|---|---|
| 56133 | 9th September |
| 56134 | 12th September |
| 56127 | 19th September |
| 56134 | 3rd October |
| 56088 | 31st October |
| 56115 | 7th November |

The year rounded off with 56064 at Millerhill on a cement working on 23rd December, one day after Romanian 019 had appeared at the same location.

Meanwhile, on the London Midland Region, the 56s' sphere of activity continued to spread in 1985. Crew training was underway in the north-west and 56093 reached Barrow on a light engine working from Carlisle on March 8th. It then left for Carnforth on what was believed to be the first appearance of the type on the Cumbrian coast route. Newton Heath also received a crew trainer in March, but 56066 failed and its replacement, 56024, didn't arrive from Tinsley until the end of the month.

56099 made itself equally unpopular on Merseyside in May when it derailed all wheels at Allerton depot on the 7th. Astonishingly, the same loco suffered the same 'earth fault' at the same depot only a fortnight later!

As more crews became familiar with the class, examples would appear at more and more unusual locations. For example, Gateshead's 56079 worked 6P87 Walton Old Yard-Burn Naze on 11th July and during its layover before the return 6F87 was put to work as the Blackpool North shunter! What a difference a decade makes - by 1994/95, when Transrail operated the service, 56s were almost mundane on this duty.

Probably on another training mission, 56119 ran light engine to Castleton on 14th February 1985. In later years, trains to and from the CWR depot were often used to test locos coming off repairs at Toton as it was an out-and-back turn with little chance of the loco finding itself allocated to another diagram once it reached Castleton. One wonders how often that went wrong?!

Despite all this wing-spreading, the class as a whole reached another low point in September 1985 with some 30 stopped for

*Above:* 56001 heads west through Langley with 6V17 10.00 Allington to Stoke Gifford ARC stone empties on 6th November 1986. *Photo: Martin Loader*

attention, partly because of a spate of camshaft failures. Availability dived below 80% and the miles per casualty figure dropped to the previous low of 6,000. As if that weren't bad enough, the propensity to self-combust had shown itself again earlier in the year when 56014 caught fire at West Burton while working 7D43 Worksop-Immingham.

The LMR suffered particularly badly, sometimes with only eight locos available to cover thirteen duties - no doubt the reason why Tinsley's 56095 appeared on the Toton-dominated 6H52 West Burton-Fletton flyash on 7th September. The Toton-Northfleet coal trains were frequent victims of these shortages, ending up with a 47 or, as a last resort, a 58. The 'super' Type 5 was not a popular replacement as it had to come off at Cricklewood, where traction knowledge of the class ran out. If a slow-speed-fitted 47 couldn't be found to take the train forward, Cricklewood had no choice but to terminate the working.

Of course, availability of Class 56 was never an issue at weekends, so they continued to appear on various unscheduled passenger turns during this period. On 15th February 1985, 56091 dragged WCML electric services in both directions through Warrington Bank Quay during an OLE power outage, most likely working between Crewe and Preston. The following June, 56070 rescued a failed 47541 at Stalybridge on 1E59 Liverpool-Newcastle and worked the train as far as Leeds, where 47189 took over.

In the first month of 1986, bogie rebel 56042 dragged the 11.05 Glasgow-Euston around the back of Carlisle Citadel on the freight-only lines after another overhead line incident at Upperby. Later the same year, on 8th August, 042 took over a Fareham-York excursion at Derby after 47315 expired. There is no record of the return run, so the York controller must have found something less contentious to take the trippers back to Hampshire.

Barely twenty-four hours elapsed before 56066 was called up to work the weekday 08.20 Newcastle-Llandudno forward from Chester when 45135 failed. As it was mid-August and the non-heat season, the 56 could also have worked the return from Llandudno, but it didn't. Enthusiasts often wondered why 56s were replaced like this, but of course 066 wasn't standing at Chester just in case a 45/1 failed. It would have had a diagrammed freight train to work, and the Peak, even if Chester had fixed it, would have been unsuitable for the duty as it had no slow-speed control, never mind the thorny issue of traction knowledge.

*On 22nd June 1986, 56083, the last loco out-shopped in all-over rail blue, finally gets a large logo after a visit to Doncaster for an Intermediate overhaul. Photo: Paul Bettany*

*Above: Between January 1987 and August 1988, the 1D43 09.20 Euston-Holyhead was used to test locomotives after their overhaul at Crewe. The 56 piloted the rostered Class 47, which only provided electric train heat. On 26th June 1988, 56088 passes Prestatyn. Photo: John Powell*

39

*Above:* On 31st July 1987, 56090 departs from Rhyl with 1D43. This was the loco's second appearance in five days on the train. Its first run on 26th July highlighted that further work was needed - hence the second. In between the actual tests, 56049 worked the train three more times to prove it was fit to return to traffic! *Photo: John Powell*

Whatever happened to the concept of the truly mixed traffic locomotive?

A month of hyper-activity on the passenger front rounded off with 56072 on a Lostock drawback during weekend engineering work. The 56 was attached to the non-powered end of 1P06 Birmingham New Street-Blackpool North, which it dragged to Lostock Junction so the 47/4 at the sharp end could continue without having to run-round.

Although Class 56 appearances on the Southern Region became commonplace in later years, sightings apart from the Toton-Northfleet workings were considered notable in 1985/86. Under that heading is 56047's visit to Hamworthy cement terminal on July 10th 1985, definitely a first.

Equally noteworthy, if a little odd, 56034 spent 14th-16th and 21st-23rd August 1985 on crew training runs around Kent, towing a pair of 4-EPB EMUs. In February 1986, the same loco appeared on the Tonbridge-Redhill line - not a first, but one of the early sightings of Type 5 power on the route.

Crewe re-entered the Class 56 story between January 1987 and August 1988 when it assumed responsibility for works overhauls of the class and this led to 1D43 09.20 Euston-Holyhead being used to test the locos - piloting the rostered Class 47. During this 20-month period, 28 Class 56s appeared on the train, some for days, even weeks on end as teething troubles were addressed. Locos usually ran all the way to Holyhead and, if there were no problems, all the way back to Crewe, with the 47 only providing services power to the stock.

Although 56s continued to appear at open days during the two years under review, organisers increasingly expressed a preference for the newer Class 58 rather than the 'old hat' loco. On 7th September 1985, 56037 did turn out for the Laira open day, but the type was conspicuous by its absence at Old Oak Common a week later. The Welsh were obviously more disposed towards the 56. A week later 56034 showed itself off at Landore, but it is more significant to note that three WR depots held events in a three-week period. We really were spoiled in BR days and we never realised it.

A week after Landore, Stewarts Lane threw open its doors to the public and featured both Type 5 variants in the shape of 56001 and 58021.

56037 flew the Welsh flag again at Newport on September 10th, along with a selection of modern freight vehicles, as part of a Railfreight publicity event.

1986 was a little quieter. 56081 and 58040 were on display at Birkenhead on 4th/5th April, while Aylesbury's open day produced 58013, but no 56.

And so, Class 56's first decade drew to a close, not without its problems but in an operational pattern now viewed with extreme nostalgia - the Classic Age of the Grid when rail blue and large logo ruled, and only a handful had appeared in the new Railfreight liveries. Thereafter, it was all change . . . repeatedly.

*Above:* On 1st March 1986, 56017 sits inside the shed at Tinsley, awaiting attention and, presumably, a trip through the depot's washing plant. This, of course, is from a time when depot visits were still possible for photographers and number-crunchers alike, and when events called Open Days were held. *Photo: Paul Bettany*

# 5. SECTORISATION 1987 - 1993

*Above:* In 1987, British Rail divided itself into business sectors as a prelude to privatisation. The majority of Class 56s were allocated to the new Coal Sector. 56029, in that sector's colours, returns east at Mytholmroyd with an MGR after delivering its load to Fiddler's Ferry. *Photo: Neil Harvey*

The breaking up of the British Rail monolith into business sectors began in 1987 as an interim step towards full privatisation of the network and its train services, as well as repair and main works functions. The stated intention was to focus common traffic-related activity under one management to create cost savings. For example, all coal trains would be operated by one division with its own pool of resources and locomotives, thus ending the days when a Class 56 or any other freight-dedicated loco could appear on other sectors' trains, such as a passenger rescue or a drag. If those circumstances arose through necessity, a payment would be made by the passenger sector to the freight sector for the loan of the locomotive. Whether this re-focussing onto 'competing' businesses would change the long-established practice of giving passenger trains priority over freight, only time would tell, but it was just conceivable that the sight of 56s standing in loops at frequent intervals in their journeys would also become a thing of the past.

A secondary motive for sectorisation (the primary motive if you're a cynic) was to prove that individual railway businesses could operate efficiently *and* profitably, thus making them more attractive to potential investors when the Railway Act authorising the sale of the network eventually passed through parliament. However, this was still some six years away when 1987 began. In the meantime, there would be many changes to operating procedures and the paper organisation of the fleet . . . not to mention a lengthy period for the new sectors to prove their financial viability.

Within each sector, locos were allocated to pools dedicated to specific areas or traffic flows. One of the first experiments with dedicated pools was in the Construction sector at Leicester, where an informal group of locos was created in March 1987 to work the area's aggregates traffic. Each pool created thereafter had a four-letter code to identify its members on the TOPS computer. Movements between pools were frequent, especially in the early years, yet locomotives often remained allocated to the same depot when they transferred from one pool to another.

The Class 56 fleet was allocated to three main sectors - Coal, Construction and Metals - in which locomotives and rolling stock were to have an individual livery applied to denote their new 'ownership'. The new 'colours' (sorry about all the inverted commas, but much of the activity at this time stretched the meaning of words) became known as Triple Grey, or in some cases Two-Tone Grey. 56001 was the first, unveiled in all its drab greyness relieved only by the colourful sector markings on the bodyside and repeated behind the cab handrails. 56036 was unique in carrying Petroleum sector branding for a short time. This and 56048 were only allocated to pool FPLW (Trainload Freight Petroleum - Cardiff Locos) between 7th December 1987 and 15th May 1988, after which they transferred to the Cardiff Aggregates pool, FAWC.

While all this reorganisation was going on, BR continued to reduce its fleet of older locomotives. 1987, for instance, saw the last of Class 25 and 27, while 45/0 and 45/1 were heavily depleted during the year. Even Class 47/0 suffered a loss of 20 members.

More relevant to the 56 story, though, was the end of Tinsley's association with the class on 18th January 1987, when 56089-56111 transferred to Toton. Equally surprising, given the repeated strengthening of its 56 allocation, Bristol Bath Road became an Intercity/ Parcels sector depot with responsibility for Class 47s allocated to these sectors. As a result, all 15 of its 56s transferred to Canton in October 1987 - the entire fleet out-based at Westbury for non-Yeoman work, comprising 56001, 031, 033, 034, 036, 039, 043, 045, 046, 048, 049, 051, 055, 056 & 057. In reality, this was the first step towards the long-planned concentration of the class at Toton where, it was hoped, superior repair work would improve reliability. Gateshead's 56112-56135 transferred to Toton at the same time, creating an interim position of 23 locos at Cardiff and the rest at Toton.

Many rare sightings of 'foreign' 56s occurred during this period of transition, but, sadly for the enthusiast, this was not to last. Strict control of each sector's allocation would soon be introduced.

Many of the initial pools were created simply by grouping the locomotives already sharing the same duties. However, a notable first occurred on 12th May 1991 when the Southern Region received its first 56

*41*

*Above: The first Class 56 to receive a new sector livery was 56001. The triple-grey 'colour scheme' was finished off with sector markings designed by the Roundell Group, cast BR arrows and depot plaques. 001 stands inside the servicing shed at Bristol Bath Road in June 1989. Photo: Mike Goodfield*

allocation. 56001, 033, 037 & 039 transferred to Stewarts Lane to create a new FASB pool dedicated to south-east aggregates traffic. All four came from Cardiff's FASK Construction pool, which received 56044 & 046 from Toton as partial replacement (almost four years on, the idea of mass concentration at Toton appears to have been abandoned). The Southern locos (strictly speaking, Network SouthEast area, as the Southern and other traditional Regions had ceased to exist officially) were serviced at either Hither Green or Westbury, while heavier repairs were carried out at Stewarts Lane. By the end of September 1991 a further ten of Cardiff's Mendip stone locos - 56031, 034, 041, 043, 050, 051, 052, 053, 055 & 056 - had also transferred to FASB.

A month later, four locos - 56035, 058, 059 & 070 - moved from Leicester Aggregates pool FAXN to FASN, a contingency pool set up at Toton to interchange duties with Stewarts Lane's FASB members at times of high demand. As FASB also contained Class 37s and 60s for Mendip-originating stone traffic, 56s were likely to appear on these workings as stand-ins. The Toton temporary pool proved very temporary. On 8th December 1991, its four locos returned to FAXN at Leicester.

Cardiff had a main pool designated FMCK for metals traffic, but a second grouping - FMHK - was established in December 1991 to work trunk flows of steel between South Wales and the West Midlands terminals as well as Teeside/Humberside. The initial allocation comprised 56032, 038, 040, 044, 046 & 064. In practice, such a specific pool was found to be too small and by the following July all five of its locos had reverted to their original FMCK. This pool finally reached its intended strength of ten locos in May 1992 with the arrival of 56048 from Toton's FAXN and 56052 & 053 from Stewarts Lane's FASB.

They joined 56032, 038, 040, 044, 046, 064 & 073 at Cardiff. The latter loco had transferred from Yorkshire Coal pool FEDN in the middle of March, reportedly for use on driver training in the Hereford and Newport areas because of its high engine hours. So much for reinforcing steel traffic.

Swops of individual locos between pools were so commonplace that it would probably take another book to detail them all. Very often they were temporary, lasting only a few weeks or months, and were mostly brought about by surges in local traffic flows or as cover for locos away for works attention. These examples are typical: In December 1992, 56121 was restricted to local jobs off Toton to keep it close to hand for an imminent call to Doncaster Works. 56112 was re-allocated to Blyth to cover 121's place in the north-east coal pool. Similarly, 56078 was drafted to Blyth the same month to replace 128 when the latter, just out of works and with only 62 TOPS hours, was side-swiped by a derailed MGR wagon while it sat minding its own business in the headshunt at Ryhope Grange. After a second, unscheduled, release from Doncaster in February 1993, 128 resumed its rightful place in the coal pool, reversing the swop with 078.

To ensure that availability reporting was as meaningful as possible (!), stored and withdrawn locos were kept separate by the internal formation of dedicated pools. Unfortunately, many of the first locos to be placed in these pools were Romanian examples. By the end of 1993, 56002, 008, 012, 013, 014, 017 & 023 would be withdrawn, along with the non-standard 56042 and collision-damaged 56122.

But it wasn't all bad news for the Romanians. As new traffic flows developed, a number of previously stored locos were reinstated for training duties in late 1993. 56025 was used at Motherwell to support the FCPA Coal pool out-based at Ayr, and Carlisle received 56029 for the FCNN north-west Coal pool out-based at Wigan Springs Branch. Others in the Springs Branch pool were 56019, 092, 099 & 132.

56014 was re-allocated to FPYX, the Petroleum-General/stored pool, and moved to Immingham depot for driver training in advance of new FPGI pool duties. 56084/094/106 & 126 were already in this pool, which took over Immingham Class 37/7 duties such as the Immingham-Glazebrook trains and some workings from the Humberside refineries. 56003 was reinstated and used for fitter training at Immingham before a new flow of imported coal began arriving through the nearby docks, and both 56009 and 004 appeared at Rugby on various occasions in December 1993 on crew training runs.

Despite the official system of rigid allocation to sectors and pools, many off-sector workings occurred in addition to the temporary swops within sectors. For example, on June 18th 1990 the Coal sector's 56002 & 014 stood in for a pair of Metals sector 37s on the 05.09 Toton-Corby steel train and 10.23 return. No sooner had they arrived back at Toton than another pair of Construction 37s failed on the 09.36 Peak Forest-Bletchley stone working, resulting in

*Above: 56008 awaits attention at Hither Green on 25th March 1990. From May 1991, Class 56s were allocated to a London depot for the first time - Stewarts Lane. Hither Green continued to service the locos, as it had always done when they visited the Southern Region. Photo: Adrian Tibble*

GRIDS

*Above:* Scrap trains came under the Metals sector's remit. 56076 heads one such working at Narroways, Bristol - the 14.20 Exeter-Cardiff Tidal on 19th June 1993. *Photo: Mike Goodfield*

more unscheduled work for the Romanian duo. They took the stone train forward from Bletchley to Toton, allowing time for another pair of 37s to be sent from Buxton to take over the onward run to Peak Forest.

Early in 1993, three of Stewarts Lane's aggregates 56s - 034, 043 & 050 - moved to Thornaby's FMTY pool to help out with an increase in metals traffic. At the same time 56087, fresh out of works, was tested on IN21/ID21 to Tyne Yard before joining the former Southern locos at Thornaby. As compensation, the Leicester stone pool - comprising 56054, 057, 058, 059, 065-070, 103 & 105 - transferred en masse to Stewarts Lane in April.

At the other end of the country, Class 56's connection with Scotland before the Sectorisation period is best described as tenuous compared with the rest of the country. Only unscheduled, one-off visits were recorded in the 1980s, like 56125 hauling the 13.00 ex-King's Cross into Edinburgh Waverley on 3rd July 1987 after rescuing it at Morpeth.

For the handful of locos which did cross the border, Millerhill on the east coast and Mossend on the west became like Exeter in the West Country - a metaphorical buffer stop where traction knowledge ran out. Typical, albeit very occasional, examples included 56059 working into Millerhill with cement from Ketton and 56120 arriving at Mossend in charge of the alumina from Blyth, which later travelled on to Fort William.

However, in May 1990 56086 went to Millerhill for staff familiarisation before the class took over coal emanating from Blindwells colliery, although 086 was declared unfit on May 24th and exchanged for 56091. 'Technical problems' prevented 56s from passing over the weighbridge at Blindwells, so pairs of Class 26s delivered the 36 wagon trains to Millerhill for the 56s to take south. By June, four were based there, allowing them to take on other work, like 56081 on 6D28 Oxwelmains-Uddingston View Park cement on 20th June and 56074 & 123 working the Ravenstruther-Leith MGR circuit. Locos were frequently exchanged, producing the following sightings: 56029, 073, 074. 081, 086, 087, 091, 095 & 123.

On the western side of the Scottish lowlands, 56092 was trialled on coal workings around Ayr on 29th October 1990 in advance of the class replacing pairs of Class 37s, allowing the Type 3s to be released to other traffic.

The Caledonian invasion continued; between Christmas and New Year 1990,

*Above:* Gateshead depot on 25th April 1987. 56132, a Coal machine since sectorisation, receives attention alongside a Class 47 and a Class 37. *Photo: Adrian Tibble*

43

*Above:* As well as carrying the experimental Large Logo scheme, 56036 was also the only Grid to appear with Petroleum branding, after its brief allocation to the sector between 7th December 1987 and 15th May 1988, whereupon it transferred to Construction. The loco sits at Wolverton stone terminal on 15th February 1990 after bringing in 6M24 from Stoke Gifford. *Photo: Mike Goodfield*

56069 was busy at Cupar in Fife in advance of 56s taking over the area's coal workings in the new year. In January 1991, 56112 appeared at Dundee for crew training; on February 1st it was spotted shunting in Dundee yard before running south across the Tay Bridge. Seven days later, the same loco hauled 6H33 Millerhill-Inverness via Grangemouth, but there is no report of it working through to Inverness.

The May 1991 timetable changes brought more 56s to Millerhill, On the 28th, for example, 56079 was on 6E70 MGR to York Yard North, 56076 on local trip workings, while 56093 & 095 and 56069 & 109 'multied up' for Ravenstruther duties.

The Millerhill turns tended to be covered by the FEDN pool, but occasional Nottinghamshire and north-east pool locos also appeared, such as 56005 on 8th July 1992 and 56008 a fortnight later. FEEN's 56120, 126 & 131 were all sighted, alongside FEDN's 56069, 072, 075, 085, 089, 090, 092, 093, 096, 097, 099, 106, 107, 108 & 111.

In May 1993, a new FCPA pool out-based at Ayr received 56104, 121, 123, 124, 125, 127, 128 & 129 for coal work. Most of the locos came from the north-east coal pool, which received 56062 & 094 as partial replacements.

Cardiff's FCKK pool, set up to cover the intensive Margam-Llanwern coal trains, was a good example of a small fleet operating on dedicated traffic. On 25th May 1993, all four were available for work - 56114, 115 & 119 working trains, 113 stabled at Newport as a stand-by.

Knottingley remained a core location and a new facility opened there in April 1993. 58043 was named after the location at the open day on April the 25th. As part of the efficiencies, Knottingley train crew also learned the road to Tyne Yard that month. 58s were the motive power of choice, but 56086 appeared on 1st April and 079 on the 20th.

As mentioned in a previous chapter, Class 56 had already lost out to imported Class 59s on the Yeoman traffic and continued to be under threat from domestic power. Following 37902's exploits on the Llanwern-Dee Marsh trial, 37902 & 905 were set a similar challenge on the heavy Port Talbot-Llanwern iron ore trains. On the first test run, they managed to restart the train on Stormy Bank, to the east of Margam, and keep time until Cardiff, where pathing problems caused a delay. And so, after many years on the Llanwern ore circuit, Class 56 gave way to pairs of refurbished 37/7s. The ballasted and alternator-fitted 37s in pairs were equal to a single 56 in terms of haulage capacity, but couldn't always accelerate to line speed as quickly.

However, this wasn't a total victory for the revitalised Class 37 over its younger rival. Spells of poor availability of the Cardiff fleet, combined with new traffic flows and increased loadings, meant that often there weren't

*Above:* 56083 departs from Healey Mills on 3rd October 1988, with a rake of engineer's wagons in tow. Note the slots cut into the sides of the wagons to stop them becoming overloaded with wet spoil at work sites. Spoil weighed a lot more than the coal the wagons were designed to carry. *Photo: Neil Harvey*

enough locos to go around. As a result, the Dee Marsh workings reverted to 56 haulage, allowing two 37s to be released to work either singly or as a pair on lesser flows.

Toton's Coal sector pools had a surplus of 56s and a number were loaned to the Metals sector, producing on one occasion the Romanian pairing of 004 & 023 on the Lackenby-Corby steelworks working.

Another of the imports, 56014, also appeared on the 02.15 Margam-Dee Marsh while on loan to Cardiff in late May 1991. The following summer, 56003 worked the 12.23 Margam-Dee Marsh and within five days had picked up the 6V37 Sheerness-Cardiff scrap movement. However, the space between the dates indicates the rarity of such appearances. Doncaster product remained the staple South Wales traction; on the same day in June 1992 as 003's surprise appearance, 56048, newly re-allocated to the FMCK pool, was in charge of

working with a 60 revealed a useful cost-saving. The test train, with the consist of 6M41 tied on the back, produced a 42-wagon load running as 6M26 Redcar-Hardendale and proved that combining two trains saved an extra locomotive and, more importantly, an extra path. Having finally realised the haulage capability of the heavyweight 60, the sector removed 56s from the Teeside train.

As predicted, control of the class became much tighter during the Sectorisation period but, when problems arose, not even the most carefully considered plan survived. So, 56s continued to appear on passenger rescues, weekend drags and, sometimes, movements of empty stock.

The weather played its part too. In January 1987, for instance, the south-east of England was hit by heavy snow, causing serious disruption on the afternoon of the 11th with many lines

Rainham, Faversham and Ramsgate over a four-day period.

Prolonged freezing temperatures returned to Kent four years later in February 1991. On the 8th, an 8-car EMU left London Victoria for the Kent Coast but came to a halt at Longfield because of a build-up of ice on the third rail. The following two trains, both 8-car, drew forward and coupled up, but failed to make any progress. 47206 had no better luck when it arrived to try and move the collection, and so it was left to 56045 to save the day. The loco arrived from Stewarts Lane at 19.35, buffered up, and shoved the whole lot - 24 EMU vehicles and the 47 - onwards to Chatham where passengers were finally able to escape!

In the ensuing days, 56043 worked two Dartford-Charing Cross

*Above:* The heavy snow of January 1987 wrought havoc on the former Southern Region, as it always does. Diesel locos were used to tow EMUs from London into Kent and 56001 was one of three 56s requisitioned. The first two views show the loco at London Victoria, in the third it's arriving at Dartford. *Photos: Phil Wormald*

the 08.30 Llanwern-Dee Marsh.

Much of the new Welsh traffic comprised scrap flows from Cardiff Tidal Sidings to Swindon, Hamworthy, Exeter and Sheerness. A newly-introduced 6V37 working from Cardiff Tidal to Sheerness steelworks was entrusted to 56046 on 29th August 1991. These trains could produce heavy loads and, eventually, some were taken over by Class 60s. The 6C14 Cardiff Tidal-Exeter Riverside scrap train, for instance, enjoyed 56 haulage for the last time on 30th October 1993.

But as one 56 duty finished, another appeared. In October 1993 locos from Cardiff's FMCK pool replaced Class 47s on the 6V26 Burn Naze-Barry (Tuesdays, Thursdays and Sundays only) and 6M45 return (Mondays, Wednesday and Fridays only) chemicals traffic.

By now, the numbers of Class 56 available for traffic were considered abundant compared with the early years and they were considered for duties they had not previously worked, such as replacing the 'long in the tooth' 47s kept in a weekends-only pool for drags and engineering work. The heavy Channel Tunnel concrete trains were considered too much for the 3 x Class 20 originally proposed, so 56s were considered for this work too.

They also began to appear on the Hardendale limestone traffic. 56034 appeared first with 6M41 Lackenby-Hardendale, closely followed by 56054. Although the occasional Class 60 continued to appear, the work became a solid Class 56 turn until a trial

blocked by the snow itself or by stalled trains. Those that were able to run were reported as four to six hours late and following no particular timetable. The disruption continued for several days; by the 15th services were operating again over the Charing Cross-Tonbridge-Ashford route and to the Medway towns, but only thanks to a fleet of nineteen diesel locos towing EMUs, among them 56001, 056 & 062! 001 worked for five consecutive days on the Faversham, Rainham, Ashford and Dover routes, while 56062 worked Charing Cross-Orpington as well as to

trips, again hauling iced-up EMU stock, and 56056 propelled two VEP units on the Ashford line. 56001 appeared at Faversham again on the 10th working late evening trains until the early hours of the next day. A week after the freeze began, 56036, 046 & 061 could still be found stabled at Gillingham in case the bad weather returned.

Because of local freight requirements, 56s had become more associated with passenger work in some areas than others. Passengers travelling between Westbury and Reading, for instance, were always reporting Type 5 rescues. There was a burst of similar activity

*Above:* All correctly turned out. Six Grids stand outside Knottingley depot on 13th July 1991. 56098 is nearest the camera. *Photo: AdrianTibble*

45

*Above:* 56108 passes Llangewydd, between Bridgend and Port Talbot, with the 6B69 Llanwern to Port Talbot coal empties on 15th April 1991. *Photo: Martin Loader*

for the same reason in the north-west in late 1991, particularly in the area around Stoke on Trent. Full details of these workings are listed in the table at the end of the book, and it is interesting to note how many times 56015 & 016 appeared because of their allocation to the Stoke pool working MGR traffic.

The sectors eventually realised there was extra revenue to be had by exploiting their Type 5 inheritance with the enthusiast market and a number of specials were organised over the Settle & Carlisle route with well-advertised freight locos piloting the, usually, Class 47-hauled service trains. On March 17th 1990, for instance, 56075 piloted 47453 on the 08.25 Leeds-Carlisle and return, while December 30th 1991 threw up 56134 piloting 31418 on the 09.47 Leeds to Carlisle, where 56117 took over for the return run.

Problems with the overhead lines continued to provide unscheduled work for Class 56 in the Sector period. An outage at Law Junction in July 1993 was one of the more notable. 56125 worked between Edinburgh and Carlisle with 1M12 21.20 Aberdeen-Euston and then took 1S79 22.03 Euston-Aberdeen forward to Edinburgh. 56077 also worked from Edinburgh to Carlisle with 1M15 19.15 Fort William-Euston, but then surprised everyone by taking 1S26 23.50 ex-Euston right through to Glasgow Central. Both trains comprised 16 or 17 coaches, but the 56 is reported to have taken them over Beattock with ease.

The most unusual working of that year, however, had taken place a month earlier, one which not even an all-line Railrover would have got you on. When The Queen travelled to Newcastle races on 27th June, the Royal Train was booked to stable overnight at Hepscott on the Blyth and Tyne Line. The Royal 47 couldn't work the short trip because Blyth men only signed 56s; so, enter 56134. Unfortunately, the loco suffered a graffiti attack only hours before this important job, but the royal party was already on its way to the races when the 56 backed onto the stock at Newcastle Central. No embarrassment there, then.

The changing nature of the coal industry continued to demonstrate the usefulness of the 56, often in ways not envisaged when the design was conceived. As flows of imported coal increased, distances between source and end-user inevitably increased. What's more, because of the ports' geography, trains conveying the imports regularly had to travel over high-speed routes. Although track capacity had been reduced, this was partially offset by the replacement of old and slow first generation DMUs with much faster Sprinter units. Even so, heavy coal trains had to be on the move quickly to minimise disruption to express services - a task for which Class 56 had more than enough power. On the right kind of train, the locos' 80 mph maximum could be fully utilised, further reducing the likelihood of delays.

As well as the diagrammed journey, extra trains also ran for short periods in the early 1990s to clear accumulated stocks of imported coal from the dockside, usually at locations like Tyne, Avonmouth and Immingham, but 56s were also sighted at the inland port of King's Lynn on coal clearance work. 56s began to appear again at King's Lynn in the summer of 1990 on the twice-weekly coal trains to the cement works at Foxton, after taking over the work from pairs of Class 20s. Toton's FCBN pool provided the traction and the same loco often worked both trains in a single week.

Another short-term operation involved Hull's King George Dock in 1990. Following a trial run with 56091, the first train from Saltend (Hull) to Ferrybridge power station was worked by 56101. The following were also drafted in to help - 56047, 067, 069, 073, 080, 081, 084, 089, 091, 092 - until the stocks were completely cleared. Hull began importing coal again in September 1991 and a number of 56s were provided to work trains from the New Sidings.

During the transition from domestic to imported coal, significant investment in new facilities took place, while older plant which had fallen out of use was refurbished and reactivated. On 14th April 1988, 56122 was named *Wilton Coal Power* before hauling the first train through the newly-installed unloading facility at ICI's Wilton power station on Teeside. The station had recently been converted to run on coal rather than oil. 56121 was close by in case 122 disgraced itself.

In a reversal of the new pattern, exports through Leith Docks began in April 1990. 56047 & 077 worked the first train on 25th, followed next day by 56083 & 108. In September of that

*Above:* Railtours were a much more convenient way to bag Class 56s for haulage, although maybe not as satisfying as 'deck-chairing' for hours on end. 56089 & 100 await departure from Sheffield with a shuttle to Cottam power station, organised as part of the Worksop open day festivities on 5th September 1993. *Photo: Duncan Jennings*

year, special coal workings began from the re-commissioned Hunterston terminal to British Steel's plant at Scunthorpe, again with Class 56 haulage. By 1992 Immingham had expanded significantly as a coal import terminal and the east coast port became the focus of coal workings to the Scunthorpe blast furnaces - work with which Class 56 was synonymous until the end of its traditional life.

Avonmouth received significant investment in 1992 when a new import facility was constructed. The Construction sector provided the stone for the work, which it delivered to site using the Redland self-discharging train. Locos involved between the 9th and the 16th of December were 56105, 070 & 037. The SDT was perfect for flows whose short-term nature did not justify investment in dedicated unloading facilities.

Once the Avonmouth terminal was complete, trials commenced. 56114 & 37887 were the first arrivals on 25th June 1993 for clearance testing with 10 HBAs from Barry. 60077 was also on site, with the intention of using all three types of traction into the terminal. Traffic began on 7th September with two daily trains, although this was expected to increase to six over time. The import of foreign coal through Avonmouth spelled the end for the long-established workings of Toton 56s and 58s with MGRs from the Nottinghamshire coalfield to Didcot.

By July 1993 Barry drivers were learning the class, using 56114, in readiness for the next flow of imported coal from Avonmouth to Aberthaw power station. 56s were also trialled on the Cumbargoed branch, although the steep grades raised many technical difficulties, not least the compatibility of braking systems on 56s and MGR wagons in such conditions - a problem which would not be resolved for many months.

By September, Port Talbot to Llanwern steelworks coal traffic was in the hands of a small pool of locos based at Canton, comprising 56113, 114, 115 & 119. These workings used canopy-fitted hoppers to reduce 'blow off' on the faster sections of the South Wales main line. A stationary MGR train could also lose a significant quantity of coal from the turbulence caused by a passing HST set!

Other 1993 developments involved Willington power station, which began receiving coal deliveries by rail again. Some 200,000 tonnes were brought in from the Lounge opencast site near Ashby-de-la-Zouch or from Denby, with the intention of building a stockpile at the station. Unfortunately the first day was disrupted by a loco failure and 58014 was the first to unload on 11th February. Class 56s which did manage the trip included 028, 070 & 092, along with 58011, 021 & 027.

Although the Southern Region had acquired a new Class 56-hauled flow in 1988, from Oxham to Ridham Dock to serve the Bowaters paper mill at Sheerness, the long-established Northfleet duties came to an end

*Above:* 56047, one of only four Class 56s repainted from rail blue into Large Logo, passes Wakefield on 14th September 1988. *Photo: Adrian Tibble*

*Above:* On 21st. February 1989, 56082 heads an MGR returning from Fiddler's Ferry at Hawksclough. These trains were re-routed away from the Diggle route after the introduction of Class 158s. *Photo: Neil Harvey*

*Above:* 56114 *Maltby Colliery* stands at the recently-completed Avonmouth Bulk Handling Terminal during gauging trials on 25th June 1993. Along with 60077 (which can just be glimpsed through the bunker in the background) and 37887, it was used with rakes of HEA wagons to check clearances through the new structure before deliveries to Didcot power station began - a switch from the home-produced coal of the Midlands to imports from all over the world. *Photo: Martin Loader*

in 1993 following the conversion of New Hythe paper mill from coal to gas. Still worked by Toton's FCBN pool containing many Romanian examples, the train's final week featured 56011 & 019 before 007 hauled the very last one on 2nd December. At the same time, the Oxcroft-Ridham traffic was re-scheduled to make it a same day out-and-back working, which often resulted in the same loco turning up repeatedly rather than the alternation seen previously. 56004 was the motive power of choice for almost the whole of November and December.

It is worth mentioning that the Coal sector was also responsible for nuclear traffic, and 56s were diagrammed to trips between Carlisle and Fairlie (near Largs) and to Torness (near Dunbar). Despite this diagramming, the class never became a common sight on such trains.

As mentioned previously, the fall-out from the miners strike of 1984 was considerable - not least in the widespread pit closures and replacement of their product with foreign coal. The ripple effect was still being felt in November 1992 when yet another new flow of imports began from Redcar to Longannet power station - the first coal traffic to run into Scotland for many years and significant because it created the sight of loaded coal trains passing each other on the East Coast Main Line. The coal from Blindwells was still being used to 'sweeten' the output from Gascoigne Wood to make it more suitable for the Yorkshire power stations - again highlighting the widely differing quality from different sources and giving the layman, at least, the impression of a wholly inefficient operation. Shades of the early 1970s, *before* the invention of Class 56!

*Above:* The Coal sector was also responsible for flyash trains. 56027 heads through Cossington while returning empties from Fletton to Ratcliffe power station on 5th November 1990. *Photo: Adrian Tibble*

GRIDS

*Above:* 56033 passes Corsham on 30th April 1993 with 4C13 11.21 Calvert-Bristol binliner empties. This train has seen a considerable variety of traction over the years, starting with 47s, then 56s, 60s, 37s, 58s and the inevitable 66s. *Photo: Martin Loader*

Not surprisingly, the class was heavily associated with the final workings at many pits before their closure.

In September 1992, for example, 56072 worked the last train from Askern to Eggborough power station, 7K93. In keeping with the colliery's reputation, the loco took 90 minutes to cover 200 yards because of poor rail conditions.

Murton Colliery in the north-east, closed in November 1992, had a railway history going back more than 150 years. The branch from Murton joined the Durham coast line at Ryhope Grange Junction, which is where 56122 was hit and seriously damaged by a derailed MGR train on 22nd November 1991 - a tenuous link with a final working, it's true. However, the final coal train along the Murton branch, from Hawthorn Colliery, was worked by 56119 on 1st April 1993.

In the same month Gedling colliery, near the former Colwick MPD north-east of Nottingham, ceased operations, its final train worked by 58012. A day earlier, 56025 had called in as a mark of respect to the colliery and its men. The final working comprised only 10 HEA hoppers, but Toton allocated Type 5 traction for the same reason.

Also of note, given its recent renaissance as a preservation centre, was the closure of Barrow Hill and its Midland Railway roundhouse on 11th February 1991. 56011 was the last 56 out the door, and 58042 the very last to leave the site under old ownership.

The pattern of Class 56 life - intensely busy during the week, totally idle at weekends - continued as before in the early years of the Sector period, but the situation was now turned to advantage in the never-ending drive for efficiency. Rather than kicking their heels for two days, the locos were used with greater frequency on weekend engineering trains, allowing the disposal of many older types like Class 31, 33 and 37. On Saturdays, locations such as Tyne Yard, Doncaster Belmont and Millerhill would often have rows of 56s lined up on engineers trains, ready for overnight permanent way work.

One rumour which did come true was the use of Class 56 on china clay traffic in Cornwall, when a trial was announced in February 1990. Although 56s were not uncommon at Exeter (56019 appeared there that month with the Cliffe Vale-Exeter china clay empties), they only occasionally reached as far as Plymouth. However, on February 27th, 56013 became the first of its class to reach Cornwall when it took part in route clearance tests and visited a number of china clay branches in the area. As an encore, it rescued 47815 and the Paddington-Penzance sleepers. After pushing them from Treverrin Tunnel to Par, it moved to the front and took the beds on to Penzance. 013 returned north on a Speedlink working

Although the class was closely identified with the bulk delivery of materials for industry, like coal, steel, oil and stone, the waste produced by industry had to be removed too - a requirement which opened up new flows for Class 56 to add to its previous movements of shale and slag from collieries.

The removal of household rubbish had become big business. In the early years, these trains were in the hands of 31s and 37s but, as loads increased, the 56s began to appear. A first sighting involved 56042, of all locos, replacing the usual pair of Type 2s on the Cricklewood-Forders 'bins' in late January 1989.

In 1991, 56s took over from Class 47s on the Calvert-Westerleigh waste trains and, in early 1993, replaced 60s on the Avon 'binliners'. All these trains were highly popular with photographers as they were liable to throw up all manner of traction, and traction combinations, so the use of Type 5s as glorified binmen was a bonus. The Northolt-Calvert trains, especially partial to different traction combinations, also used 56 power until the flow was taken over by Mainline Freight in 1994. Construction sector locos were the order of the day, with 56037, 041, 042, 051 & 065 performing single-handedly in the early months of 1993.

The north-west used 56s on its waste for a while, although it would be the late 1990s before they dominated on the flow across the Pennines to Roxby.

Waste of a different kind was lost, though, in February 1991 when Class 47s took over the Fletton flyash workings. 56022 worked the last one from Ratcliffe-on-Soar to Fletton on 28th February, roughly ten days later than the planned changeover date.

Environmental pressures also created new traffic, eventually leading to the movement of vast tonnages of limestone and gypsum recovered by a cleaner emissions policy at Drax power station - an early forerunner of the 'carbon capture' everyone talks about today. Along the same line of thought, 56086 worked a trial train of sulphur in two MEA wagons in June 1991 to the Newcastle area -

*49*

*Above:* An unidentified 56 passes Sydney Gardens in Bristol with an empty stone train bound for South Wales in June 1991. *Photo: Mike Goodfield*

preparation for the imminent introduction of flue gas de-sulphurisation equipment at Drax, aimed at reducing the effects of acid rain . . . which was mostly falling on Scandinavia.

Not quite waste because it has secondary uses, molasses became a Class 56 commodity in January 1991 when 56035 worked a train of it through north Norfolk. Anyone seeing the train would have assumed it was a fuel oil working as the molasses, a by-product of sugar-refining, was conveyed in TTA tankers. This became a regular Saturdays-only working from King's Lynn to Peterborough and back.

While parts of the country were absorbed in the task of turning Class 56s into waste disposal operatives, others remained focussed on the higher end of the locos' speed range for Freightliner work, with mixed results. In July 1988, for example, 56049 had successfully worked 4S81 Pengam-Coatbridge liner, although two days earlier 043 had failed with the same job on Llanvihangel bank, calling for a push over the summit by 37263 & 021.

Felixstowe liner traffic also produced Class 56 on occasions. 058 worked 4M73 to Trafford Park on 4th April 1993, running via Willesden because of OHL problems in the Dalston area. After recessing at Willesden, the loco worked 4L82 Trafford Park-Felixstowe as far as Ipswich. At around the same time, 056 went on top of 37079 & 225 at Doncaster with 4L79 from Wilton, although this may only have been a convenient means of moving the loco to Felixstowe after maintenance at Thornaby.

Regularly rubbing shoulders with the Felixstowe liners were the heavy sand trains from Marks Tey to Mile End. On the same day as 013's Cornish exploits, 078 was allocated to crew familiarisation at Ipswich, with the intention of using Class 56 on the sand instead of struggling Class 37s. While at Ipswich, 078 made a few trips down the Felixstowe branch with liner flats and ended up working 4L96 Coatbridge-Felixstowe to the terminal . . . but only from Ipswich. Once again, the late '90s would roll around on the calendar before Class 56 became a regular sight doing battle with Trimley bank with boxes in tow.

Although the economy was heading for recession in the early 1990s, the construction industry was still enjoying a boom, thanks to a major programme of infrastructure projects. Much of the work - roads, airport runways, even Channel Tunnels - needed vast amounts of stone, almost all of which was delivered to site by rail, providing Construction sector 56s with more work.

At the turn of the decade, various trials were held with a view to establishing new flows - hence 56063 working an inaugural Mountsorrel-Wednesbury aggregates and 56060 taking Redland's self-discharging train to Hythe near Colchester. Both 56059 and 061 were reported on stone traffic for the

*Above:* 56033 arrives at Stoke Gifford with a Yeoman train from Swindon on 18th May 1992. This loco was undergoing ATP trials at the time. *Photo: Mike Goodfield*

building of Stansted Airport's new runway at around the same time. In the south-east, demand for stone was so great that additional services operated between Whatley Quarry and Fareham in the autumn of 1991.

Despite all this new work, Construction locos' movements were reasonably predictable, although they could occasionally surprise. Twice in the space of three months, 56s were reported on single parcels vans on the Midland main line, replacing a failed DPU. 56110 appeared on one such working in January 1990, running as the 06.34 Leicester-Luton parcels and return. On the following 4th of April, 56064 worked a similar turn - the 19.53 Bedford-St Pancras after another DPU failure. Control obviously wanted the loco back hauling aggregates, so it only worked the return 00.05 St Pancras-Leeds as far as Leicester, where 31404 took over.

In later years, Class 56 would lose out to the superior haulage capacity of Class 60 but, in 1990, further delays in introducing the Type 5 Tug reprieved some locos slated for withdrawal. In the spring of that year, the Mountsorrel Redland working provided test facilities for the new build, but with the regular 56 dead in tow as insurance - for example, 60005 working with 56064, and 60010 accompanied by 56062.

Eighteen months later, ARC re-opened its Tytherington Quarry to cope with the demand for stone. 56051 worked the first train - 6Z84 14.00 Tytherington-Westbury on 29th August 1991.

The construction of the Channel Tunnel was Britain's biggest civil engineering project since the exploits of the railway pioneers of the early 19th Century. Class 56 featured alongside several other types, primarily on the Shakespeare Cliff-Sevington trains which delivered construction materials to the site as well as shifting vast quantities of spoil extracted during the tunnel boring phase of the project. 56036 was the first of its class to appear, noted at Dollands Moor on 2nd April 1990.

56s also proved their worth during Operation Dollands Storm (shades of the first Iraq War!) when an intensive series of weekend possessions relayed many miles of existing track. During this work, the Redland self-discharging train was able to deliver ballast very precisely thanks to the 56's slow speed control.

Like many flows supported by the Construction sector, Channel Tunnel work decreased as the project neared completion. 56055 worked the last BR train associated with the project on 25th June 1993, shifting a train load of removed narrow gauge rails to the Queenborough steelworks for scrap . . . a word which would soon rear its head again.

*Above:* 56056 passes Crofton with a stone train from Westbury to Harlow Mill on 5th November 1990. *Photo: Mike Goodfield*

*Above:* In the early 1990s, a pair of relief lines were reinstated between Wantage Road and Challow on the Great Western Main Line, principally to cater for the, then, new Avonmouth to Didcot coal trains. On 21st February 1993, 56105 & 054 stand on the recently-laid down relief line near Grove with a Redland stone train after ballasting operations further up the line. The up relief line has yet to be laid. *Photo: Martin Loader*

# 6. SLIMMING DOWN

*Above:* 56124 passes Hebden Bridge with the 6M21 Blyth-Ellesmere Port Cawood coal containers on 20th May 1988. *Photo: Neil Harvey*

In the run-up to privatisation, many changes to working practices had been introduced. On the fleet side, reductions in business because of the recent economic recession had created a corresponding drop in locomotive requirement. With a surplus of traction on its books, Railfreight adopted a policy of standardisation for the loco types it allocated to each sector. A main benefit of this policy was expected to be an improvement in reliability as depots became more skilled in maintaining particular types through having fewer classes of loco to attend to. By the same token, savings were expected from holding a reduced stock of spares and from more focussed use of training time.

Higher-powered locos could obviously haul heavier trains, allowing some workings to be combined, further reducing loco requirement. As one example, the two daily limestone trains between Hardendale and Teeside were combined once a Class 60 was allocated to the work. Generally the lower-powered types were eliminated altogether or used in pairs on secondary work.

Many coal services working on the ECML to Milford had been double-headed by 56s from Knottingley's pool but, by December 1992, the number of pairs became noticeably fewer, again because a single Class 60 could cope with the load.

As well as the changes to working practices, some of the more out-dated were eliminated. For example, the age-old policy of changing locomotives at Regional boundaries was dispensed with. Yards such as Doncaster Decoy, York North and Barrow Hill suffered a huge reduction in activity as the same locomotive that had begun the journey worked the train straight past the yard. Traincrews were working much longer distances, which meant that trains no longer needed to stop for a crew change. Worksop men, for example, would previously have worked coal into Barrow Hill with a 58, where a Toton 56 or 58, crewed by Toton men, would have taken over.

Some workings remained typical of the old world. Trains on the Denby branch, instantly recognisable by the brake vans at either end of the MGR rake, were tortuous affairs because of the many crossings. Stopping repeatedly to open and close gates was not merely slow but labour intensive, as the number of trips completed in a shift was severely limited.

Other infrastructure problems also caused inefficiencies. For example, the lack of a crossover could mean trains having to leave a site in the wrong direction, run round and then pass the loading point again en route to their destination. Investment was made at some locations to alleviate this problem, such as the Plenmellor opencast site. From May 1993, trains could gain direct access to the eastbound line thanks to a new crossover, saving a lengthy trip via Carlisle. 56126 was the last loco to take the scenic route; thereafter, its classmates saved 56 miles per visit!

Use of the self-discharging train in traffic has already been mentioned several times, and this too came under the heading of efficiency. The Redland company helped to develop the system in the early 1990s - a series of under-slung conveyer belts which carried stone to a specially-designed discharge vehicle at the end of a rake of hoppers. Trails took place initially between Mountsorrel and Chesterton, with the locomotive running round at Cambridge. The first mishap occurred in September 1992 when 60006 ran into a landslide at Sharnbrook. The SDT may be a wonderful piece of technology, but it was unable to dig itself out of the mud and needed a recovery drag from 56070.

Containerisation was also being explored in the quest for greater efficiency. Cawoods pioneered this method, which eliminated the need for expensive loading and unloading equipment. The distinctive yellow containers were filled with coal by mechanical shovel and craned onto a vessel for shipment to Ireland. The coal could arrive at the ports from many sources, but the established flows ran from Blyth to Lynemouth, Grimethorpe to Ellesmere Port and, later, to Seaforth. Another later flow ran from Immingham to the Russell terminal near Inverness, via the Settle and Carlisle route.

Despite the higher speed of the 56, Ellesmere Port-bound trains were routed over the Pennines via Todmorden to prevent them getting in the way of the intensive trans-Pennine Sprinter service on the Diggle route.

The introduction in 1990 of two Westfield opencast to Drax trains, staging at York yard en route, provided Class 56 with long-distance coal work hauling 36 wagons, although the efficiency aspect of this operation is questionable. Because of weight restrictions on the Forth Bridge, the two 36-wagon formations had first to be tripped to Thornton Yard and split into three 24-wagon trains. Once at Millerhill, where Class 56 took over, three became two again for the onward journey south. Special local instructions were eventually put in place to ensure the 56 was given a good run at Cockburnspath bank, with no restrictive aspects to be shown on the bank itself and on the approach. This instruction meant that the one-time assisting loco, usually a Class 26, could be dispensed with, thus saving fuel, traincrew, and the time spent detaching it at Berwick.

In July 1990, trials on the Bootle branch on Merseyside featured pairs of 56s on 45 wagon MGR rakes over the difficult section from Gladstone Dock to Edge Hill, which involved a section at 1 in 60 on a sharp curve. Previously a pair of Class 20s had taken 30 hoppers over this section, but the addition of another pair allowed an increase to 45. Replacing four locos with two was clearly the aim, although 56025 & 026 began cautiously with a light engine run over the branch. As if to emphasise the need for more power, on the day of the trial 20141 & 013 stalled on the gradient with only 30 hoppers and needed the assistance of 20166 & 007 to complete the climb.

On the following Saturday 56014 & 023 successfully made a round trip with a reinforced rake of hoppers and, from August 25th, the four Class 20s were replaced by Type 5s, initially 56009 & 011. 56008's stint on this work was short; it had to be returned to Toton as its large, round Oleo buffers caused problems because of the nature of the branch's trackwork.

Often, simply making better arrangements and issuing instructions to signalmen allowed a second locomotive to be dispensed with on some flows. On a journey with only one or two gradients where an extra loco might be needed, a single loco could perform the task if it wasn't cautioned on the approach to the banks, as at Cockburnspath. South Wales was an ideal territory to try this out, especially on the Margam to Dee Marsh workings. On 1st December 1992, 56053 set off with the 1600 tonne trailing load of 6M85 to Dee Marsh and coped well with the notorious Stormy Bank, and then Llanvihangel on the Welsh Marches route after signallers were instructed to give the train clear aspects as it approached them.

Further load tests took place in January 1993 when 56048, with 56040 as assisting engine only, tackled the 36 wagons of the 21.15 Swindon Cocklebury-Cardiff tidal scrap, weighing in at 1672 tonnes with the dead classmate. This time a clear run was organised on the approach to the Severn Tunnel from Pilning so the train could be at full speed before the 1 in 90 climb out of the tunnel. The next day, 048 worked a similar test. After running from Cardiff Tidal to Temple Mills as 6Z37, it returned with a load of 1530 tonnes and succeeded for a second time in climbing from the tunnel unaided. The simple expedient of efficient signalling allowed a new benchmark to be set for 56-hauled trains running on this route.

The success of many of these efficiency improvements allowed all Railfreight sectors to reduce their locomotive and traincrew requirement. Many of the surplus locos were stored, as the sectors 'slimmed down' before their next incarnation as Trainload Freight companies.

In advance of the 1993 timetable, the Construction sector's fleet reduced from 60 to 42. This included the loss of seven Class 56s and the release of all 37/4s and 37/5s, allowing the sector to consolidate on only Class 60 and the remaining 56s.

The Metals fleet declined from 63 to 43, although it did gain two 56s while consolidating on Classes 37/9, 56 and 60. Like Construction, it lost its other 37s of /0, /5 and /7 variants.

The mighty Coal sector experienced an overall drop from 223 to 198 locos (11%), but gained three 56s to take their total to 84. However, it lost all locos of Classes 20, 37/0 and 37/3. During this process, Coal re-allocated six 56s to Scotland, where they replaced all but three 37/7s which were retained for vacuum-braked work to and from Methil power station.

In South Wales the 37/7 fleet declined by four to 16, with a plan to replace the remaining refurbished 37s with 56s by mid-1994.

For a short time, Petroleum sector received four extra 56s for its Immingham FPGI pool, 56084, 56094, 56106 & 56126. Despite this, the overall fleet reduced in line with the trend - from 77 to 65 locomotives.

Cutbacks notwithstanding, Class 56 was clearly back in favour and seventeen, including a number of Romanian examples, were provisionally earmarked for CEM overhaul at Toton.

All this shuffling even produced two spare locos, 56048 & 052, which were eagerly

*Above:* 56131 works 6M21 09.33 Blyth Dock Reception-Ellesmere Port Cawoods coal at Moore near Warrington on 22nd March 1991. *Photo: John Hooson*

*Above:* 56090 emerges from Elland Tunnel on 13th May 1992 with 6E64 Fiddler's Ferry-Milford empties. *Photo: Neil Harvey*

*Above: 56094 soon after emerging from the Doncaster paint shop. Photo: Derek Porter*

snapped up by Network SouthEast for its new Meldon infrastructure pool - dealt with in detail later in this chapter.

Enhancing Class 56's reputation still further, reliability problems were also arising with the power units in much newer Class 60s. As a result, a number of the surplus 56s were placed in store rather than being scrapped - the start of an on-going policy of secondary insurance which continues to this day.

Although the first Class 60 had worked a revenue-earning train at the end of 1989 (60005, on 11th December), numerous faults with the new build would delay their mass introduction for some eighteen months.

Even so, as 1990 began, there were murmurings about reductions in the Class 56 fleet when the new build finally became available. Four had been mentioned, so speculation was rife as to which four locos would be stored or withdrawn. If any *were* to go, 56002 was an easy one to pencil in because of its major collision damage.

The plan - if that is the right word when the facts on which the plan is based constantly change because of accidents, spares shortages and financial considerations - was that 56002, 005, 016 & 018 should go to Doncaster and surrender their power units for the classified overhauls of 56033, 106, 103 & 109. As well as those four, another fifteen were scheduled for 'F' exams during the 1990/91 financial year - 56007, 077, 035, 009, 086, 041, 084, 060, 083, 045 & 085, in that order, with 56069, 089, 038 & 096 following in the period up to April 1991.

The situation was clouded further by 56042. The hybrid had been out of traffic since 3rd December 1989, requiring two replacement wheelsets which, you'll recall, could not be provided by classmates. In February 1990, the Leicester aggregates pool loco was deemed surplus and, having surrendered its defective bogies to Derby, its fate seemed sealed when the power unit was removed for re-use in 56103. The remains were put into store until 29th September, when 042 became the first confirmed withdrawal.

Meanwhile, the writing on the wall appeared a little larger for the rest when various depots - Thornaby, Old Oak Common, Cardiff and Stewarts Lane - received examples of the first ten Class 60s for crew training.

With so much focus on how each sector managed its expenditure, and whether it was operating efficiently, speculation about possible traction surpluses was inevitable. The Construction sector was first in the spotlight when stories surfaced that aggregates locos 56105 & 110 were to be set aside. Similarly in February 1990, the Metals sector's 56033 & 045, based at Cardiff, arrived at Doncaster but had their overhauls delayed until the new financial year began in April because their owners wanted to conserve cash flow. Once the 'F' exams were complete, the intention was to re-allocate them to the Leicester aggregates pool (begging the obvious question of which sector would actually pay for the work), allowing the possible withdrawal of Leicester's 56058, 059 & 064 sometime during March.

Given all this, it is surprising that the end of 1991 rolled around before hard evidence emerged that *any* 56s would be joining 042 in the scrapline. By then, 56017 was 'stored unserviceable' at Crewe, and it was joined in that category by 56122 at Toton in March 1992. 122 had already been cannibalised and its bogies earmarked for 56031. Long-standing Doncaster resident 56002 was also 'stored' and, with 56017 from the FEXX Coal pool, was moved into FEZX withdrawn pool in May 1992. Their places in the stored pool were taken by 56012 & 016, both previously allocated to Nottinghamshire Coal FECN. 012 had its nameplates removed around this time.

It is also worth recording that the Class 56 and Class 58 test-bed loco 47901 was noted on a low-loader near Doncaster on 18th February 1992, en route to MC Metals, Glasgow, for scrapping.

Few of the stored locos returned, and by the end of 1993 Trainload Freight (as we must now refer to it) had withdrawn the following from all sectors: 56002, 008, 012, 013, 014, 015, 017, 023, 028, 030, 042 & 122.

Before we move on, it's worth pausing to consider Trainload Coal's plan for its 56s from the summer of 1992, not least because it shows that serious thought had been given to efficient use of resources:

56002, stored at Doncaster, to donate its power unit to 114 at Doncaster and its bogies to 125 at Toton. 56017 stored at Crewe, 56122 stored at Toton.56022 to be scrapped, its place in the FEDN Yorkshire Coal pool to be filled by 56094 ex-works from Crewe after collision repairs. 56004 & 026 (both stored 6/7/92) to be scrapped.

*Above: On 22nd November 1991, 56122 was waiting at Ryhope Grange Junction when a passing MGR train derailed and struck the No 2 end cab, causing severe damage. It was subsequently withdrawn, cannibalised for spares and never ran again. 122 had been in service for only slightly more than eight years. On 18th October 1992 the loco stands outside Toton, looking very much the worse for wear. Photo: Adrian Tibble*

*Above:* 56016 was chosen for early withdrawal in 1990, but carried on working until May 1992 when it was placed in store. Its power unit was subsequently re-used, but this Romanian never worked again. Five years before its demise, 016 emerges from Sowerby Bridge Tunnel with 6E56 Fiddler's Ferry-Healey Mills empties on 8th May 1987. *Photo: Neil Harvey*

In addition, the following would go to Doncaster and surrender major components for the overhaul of others:

```
56008  for  56113
56016  for  56123
56024  for  56125
56069  for  56119
56015  for  56121
56014  for  56129
56092  for  56128
```

It is immediately obvious that Romanian examples were high on the list for sacrifice, not least to keep British-built locos in traffic.

Fortunately for the intended victims, the possibility of increased domestic and Channel Tunnel traffic encouraged the BR Board to review its expenditure plans and assess a number of locos for overhaul which were originally to have been side-lined. As a result, all talk of withdrawing 56033, 110, *et cetera*, fizzled out and a check of the plan above shows that some, once earmarked to yield parts to others - like 004, 069 & 092 - went on to enjoy long careers. Ironically, many years later at least one of the 'recipients', 56123, would be cut up while several of the 'donors' were still going strong.

Others weren't so lucky, while some had close calls after suffering collision damage. Nine days before Christmas 1992 was a bad time for 56108 and 111 to drive into each other in Knottingley depot yard and sustain bogie and cab damage. Despatched to Toton for assessment, they were fortunate that their repair at Doncaster was authorised.

The collision-damaged 56002 moved from Doncaster BRML to Doncaster Carr in January 1993, where it sat on timber piles because its bogies had been removed for a luckier classmate.

Meanwhile, 'hopeless cases' 026 & 122 were suffering parts recovery at Toton. 56017 joined them from Crewe Works and 56015 came from Doncaster for the same purpose. 017 was in such bad condition that it had to be moved by road. In August 1993, 56028 came out of traffic from Knottingley's Aire Valley coal pool and was stored unserviceable.

Although once under a cloud, 56033 became the Automatic Train Protection test locomotive and in the summer of 1991 was fitted with ATP equipment at Derby research centre in preparation for a week of trials. The loco remained allocated to Stewarts Lane but was assigned the unique pool code FXXC - Trainload Freight General, SL Class 56, ATP Trials. As temporary cover, 56116 was re-allocated from the north-east pool to Stewarts Lane FASB while 033 was away.

Despite their new responsibilities, both locos occasionally strayed onto other work. 116, for instance, was used for a month on

*Above:* 56017 was another Romanian accident victim. It collided with a Class 31 at Ashby-de-la-Zouch on 12th November 1991 and initially moved to Crewe. In August 1992 it moved on to Toton, where its bogies were re-used and the rest of it became a 'Christmas tree' donor, until the remains were broken up on-site in May 1994. This was the state of the loco on 18th October 1992. *Photo: Adrian Tibble*

*Above:* 56041 heads for Kent at Kensington Olympia with a Foster Yeoman train in February 1994. Photo: Adrian Tibble.

crew-training at Swindon from late-February 1992, but had to be temporarily replaced by 033 because of a turbo-charger defect.

The ATP trials began again in April with 033, although 56039 had also been fitted with the equipment by then. 18th May was typical, when 033 made two runs between Swindon and Stoke Gifford with FY bogie hoppers in tow. It even managed to stray onto the 08.00 Paddington-Paignton relief on June 21st as far as Exeter, where 37672 took over. 033 brought the return working back in the evening. 56116 also made a name for itself the following November when it piloted 47351 on the 01.20 Dover-Willesden as far as Hither Green.

Normality returned in May 1993. 116 went back to Toton and 033 reclaimed its former position in Stewarts Lane FASB, effectively replacing the 'first-born' 56001 which had gone into store.

The surplus of Class 56s created by the re-shaping of the coal industry and increasing numbers of Class 60s did not pass unnoticed at Network SouthEast headquarters. This giant sector comprised the whole of former-Southern Region territory, but also extended to Norwich and King's Lynn in the east, over parts of the former London Midland and Western Regions, as well as the line from Salisbury to Exeter and, partially, beyond. The 'beyond' included the quarry at Meldon on the Okehampton branch, which produced vast quantities of ballast for the railway network. The heavy trains from the quarry had been worked by pairs of Class 33s since long before NSE's creation, but the much-loved 'Cromptons' (at least on the Southern) were by now years out of works and showing their age. Class 56s were clearly ideal replacements, having demonstrated their haulage credentials on the WR stone traffic, and so NSE 'placed an order' for twelve.

NSE planned to 'shop' all the locos before they took over the Meldon traffic, but the aspirational number of twelve was reduced to six, allegedly when NSE Director Chris Green saw the invoice from Doncaster - £1.5 million for the first six 'G' exams! Whatever the truth, the overhauls delayed the appearance of 56s on the new work until January 1993. To a large extent, NSE was at the mercy of Trainload Freight as to which locos were supplied (two of those offered were in store), although the request did stipulate that Romanian examples be excluded. Obviously, the imports in FASB pool (001, *et cetera*) had gained a bad reputation.

56031, 036 & 049 were the first three selected and they were placed in a new pool - NKJM Network SouthEast Infrastructure pool, Meldon Quarry - in November 1992. 56036 was one of the stored locos, parked at Toton needing two new wheelsets. Work began at Doncaster amid speculation about the identity of the other three and whether the locos would carry the garish NSE livery (the "upside-down Amtrak", as someone once called it). There was even a suggestion that the six locos would receive names of RAF aircraft in the tradition of the 'Battle of Britain' Class steam locomotives, but this turned out to be mere hankering for the past. In reality, the six appeared in the civil engineer's 'Dutch' livery of yellow and grey and only one carried a name - 56031 *Merehead*, a rather strange spelling of Meldon.

56049 emerged from Doncaster on 23rd January 1993 and, after a test run to Tyne Yard, appeared at Hither Green soon after. Its first working was 6Z69 Willesden-Hoo Junction ballast on 26th January but, barely twenty-four hours later, it collided with 47345 at Hither Green and had to be sent to Stewarts Lane for attention. With minor repairs completed, the loco next appeared at Stratford's fuel point on 29th January on crew training duties. Stratford would serve as a filling station, if required, when the locos worked trains to Leyton civil engineer's sidings.

56046 appeared next on the radar. This one had been stored in November 1992, closely followed by the ominous move into the 'stored unserviceable' pool - a status often indicating that a loco needed major repairs before it could work again. Even so, 046 was transferred into NKJM in January 1993, amid rumours that 56048 & 052 were to be NSE's numbers five and six.

After a tortuous journey involving 6E47 Cardiff-Scunthorpe steel, a tow to Frodingham depot and then Doncaster Carr, 046 arrived at the works on 30th January where it took the place recently vacated by 049.

Two days later, 56036 emerged from Doncaster in its new Dutch colours (the point at which Trainload Petroleum livery became obsolete on Class 56) and ran light to York to collect the works test train. After an out-and-back run to Tyne Yard, the loco ran light again to Doncaster and then to Toton on 3rd February, where it was commandeered to work a New Bank to Denby MGR before Toton finally sent the loco on its way to Stewarts Lane via Cricklewood. 036 took up residence in south London on the afternoon of 4th February and was noted on a Leyton CCE-Chesterton Junction trip eight days later.

56031 came out of Doncaster on April 7th 1993 and also worked 1N21/1D21 return test to Tyne, followed by 56046 in similar fashion on 23rd April.

A few days later, 56049 worked the Hoo-Forders spoil train, the only occasion a NKJM loco appeared on this Construction sector service. Appearances of the locos at Hoo normally indicated they would be moving on to ballast duties centred at the yard at Tonbridge.

The first of the revitalised 56s was commandeered for a railtour on 15th May, when 56031 worked the "Merry Wives' charter . . . . for Pathfinder, naturally.

The next day 56052 was allocated to the NKJM pool. Although it didn't go through works, it had been one of the 'rumours' and replaced 56047 - not rumoured but officially chosen as one of the six to join the fleet! 047 suffered derailment damage only weeks before it should have transferred and was actually 'on decision' for a week before a sympathetic soul pronounced it fit to continue. 047 transferred to NKJM on 23rd May, but 052 remained in case unexpected problems arose with the first choice locos.

Despite this official explanation, the rumours persisted about 052's inclusion (prompting the question why?) and only ended when the loco was hastily recalled to Cardiff's FMCK pool the following August because of an acute shortage of serviceable 56s at Canton (56038 had been stored that month with major faults in its non-standard Brown-Boveri exhaust system - it was out of traffic for four months - while 56054 had suffered a seemingly-endless list of faults which inevitably sent it into store).

Meanwhile back at Stewarts Lane, the first three locos had been at work for roughly six months. Typical of their varied duties were 56031 working Leyton CCE-Chesterton Junction trips on 19th & 21st May, and 56046 hauling a railtour across the Bletchley flyover on 29th May - the last train to travel the route. And they also became the mainstay of the Meldon traffic - wholly routine work which was rather overlooked at the time, such was the fascination with watching them do something unusual.

By 1st July 1993, the fifth of NSE's sextet stood complete at Doncaster - 56048,

*Above:* 56010 passes through Colchester on 29th March 1994 with 6M83 Ipswich-Ditton carbon dioxide tanks.
*Below:* 56052 at South Moreton on 26th March 1993 with 6V99 Hamworthy-Cardiff Tidal sidings. *Photos: John Hooson*

*Above: 56039 at speed through Grateley, east of Salisbury, with 6O89 06.45 Whatley-Woking ARC stone train on 14th November 1991. Photo: Martin Loader*

rumoured and actually chosen. This loco and 049 had been two of the last five 56s to carry the redundant redstripe version of Railfreight grey livery. Once those two were 'Dutched', only 56011, 019 & 108 remained. 56048 worked 1N21/ID21 Tyne test on 2nd July, followed by the last of the batch, 56047, on 27th July.

The NSE NKJM pool as a fully-formed group lasted barely six months - not much of a return for £1.5 million of overhaul investment. The Railway Act authorising the sale of the rail network had received Royal Assent in 1993, clearing the way for the setting up of three independent companies in April 1994 as a prelude to full private ownership. All six locos allocated to NSE infrastructure work transferred back to Toton at the end of January 1994 and once again became part of the main fleet, although this was merely a temporary move before the mass re-allocation of locos to the three companies. The former-NSE locos were split into two groups: 56031, 046 & 048 went to Trainload Freight-North (soon to become Loadhaul), while Trainload Freight-West (soon to become Transrail) picked up 56036, 047 & 049.

Some of the Stewarts Lane Six jumped the gun. 56049, for instance, was noted on a Milford-Fiddler's Ferry MGR on 2nd February, but by the 13th March had moved to an area more appropriate to its new owners when it was spotted at Bescot. Others were more attached to the south-east and seemed reluctant to leave. 56048 was at Willesden Brent on 4th March, while 56036 was still clinging to Stewarts Lane depot on 5th March.

Naturally, new pool codes arose with the new companies. The official day of locomotive transfer to them, 21st March, was referred to as D-Day, yet 56047 could still be found loitering in the south when the button on the computer was pressed, working 6O76 Willesden-Sheerness and 6M87 return. Twenty-four hours later, 56047 had charge of 6L76 2106 Ditton-Ipswich tanks and 6M83 return.

As for the 'new northerners', from early April anyone wanting to see 56031, 046 & 048 needed only to visit Knottingley or Milford Junction, as they rarely strayed far from their latest home. That said, 048 appeared at Toton on 18th April along with 56035, and these two operational locos provided a stark contrast with the numerous, derelict and stored examples scattered around the site, never mind the days when Toton positively shook to the sound of vibrating 56s.

Apart from the added decoration of a company logo applied to Transrail's trio, all six of the Stewarts Lane pool carried their unspoiled Dutch livery until withdrawal . . . or, in the case of 56049, until Fertis colours were applied. As such, they became famous in their own right and their travels were widely reported - quite a legacy from only a year of hauling Devon ballast.

Before moving on to the period immediately before full privatisation, here are some of the accidents and mishaps to befall Class 56 during Sectorisation - always a tricky subject as, sometimes, serious injury to traincrew and even death results.

56019 was involved in only a minor incident in April 1989 when it derailed at Lee Spur Junction near Hither Green after running through catch points, Although the loco came to rest at a precarious angle, damage was slight and repairs quickly ensued.

56062 wasn't so fortunate. On 14th June 1988 it derailed at Copyhold Junction, Haywards Heath while working the 09.55 Ardingley-Westbury ARC train. The loco rolled down an embankment and came to rest rather precariously after some saplings arrested its progress. A major civil engineering job was needed to recover it, involving earthworks, airbags, and the removal of the power unit before the locomotive body was lifted onto a fresh set of bogies. The recovery operation lasted until the 2nd of October, whereafter 062 sat in Three Bridges yard until the 29th before moving to Doncaster at no more than 45 mph. The manager of Doncaster BRML was famously quoted as saying he could repair it in less time than it had taken to recover. Fortunately, his staff responded and restored the loco to full working order by the end of February 1989, saving their manager much embarrassment. The power unit recovered from site went into 56032, the bogies into the works float.

Repairing 56062 was good practice for Doncaster, as there seemed to be a queue of 56s with major accident damage in the ensuing years. The next to arrive was 56002 with a badly-damaged No 2 end caused by the following MGR hoppers when the loco derailed while leaving Caverswall loop near Blyth Bridge with the 1500 tonne Trentham-Toton MGR. The incident occurred on 17th June 1991 and the damage was probably made worse by 56016 shoving at the back. Recovery took three weeks and, on arrival at Doncaster in early August, a decision was immediately taken to put 002 into store. The loco had only received a CEM overhaul three months earlier and in the interim had worked what would be its last passenger train - the 19.05 return footex from St Pancras to Nottingham on 18th May.

November 1991 was another bad month. On the 12th, 56017 collided with 31459 at Ashby-de-la-Zouch, closely followed by 56122's disastrous encounter with a passing MGR train at Ryhope Grange mentioned in an earlier chapter. No 2 end cab was seriously damaged and brought about the loco's premature withdrawal. Around this time, 56094 was noted being dragged through Doncaster station with tarpaulins over a damaged cab. This one had been a victim of a failure to observe the operational requirement for locos at Gascoigne Wood *not* to pass under the loading bunker because of clearance issues caused by subsidence during construction. 094's No 1 end cab was scalped.

Far more serious, 56066 suffered severe collision damage in a fatal accident at Morpeth on 13th November 1992. The 56 ran into the back of a pipe train hauled by 37717, which had stopped at a defective level crossing. The loco was towed to Blyth Cambois with the damaged cab sheeted over and, given the coal industry cutbacks announced earlier that year, it was widely assumed it would not be repaired. However, the reprieve of some collieries created an extra demand for locomotives and 066 was put through Doncaster works in 1994 and returned to service in July 1995. It was reported that InterCity, the sector responsible for the maintenance of the crossing equipment, contributed to the repair costs.

56128 had only been out of works a matter of weeks when it was involved in a shunting accident at Sunderland South Dock on 4th December 1992. As usual, the MGR hopper inflicting the damage came off best, leaving 128 with a heavy score mark down one side. The loco was re-allocated to FEXX pool on 13th December and later moved to Doncaster where it joined 56108 & 111 awaiting similar repairs. One good thing about this accident was that it put 56128 in the right place at the right time to receive the *West Burton Power Station* nameplates removed from a recently-condemned 56028.

On 6th February 1993, 56057 & 058 were working a southbound aggregates train through Dorridge when the train's fourth hopper derailed and damaged about a quarter-mile of plain track and ripped up a crossover before coming to a stand 400 yards past the pointwork. The incident occurred at around 12.30 pm and the train was cleared by 10.30 that night. Unfortunately, the track wasn't reinstated for another two days.

While travelling down the dead-end Bates branch on 14th February 1994, the last wagon in 56117's train derailed. Because of the low speed, the wagon remained in line and upright, and the continuous brake pipe didn't separate and apply the brakes until half-a-mile of track had been badly damaged. 117 was effectively stranded, but the demand for serviceable 56s was so high at the time that it was thought justifiable to recover it by road rather than wait for the track to be re-laid. The movement took place on 21st February to return 117 to the main rail network - not quite as dramatic as the locomotives stranded on Anglesey after the Britannia bridge fire in the 1970s, but a good story all the same.

*Above:* 56002 came to grief while working an MGR train in June 1991. The loco awaits recovery at Caverswall, near Blythe Bridge, north Staffordshire, on 13th July 1991. *Photo: Paul Bettany*

*Above:* 56050 pulls away from a signal check at South Moreton on 16th November 1988 while working 6V17 10.00 Allington-Stoke Gifford ARC stone empties. *Photo: Martin Loader*

# GRIDS 7. PRE-PRIVATISATION 1994 - 1996

*Above:* 56048, now part of Trainload Freight North-East, pulls away from Milford with an MGR on 9th May 1994. At this time the loco was allocated to Immingham's FDBI pool for working Construction, Metals and Petroleum traffic! *Photo: Neil Harvey*

The three 'Trainload companies' - Transrail, Loadhaul and Mainline Freight - officially came into being on 1st April 1994, but they did not become truly independent until the following September when their trading names were officially announced. In the interim, they kept their temporary names - Trainload Freight West, Trainload Freight North East and Trainload Freight South East. From September, they were meant to compete with each other for traffic, rather than operating as protected divisions of British Rail. They would also actively (rather than passively) compete with the road haulage industry and any new rail freight operators entering the market under the 'open access' policy enshrined in the 1993 Railway Act.

At the same time, railway infrastructure, including all the track, was taken over by a new private company called Railtrack, which would administer the requirements of open access, provide paths and timings to operators, and invoice them for the emotive 'access charges'. In return for the cash, Railtrack assumed responsibility for the maintenance and improvement of the entire rail network - an arrangement which inevitably ended in tears.

For the first time in Britain's railway history, companies running main line freight trains were not the owners of track or the yards in which they operated - a principle also extended to the passenger sector, which lost both track and the ownership of stations.

The remaining non-passenger sectors in British Rail's portfolio - Railfreight Distribution (international and wagonload trains), Freightliner (container trains generated by port traffic) and Rail Express Systems (parcels and mail trains) were similarly re-structured and would ultimately be offered for sale to the private sector alongside the Trainload companies.

The period of 'phoney privatisation' between April and September 1994 was deliberately engineered to allow time for things to settle down after the restructuring and to thrash out the initial allocation of traffic flows to each company - mostly determined by where the flow originated. The exception was coal. Because the origin of the product could change, it was decided that this traffic belonged to the company in whose area the destination power station was located. From September, however, the gloves were off and the flows of each company became fair game for the others to bid for.

To position themselves to take maximum advantage of this 'opportunity' - not to mention deflecting the threat of having their own traffic poached - the three companies had to reduce their costs. This inevitably raised a very big question mark over the 56s. One phrase that could never be applied to them was 'cheap to maintain'. Any work other than routine 'A' and 'B' exams was immensely time-consuming and therefore costly. Toton, for instance, documented that merely removing the roof panels to gain access to components on top of the power unit took two men an entire shift, while fitters in the north-east claimed to have built home extensions and enjoyed exotic foreign holidays purely on the back of overtime payments generated by the 56s in their care. In its favour, the class remained numerically large and therefore difficult to eliminate without creating new problems. Perversely, a large fleet was also cheaper to maintain because, if reduced, the economies of scale would be lost - precisely what had happened, the cynics pointed out, by dividing the surviving 56 fleet between two of the new companies.

One solution was the companies' eventual concentration on heavier trains at the expense of service frequency. Two well-loaded trains per week would often replace lightly-loaded daily services - a policy which created increased demand for Type 5 locomotives. Such are the fine balances of modern-day cost accounting and their effect on our favourite locomotives.

Another innovation was the creation of 'super depots' - one each, as it turned out, at Cardiff Canton (Transrail), Immingham (Loadhaul) and Toton (Mainline Freight). The surviving smaller depots were used solely to out-base locomotives for local work although some, such as Blyth and Springs Branch, continued to have a permanent allocation. For the rest, the restructuring brought closure.

Here is the original plan, showing the three super depots with their designated out-bases:

**Cardiff** - Bescot, Springs Branch, Motherwell, Ayr, Buxton, Carlisle Upperby, Gloucester, Margam, Millerhill and St Blazey.

*Above:* 56090 & 135 pass Colton Junction with 6D11 *Tees Yard-Scunthorpe steel empties. 135 has already lost its sector branding. Photo: Neil Harvey*

**Immingham** - Thornaby, Knottingley, Doncaster Carr, Blyth, Sunderland South Dock and Healey Mills.

**Toton** - Stewarts Lane, Eastleigh, Stratford, Shirebrook, Didcot, Hither Green, Leicester and Peterborough.

Lack of maintenance facilities in the north-west was a potential problem for Transrail's Cardiff fleet out-based at Springs Branch, but deploying 56s on the Irving-Burngullow china clay service was projected as a convenient method of moving them to and from Cardiff for maintenance. 'Buying in' maintenance from Rail Express Systems at Crewe Diesel was also considered.

No sooner had the plan been published than Loadhaul (or Trainload Freight North-East as it still was) decided to close Sunderland South Dock. Its final day was the 9th of April and 56051, 081 & 094 were the last locos to use the facility. 051 was the last to depart.

In the new spirit of privatisation, each company planned to charge for servicing and fuel supplied to visiting locos. This arose from the lessons learned during the Sectorisation experiment in 1987, when original policy had dictated that each sector's locos must be serviced at a facility 'owned' by that sector. It proved both inefficient and wasteful; convoys of up to five Class 47s, for example, regularly ran from the Stanlow area to Healey Mills, when both Springs Branch and Crewe Diesel were much nearer. The disincentive was that they were operated by a different sector, which would have charged for servicing.

In advance of the new era, and with traffic growing, it was decided to put more 56s through works. Most of the work went to Doncaster, although in March 1993 Toton began a programme of Light overhauls. In the year, Doncaster turned out 56121, 073, 097, 124, 134, 087 & 129 - in that order - as well as the last four locos for NSE's Meldon pool. Between March 1993 and the year-end, Toton processed 56094, 062, 127, 091, 135, 081, 078, 071 & 092.

By the end of 1993, Doncaster had cleared out all of its 56s except the collision-damaged 066, but the next wave soon arrived. During early 1994, there was a steady stream needing attention including, interestingly, two of the Romanian examples previously side-lined:

| | |
|---|---|
| January | 56131 |
| February | 56004, 043, & 093 |
| March | 56022, 082, & 029. |

It soon became apparent to the new companies that this work was expensive (as NSE had discovered a year earlier) and that works capacity was liable to become a constraint in itself. Transrail's solution was to begin a programme of light overhauls at Cardiff Canton. In the early months of 1994, 56052 & 053 were dealt with but work on the next, 56101, did not begin until October.

With no 56s allocated to Mainline Freight (or TLF South East), Toton's involvement ceased by April 1994, but not before 56011, 080, 108, 102, 081, 133 had been partially overhauled like the earlier batch. Each was released in two-tone grey without sector markings. In time the locos' change of ownership would involve new liveries and logos, but not before the company names were officially announced in September. Given the present day obsession with paint and plastic stickers, it is surprising that none of the overhauled locos ran around with Trainload Freight-something-or-other on their bodysides in the five-month 'ghost' period. Obviously, cost was being taken very seriously.

The mass re-allocation of locomotives produced a few unexpected results. TLF South, for instance, received no 56s but took over the entire fleet of 58s. Given that a significant proportion of the company's work was aggregates traffic in and around the former Southern Region, where all traincrew were familiar with Class 56, this looked a little odd at first glance. The fifty locos of Class 58, of course, had only ever been allocated to Toton and it was thought that transferring them elsewhere could have raised reliability issues.

The initial plan for Class 56 involved a two-way split - 57 going to TLF West at Canton, and 74 to TLF North at Immingham. These figures included stored and withdrawn examples and almost immediately some of the stored Romanian locos were reinstated and included in the overhaul programme.

Before the official start of Trainload on 1st April, a number of transfers into the new loco pools took place at the end of February and Class 56s immediately began to appear on flows and at locations where they were hitherto unknown. This created some interesting workings for the class, especially on what had been known as contract services workings, i.e flows which did not fit in with any of the TLF sectors' portfolios.

The Elgin-Dee Marsh logs, English China Clay's St Blazey-Cliffe Vale, the Willesden-Cameron Bridge carbon dioxide tanks, and Earles-Widnes cement traffic all switched to Class 56 haulage in advance of the April date. Purely by chance, most of these originated in the TLF West area - the yardstick, you'll recall, by which non-coal traffic flows were originally allocated. This good fortune allowed TLF-W, and later Transrail, to develop a new 'Enterprise' network, handling wagon loads in a well-managed system of collection and delivery trips feeding into main trunk flows between Mossend, Carlisle, Warrington, Bescot and Willesden.

The mass locomotive re-allocation of 'D-Day', the 21st of March, produced the following starting positions for Class 56:

### Trainload Freight North
*Blyth* (pool FMBB): 16 locos for 12 north-east coal diagrams - 56051, 062, 081, 107-112, 117, 118, 120, 130, 131, 134 & 135.

*Thornaby* (pool FMBY): 10 locos for 7 diagrams - 5 for Metals and 2 for Boulby traffic - 56034, 039, 045, 050, 061, 063, 069, 087, 097 & 116.

*Knottingley* (pool FDBY): 22 locos for 17 Aire Valley power station diagrams - 56005, 006, 011, 021, 031, 043, 046, 055, 067, 068, 070, 074, 075, 077, 078, 080, 083, 091, 095, 098, 100 & 102 (working alongside Class 60s).

*Immingham* (pool FDBI): 12 locos for 9 diagrams covering 3 Metals duties, 3 Construction and 3 Petroleum (including Glazebrook) - 56035, 041, 048, 082, 084, 085, 088, 089, 090, 094, 106 & 126.

### Trainload Freight West
*Wigan* (pool LWBK): 24 locos for 19 diagrams -3 for Fiddler's Ferry coal, 4 contract services (RfD traffic), 4 Deanside pet food, 4 for Burn Naze and Enterprise network, 1 driver training at Ellesmere Port, 1 driver training at Wembley, 2 for Stanlow petroleum duties - 56004, 010, 018, 019, 025, 029, 033, 036, 037, 049, 056-059, 065, 072, 086, 092, 093, 096, 099, 101, 132 & 133.

*Bescot* (pool LBAK): 7 locos for 5 duties including 3 Ironbridge coal and some construction traffic from Witton - 56007, 009, 047, 071, 079, 103 & 105.

*Cardiff* (pool LNBK): 15 locos for 11 duties including 5 for south-west metals traffic, 4 for south-west-Midlands metals traffic and 2 to replace 37/7 on metals duties - 56032, 038, 040, 044, 052, 053, 054, 060, 064, 073, 076, 113, 114, 115 & 119.

*Ayr* (pool LGAM): 8 locos, plus 4 x 37, for 7 duties - 5 Ayrshire coal, 1 FCPM, 1 spare - 56104, 121, 123-125 & 127-129.

Between May and July TLF North carried out some shuffling between depots, moving 56034, 039, 045 & 050 from Thornaby to Immingham's FDBI pool, 062, 081, 084, 085 & 090 from Immingham to Thornaby's FMBY pool, and an inter-company transfer of 56065 from Cardiff to FMBY.

The new company identities were announced during the summer, at which point the paint and plastic began to appear. Transrail opted for the original Trainload Freight grey as its base livery, rather unimaginatively, with Transrail logos added to the bodysides. 56025 was the first to be treated, closely followed by 56044, 072, 073 & 099. On 9th September 1994, the staff launch of Transrail at St Blazey enjoyed the sight of 56044 and a Class 60 working into Cornwall with a rake of Transrail-branded freight stock.

Loadhaul adopted a new and startling black/orange livery, which it first applied to display locomotive 56039. There was no mass outbreak of re-painting. Many locos, no matter what their new ownership, worked out the Trainload era in the freight grey, with only the occasional coloured logo to relieve their drabness.

Those that were re-painted sometimes threw up variants. In August 1994, the second of Loadhaul's examples, 56034, appeared in a slightly different scheme, with a reversed application of the orange wrap-around on one cab. Obviously, scheme two received more votes, as the 'reversed' wrap wrap was adopted on subsequent repaints.

56074 was the next to appear in new colours, with 56006 & 050 expected to emerge from works in similar guise. Curiously, a shortage of Loadhaul logos resulted in some locos running with either one or both bodysides in plain black.

For the sake of 'image' - something all privatised railway companies have embraced fervently - the first loco in any new livery is often requested for special events or workings. 56039, for instance, showed off the new Loadhaul image on 14th February 1995 when it handled the first working from the newly-opened Kingston Terminal in Hull. The train comprised 30 HAAs of petroleum coke for Foxton cement works. Six weeks later, the same loco worked the first train out of Markham Main colliery since rail traffic temporarily ceased there three years earlier.

In the south-east, Mainline Freight initially only re-branded its locos and the end of 1994 rolled around before the attractive Mainline Blue livery was unveiled.

Although Mainline had no formal Class 56 allocation, three locos continued to reside at Toton after their withdrawal in late 1993. As such, 56013, 023 & 122 were briefly allocated to Mainline's ENZX 'locos for withdrawal' pool.

Of course, Class 56-hauled trains continued to visit the south-east from the areas of Transrail and Loadhaul - workings such as the Cameron Bridge-Brent carbon dioxide tanks and the Ditton-Ipswich liquid oxygen tanks, as well as the traffic to paper mills in the south. The-soon-to-emerge Enterprise network, part of which linked Quidhampton near Salisbury with Port Elphinstone in Scotland, also produced 56s. Terminals at Thurrock in Essex and Corkickle on the Cumbrian coast exchanged sodium tripolyphosphate traffic on which 56s were regular performers too.

Typical of the free-roaming nature of the fleet at the time, 56010 worked the 09.18 Corkickle-Willesden as far as Crewe on 2nd April but, three days later, could be found stabled at Motherwell in the company of 56094, 103 & 124. By the 18th, 56010 was at the opposite end of the country, paired up with 132 on china clay workings into Bowater's paper factory at Sittingbourne in Kent.

As the paper re-allocation of locomotives had taken place nine days earlier as a precautionary measure, nothing much physically happened on 1st April 1994 when British Rail ceased to exist. Many 56s remained in their former areas, working the

*Above:* Transrail took the cheap option when it came to 're-livery'. It kept the existing triple-grey scheme and simply replaced the sector brandings with its own logos. 56119 shows off the new 'scheme' while working 6M29 Llanwern-Dee Marsh steel coils at Onibury. *Photo: Martin Loader*

*Above:* In stark contrast to Transrail, Loadhaul came up with this startling livery. 56039 was the first to receive the new colours, although the outline shape of the orange panels was slightly modified on later locos. This one made its first public appearance at the Railfair 800 Open Day held at Doncaster Works on 9th July 1994. *Photo: Derek Porter*

same trains, such as the Scottish and north-east coal traffic. The class also continued shipping coal for Cawood's containerised service to Ireland; the only change was that coal later originated from South Wales as well as the locations mentioned earlier.

Also on-going at the start of 1994 was the plan to replace 37/7s with 56s on the Cwmbargoed branch and its six mile section of 1 in 40 descent. This was not going well; after damage to loco tyres because of the severe braking required, a number of modifications were applied to the wagons to try and encourage the train to take more of the braking strain. Trials took place throughout 1994 - 56114 appeared on 23rd February, 56038 suffered worn tyres during trials on 29th May and, finally, pairs of 37s were temporarily reintroduced in August simply to avoid the need for Barry depot to cope with two types of MGR rake with different brake characteristics for the Tower and Cwmbargoed traffic. Trials continued with wagon sets with modified brake distributors; on 23rd November, for instance, 56071 worked one such trial and better results were obtained. Thereafter, the class began working regularly on the 26,000 tonnes of coal despatched from Cwmbargoed to Aberthaw power station each week, although increased maintenance costs inevitably ensued for both wagons and track. On 13th March 1995, 56073 worked an engineering train along the Cwmbargoed branch, probably repairing some of the damage caused by the severe braking needed to keep heavy trains in check during the descent.

As the dust began to settle after the upheaval of the Trainload companies' creation, 56s regularly began to appear on other new flows. The Glazebrook to Haverton Hill and Port Clarence tanker trains, for instance, brought locos of the class to the Manchester suburbs. The 6E50 Immingham-Glazebrook tanks also regularly produced a 56. Although this work should have been covered by Immingham's FDBI pool, Blyth and Thornaby locos appeared just as often as the correct pool. 56050 worked one such train on 4th June, 56062 on the 5th and 56108 on the 29th. The Stalybridge-Immingham tanks was also a regular turn and threw up Dutch-liveried 56031 on 9th May 1994. Other potential chemical flows were also being explored, producing 56036 on a caustic soda train trial along the Seal Sands branch on 20th August.

Immediately on its creation, Trainload North East decided to roster 56s to the Boulby potash and rock salt traffic. Changes to loco diagrams on 27th March resulted in 56s taking over workings from Boulby to Tees Dock from Class 37s. 56097 was one of the first, sighted on 6P24 11.24 Boulby-Tees two days later. This change not only provided an opportunity for some spectacular cliff-top photography, but also increased the operation's productivity by adding two extra bogie hoppers, taking the Grid-size load of each train up to ten. On a typical day, two 56s worked along the branch.

The Immingham-Leith Docks fertiliser traffic - 6S33 21.18 northbound and 6E26 11.50 return - also became a regular working for TLF North's 56s. 56031's appearance on November 11th 1994 brought a former-NSE loco into Scotland. In fact, traction seemed to come from all of TLF North's pools except the Blyth allocation. Another Anglo-Scottish 56-hauled working began on 19th August, running from Gascoigne Wood to Inverness via the S&C.

Meanwhile in the TLF West area, the Cliffe Vale-St Blazey china clay trains had become solid turns for 56s from the start of 1994, a practice which continued for a time under the new company, usually with the Type 5 working to and from Exeter Yard. At the end of that summer, however, Class 37s reappeared and worked throughout. Inevitably, the failure of a Type 3 pairing brought a 56 back onto the clay - 56113 on October 4th, following the rescue at Whitchurch of 37413 & 696 on a Burngullow-Irvine working. The 37s were towed dead as far as Crewe, from where 113 took the train forward to Irvine.

The Deanside-Wisbech petfood trains were also booked for 56s from 29th March 1994 - workings with which the class would be associated almost to the end of their service on the network. RfD 47s had previously dominated this flow and initially 56s ran only as far as Doncaster because of clearance issues on the final section of the branch. Perhaps as a precaution, 47298 piloted 56103 from March on the first day with the

63

*Above:* On 3rd October 1995, 56086 departs from Cardiff Canton for London Euston the day before its naming there as *The Magistrates' Association*. Photo: Adrian Tibble

northbound Deanside working. However, the meaty chunks soon settled down to, frankly, monotonous 56 haulage, often with the same Scottish-based locos passing each other day in and day out.

The full duty, calling for two locos from the Motherwell/Ayr LGAM pool, comprised:

*6L80* 14.45 Deanside-Wisbech arriving at 02.30
*Light engine* Wisbech-Peterborough for fuel and stabling
*Light engine* 15.00 Peterborough-Wisbech, to work...
*6S93* 18.50 Wisbech-Deanside.

TLF-W/Transrail went to great efforts to ensure these trains were 56-hauled throughout. A good example is October 4th 1995 when 56072 worked the southbound train as far as Warrington Arpley, where 047 was waiting to take over, releasing 072 to take fuel.

The change to operating less frequent but heavier trains resulted in some traffic being combined. Scrap from Shotton to Llanwern, for instance, was conveyed in one of the Dee Marsh-Llanwern coil trains. The increased loadings also brought an increase in double-heading on metals trains. A memorable example occurred on 18th August 1994 when 56032 & 053 hauled a heavy scrap working up the Camp Hill incline in Birmingham, banked by 56097!

The diagramming of pairs to the 6M45 Barry ICI-Burn Naze also proved a handy way of getting Springs Branch locos to and from maintenance appointments at Canton. 56010 & 125 on 26th April and 56007 & 070 on 11th July are but two examples. Normally the train was booked for a single 56 and a month of observation of 6M45 and 6V26 return in January 1995 revealed the dominance of LNBK locos 56053, 073 and 076, but with LWBK's 56037 also doing its fair share.

In advance of the handover on 1st April 1994, the Stanlow-Dalston oil tanks also became a new flow for 56s - 6P42 08.20 outward and 6P44 17.25 return. The former 37/7s had earned a reputation for failure with this working on Shap. It only ran twice a week, on Tuesdays and Thursdays, but in the week before 56s took over, Type 3s had failed twice! 56099 appeared first, on 23rd March, followed by 56025 on the Thursday service. Both train crews remarked on the ease with which the extra power ascended Shap. Following the trend, in September 1994 fuel trains between Dalston and Grangemouth went over to 56 haulage, a duty which included the Fridays only Grangemouth-Motherwell TMD tanks.

A new timetable introduced on 25th September produced another new 56 flow from Transrail - the twice-weekly train between Ordsall Lane, Salford, and Park Royal in west London. Probably better known for what it carried rather then the traction provided, the Guinness Train appeared in the timetable as 6V15 and 6M77 return. 56s consistently worked the 'other black stuff' for nine months, until the traffic ceased in June 1995.

With the new September timetable came Transrail's introduction of the Enterprise trains, aimed at filling the gap left by Speedlink three years earlier. Unlike Speedlink the new network was more efficient in reducing duplication of core flows and making maximum use of resources which would otherwise be idle. As one example, previously a short rake of timber-carrying OTAs would have run from Scotland to Chirk, near Wrexham. Under Enterprise, the same wagons would form part of a trunk train between Mossend and Warrington, with tripping to and from both locations by dedicated locos. Often, the train engine would be similarly used to convey wagons to customers' sites rather than using a smaller loco. Intensive working, coupled with reduced down-time, ensured Enterprise became one of the big successes of the Trainload period.

Given the increased train weights that resulted, Enterprise also reinforced the case for keeping 56s in front-line service. For example, the Aberdeen-Willesden working, originally timed as a Class 6 service with a maximum speed of 60mph, was re-timed as a Class 4 running at 75mph. This allowed the former 10am departure from Aberdeen to be put back to 16.00 - much more convenient for customers needing to despatch goods south at the end of the working day.

56s performed on Enterprise feeder workings as well as the main trunk flows, conveying all manner of goods in the consists. One of the more unusual occurred on 18th October 1995 when 56047 had 50021 as part of its load. The 50 was heading for a new life in preservation at the Bo'ness Railway.

Until the contract services trains mentioned previously were absorbed into the Enterprise network - such as Cameron Bridge-Willesden $CO_2$ tanks, Port Elphinstone-Willesden and 6M37 Quidhampton EEC-Willesden Brent - 56s continued to work them as separate duties.

One of the few exceptions at the time was the heavy Warrington-Mossend Enterprise which needed extra power over Shap and was normally entrusted to a Class 60. However, all other sections of the trunk flows and almost any of the feeder services could be, and very often were, worked by 56s.

Enterprise's ability to move any customer's wagon to any point on the network wasn't lost on Transrail's maintenance controllers, who often used it as free transport for shifting locos to and from servicing points. Like 50021, 56s could often be found dead in tow as part of an Enterprise consist, such as 019 hitching a ride on 2nd February 1995 behind 60085 between Mossend and Warrington. Another powerful motivation was the dreaded access charge which arose from each and every light engine move; as well as the use of Enterprise, the instances of multiple engine moves increased, often with three or four coupled together en route to fuelling points or maintenance facilities. Further sneaky moves around Railtrack's invoice generator involved other sectors; on at least one occasion, a Class 56 was coupled inside a Virgin passenger train at Euston to transfer it north. As Virgin faced the same charging situation, there were undoubtedly instances when its stock was moved free of charge by Transrail by way of repayment.

The cost-saving implications of maximising resources also led to 56s appearing on what had previously been purely Type 2 and Type 3 work. Fuel oil deliveries to locomotive depots were a good example; many of the trains run on Saturdays, such as the Toton-Stanlow tanks, utilised Type 5s which would otherwise have been idle. In the same spirit, 56071 & 056 appeared at either end of a ballast train on the Bootle branch on 1st August 1994, probably repairing track they had helped to damage the previous week. Trips to the CWR depot at Castleton provided Toton with a convenient out-and-back working, which was often used to test locos straight after maintenance. Type 5s regularly appeared on this working.

The new timetable of September 1994 encouraged Loadhaul to re-assess its requirement for maintenance depots. The immediate result was the closure of Blyth Cambois on the 17th, only a week after the 'Blyth Spirit III' railtour had visited the area with 56090 as train loco. Previously, Blyth had carried out maintenance on the FMBB pool up to and including 'C' exams.

*Above:* 56112 heads past Freemans Crossing at North Blyth with an empty MGR train for Tyne Yard. The depot at Blyth closed on 17th September 1994 after Loadhaul re-assessed its requirement for maintenance facilities. *Photo: Martin Loader*

As another example of a small depot servicing only one type of locomotive, it too had returned impressive availability figures, but there was no place for sentiment in the great quest to save money. The work moved to a new facility opened on 4th September at Tyne Yard, where the FMBB pool had been officially out-based since the middle of August. Although nothing changed on the ground, the fleet was soon re-allocated on paper to Immingham.

The spread of the class required intensive crew training and on 8th June 1994 56007 went to Eastleigh to replace 56059 on this work. While returning light engine to Wembley on the following June 28th, 007 caught fire at Winchester. It eventually arrived back at its Cardiff home on 11th August, dead in tow in a Dover-Cardiff freight and curiously sporting collision damage as well as the scorch marks.

Despite all the changes of 1994, 56s continued to stand in for failed locos as they had in previous years. On 11th June, 56113 made a return to old duties when it appeared instead of the more usual Class 60 on a Dee Marsh-Margam empty steel train. On 3rd September, 56111 worked the Bedworth-Humber *vice* Class 60; the following week, 56071 & 093 worked in multiple on the Ipswich-Ditton tanks. On 27th November, 56010 worked the Saturdays only coal train from Toton to Bicester army base.

The reorganisation of freight traffic became such a focus during this time that the diagramming of 56s to drag the 1S77 sleeper from Euston between Carstairs and Edinburgh - via the suburban lines! -passed almost unnoticed. This work came about because of OHL maintenance, and in the period 29th May to 6th June produced a 56 every night. However, only three different locos appeared - 56058 and 56079, both twice, and 56072 five times. Later the same month, 56114 enjoyed a run over the Welsh Marches with 1M89 16.45 Cardiff-Manchester after the inbound working arrived with a sick 37408 (assisted from Bristol by 47709). 114 took over from Cardiff as the 47 was considered unsuitable for the return working. Curiously, the 56 was replaced by 31452 at Crewe.

In July 1994, OHL problems at Penrith prompted the despatch of 56022 to rescue the 09.05 Birmingham-Glasgow and take it forward to Carlisle where the AC electric regained the juice. 022 made two more trips between Carlisle and Preston, southbound with the 17.10 Edinburgh-Birmingham and back with the 18.30 Euston-Carlisle. A week later, 56124 was hired by InterCity to haul the 20.10 Polmadie-Edinburgh ECS; it later assisted 87030 between Carstairs and Glasgow on the 23.55 ex-Euston. In August, two Class 56s notched up the first visit of the class to Inverness, when 56101 and 104 worked various legs of the 2-day 'Grampian Highlander' railtour on the 6th & 7th.

Crew training stints continued as 1995 dawned. In the first week of February, 56071 set out from Bescot on a route learning special via Basford Hall to the recently-reopened Silverdale colliery link. This was followed on the 7th by 56022 working 7P67 10.45 Silverdale to Oakleigh. After discharging the load, 022 returned the empties to Warrington Arpley via Chester. 56132 repeated this pattern on February the 9th.

The summer of 1995 produced an interesting development in East Anglia. Freightliner traffic to and from the Felixstowe terminal had been in the hands of pairs of RfD Class 47s, but they were replaced by single 56s from 24th July. Mainline Freight had earlier supplied Class 58s for trials on this work, but it was Loadhaul who eventually hired 56s to RfD. On the first day 56003, 107 & 106 appeared. As before, one loco tripped the containers from Ipswich to the port, but single locos also worked back to inland terminals such as Lawley Street, Wilton and Stourton. The Wilton trains were regularly used to exchange 56s when they became due for maintenance at Thornaby.

Some unusual diversions occurred. On 28th October, for example, all Felixstowe Freightliner traffic, including the electric-hauled services, was diverted via Cambridge, producing the sight of 56109 hauling 90147 and its train, and 56061 hauling 90148. In the week commencing 25th July, the 00.18 Lawley Street-Felixstowe was diverted via South Tottenham. The list of 56s involved makes interesting reading, as all but 56048 remain technically operational in 2009: 56003 - 25th July; 56045 - 26th; 56003 again - 27th; 56097 - 28th; 56048 - 29th.

Despite fears that 56s would be removed from Felixstowe traffic by the autumn of 1995, 031, 045 & 107 could still be found at Ipswich

65

*Above:* From 24th July 1995, Loadhaul began supplying 56s for Freightliner workings over the non-electrified branch between Ipswich and Felixstowe, as well as some of the inland workings. The first Grid on the branch was 56003, here captured at Levington. *Photo: John Hooson*

on liner duties on 25th October, and 035, 085, 107, & 117 on November 18th.

Freightliner also borrowed Transrail 56s on occasions. 56119 worked the Pengam-Coatbridge liner on 27th September 1995 as far as Crewe, where 86634 & 638 took over. On 17th November, Loadhaul's 56080 & 083 ran light from Knottingley to Basford Hall to assist during OHL maintenance. Over the next three days, the locos worked various liners between Basford Hall and Carlisle, running via Newcastle and York.

Trains continued to operate in and out of collieries after their closure to shift the massive stockpiles of coal still on site. Westoe, for example, a mine with seams running far out under the North Sea, brought its last coal onto dry land in 1993, but the stockpile was only cleared by operating three trains each weekday to Tyne coal terminal until February 1995.

Other freight developments in 1995 included a new steel service from the Cobra plant at Wakefield and steel slab from Tinsley to Seaforth for export to Ireland. An occasional working for Class 56 conveyed gas oil tanks from Harwich Parkeston Quay to Aberdeen Guild Street. Running as 6Z15, 56126 worked the northbound train on 22nd September. Seven days later, 56048 worked the southbound train as far as Tyne, where 56126 took over to return the empty tanks to Harwich.

A single 56 from the LWBK pool (a Cardiff loco out-based at Springs Branch) remained allocated to the 6H33 14.00 Widnes-Earles Sidings cement train.

On 3rd October, 56060 hauled a containerised coal train from Coedbach to Roath Dock. Previously this coal had gone to Seaforth for shipment. The fact that it was containerised meant it could be easily handled by road vehicles, and on 30th October 56027 worked a trial of domestic coal from Gascoigne Wood to Stourton Freightliner Terminal, from where the load was distributed by road to houses in the Leeds area.

The Waterston-Heathfield oil train took a 56 deep into Devon for a few weeks late in 1995. 56076 was the first on November 1st, followed a week later by 56010. The class missed a week before 56119 turned up on the 22nd.

As stockpiles at long-closed collieries were finally shifted, attention turned to the further development of facilities for imported coal. As one example, on 5th October 56119 carried out additional tests at the Avonmouth import terminal. In another departure from the norm, the Immingham-Coedbach MGR was regularly powered by either 56113, 114, 115 or 119 in the middle of 1995.

In an earlier chapter, mention was made of the significant variations in coal's calorific properties, resulting in the long-distance movement of 'suitable' product when there appeared to be resources much closer to hand. After the pit closures of the late 1980s/early 90s, many customers with special requirements, in terms of calorific value, moisture content, clean burning properties, *et cetera*, found that the nearest and most convenient colliery had closed. One example of a special requirement creating long-distance movements was the Killoch-Ketton working. Killoch's output had properties which made it more suitable for the energy-intensive cement rendering process, a requirement which created a new long haul for 56111 on October the 8th. The train normally ran with a pair of 37s from Killoch to Carlisle yard, where a 56 took over for the run south via the S&C, Leicester and Peterborough.

On the works front, Loadhaul provided Doncaster with the lion's share of its work in 1995, but not exclusively. The company obviously had ambitious plans for the class because, in late December 1994, 56084, 085, 110 & 116 were despatched to ABB Crewe for major overhaul. By February 1995, Loadhaul was also investigating the possibility of overhauls at Brush's Loughborough works. 56107 arrived there for assessment and was eventually released in July after a General. The work on this loco was the development stage for the 'mini mod' programme of reliability improvements carried out on subsequent overhauls. 56041, 068 & 102 were dealt with during 1995. Meanwhile, Transrail continued Light overhauls at Cardiff, but can hardly have been happy with the rate of output. 56101 was still there almost a year after arriving, while 56064 spent six months undergoing overhaul.

Long-term Crewe resident 56127 eventually emerged on 6th March 1995. This loco had arrived for engine repairs in the summer of 1993, only months after a Light repair at Toton. 31235 was provided to tow 127 the short distance to Basford Hall, but a brake fault sent it back to works the next day. At the second attempt, the loco made it as far as Warrington behind 31190 on 13th March and subsequently reached Transrail HQ at Cardiff. Following attention to a traction motor defect, 127 then worked as far as Bescot on March the 23rd . . . and failed again. It was towed back to Cardiff by 56036, along with 009 &

*Above:* 56134 hauls 4L79 Wilton-Felixstowe liner through Milford. This flow was used to swop over 56s when they became due for servicing at Thornaby. *Photo: Neil Harvey*

099. Canton sorted her out by the end of the month and on 29th March she appeared on an MGR working from Cwmgwrach to Aberthaw, before returning with the empties to Jersey Marine yard.

Exactly why 127 remained at Crewe for so long is unclear. It is thought the work had been completed many months before her eventual release, prompting the theory that the newly-created Transrail had no immediate need for the loco and was therefore in no hurry to pay the bill. An alternative line of thought suggested the engine repairs had become part of a protracted warranty claim against the engine manufacturer. Whatever the truth, we shall probably never know the full story of 127's two years in limbo.

The four locos that arrived at Crewe in December 1994 were dealt with much more quickly. By 3rd April 1995, 56084 was out on test with 47467 and seven Res vans along the North Wales coast. Two days later, 56085 followed with the same test train and 47467. On April the 20th, 56116 ran a test accompanied by 47625, but 56110 did not emerge from works until 30th July.

Meanwhile, Doncaster continued to churn them out and the summary of arrivals and departures at all works during 1995 makes interesting reading (see next page). Test train details have been included where verified.

The quick turn-around times demanded of Doncaster and Crewe created problems of their own. 56003, for example, soon suffered a suspected seized wheelset and had to be towed from Tyne to Thornaby by 37519 on

### The 'Mini Mods' programme

This package was aimed at improving the locos' reliability by tackling persistent problems with the contactors in the electric compartment by:

1. Replacing old contactors and relays with new (a complex wiring job for the Brush engineers)

2. Ensuring the clean-air compartment was truly clean to reduce the instances of oil mist and dirt deposits (especially coal dust) building up on the contactors. The whole of the clean air compartment roof was removed and new filtration panels fitted at cantrail height.

The first three locos treated - 56041, 56068 and 56102 - had additional filters positioned amidships. Thereafter, EWS relied on notices either side of the clean air compartment, asking drivers to keep the walkway doors closed!

By April 2001, all but three of the surviving locos - 56019, 097 & 125 - had been treated in this way, although 125 would later receive the modifications while undergoing conversion to 56303 at Brush.

*Above:* 56079 pulls away from Waldersea on the Wisbech branch with a petfood train to Deanside on 25th July 1995, one of the longest-running freight flows associated with the class. *Photo: Janet Cottrell*

*Above: 56095 Harworth Colliery rescues 56091 Castle Donnington Power Station and its MGR wagons at Milford on 25th October 1995. Photo: Martin Loader*

31st March. Three weeks later, 56084 & 085 arrived at Immingham fresh from Crewe but, by 26th April, 084 was under repair at Immingham for hydrostatic oil leaks after failing in the Reception sidings the day before. Ideally, the loco should have been returned to Crewe under warranty, but the urgent need for Type 5s probably prompted Loadhaul to reach an agreement to carry out the repairs itself and back-charge ABB.

Following the repair, 084 ran for only a short while before failing again. It was towed back to Immingham on 3rd May by 56039 but, despite the local fitters' efforts, Loadhaul waved the white flag a week later and asked Crewe to have another go. 37694 towed 084 to Healey Mills, where the Type 3 hitched a lift back, rather optimistically, behind the latest Crewe release, 56116. The recalcitrant 084 eventually joined 116 on Immingham-based workings on 5th June.

Similar problems arose elsewhere. On 15th July, 56044 returned to Cardiff Canton with a seized wheelset, only a week after release following a 'G' exam there.

The reliability of Class 56s remaining in day-to-day traffic in 1995 was subject to equal variation. On 12th April, 56102 was restricted to local workings from Immingham because of oil system problems. Three days later it failed with low oil pressure. Immingham fitted a new oil pump, but the loco was still restricted to local trips on April 19th. By the 1st of May it was noted dumped in the yard, reportedly with a defective camshaft - an inevitable result of poor lubrication. 102 entered Doncaster for Unclassified attention, but was later reassigned to an Intermediate overhaul. In another burst of indecision, the loco moved to Brush for the work to be carried out in August.

Unusual workings arose throughout 1995. On 13th April, for instance, 56019 dragged failed EMU 309616 from Bescot to Longsight. On 1st September, 56104 had to propel EMU 305502 from Longniddry to Drem after the unit failed on a North Berwick service. And on the penultimate night of the year, 56101 worked both sleeper trains - 1M16 and 1S25 -

## Locos receiving Works attention during 1995.

| Loco | Arrived | Works | Reason | Released | Return | Reason | Released | Details of test trains worked where known: |
|---|---|---|---|---|---|---|---|---|
| 56127 | mid '93 | Crewe Wks | Intermediate | Mar | | | | |
| 56003 | late '94 | Donc. Wks | Intermediate | Jan | April | power unit | May | 14/1/95- 6G37 0704 Doncaster-Tyne test train |
| 56045 | late '94 | Donc. Wks | Intermediate | Jan | | | | 27/1/95 - 6G37 09xx Doncaster-Tyne test train |
| 56027 | late '94 | Donc. Wks | Intermediate | Mar | | | | 25/2/95 - 6G37 0704 Doncaster-Tyne test train |
| 56066 | mid '94 | Donc. Wks | Collision damage | Jul | | | | |
| 56084 | Jan | Crewe Wks | Intermediate | Apr | May | Hydrostatic leaks | Jun | 3/4/95 - 5D06/5K06 Crewe test train with 47467 |
| 56085 | Jan | Crewe Wks | Intermediate | Apr | | | | 5/4/95 - 5D06/5K06 Crewe test train with 47467 |
| 56106 | Jan | Donc. Wks | Intermediate | Mar | | | | |
| 56110 | Jan | Crewe Wks | Intermediate | Jul | | | | |
| 56116 | Jan | Crewe Wks | Intermediate | May | | | | 12/4/95 - 5D06/5K06 Crewe test train with 47625 |
| 56006 | Feb | Donc. Wks | bogies | Mar | | | | |
| 56055 | Feb | Donc. Wks | Intermediate | Jul | | | | |
| 56079 | Feb | Donc. Wks | Intermediate | Apr | | | | |
| 56107 | Feb | Brush | General | Jul | | | | |
| 56109 | Feb | Donc. Wks | Intermediate | Apr | Apr | wheelsets | Sep | 20/3/95 - 6G37 09xx Doncaster-Heaton test train |
| 56064 | Mar | Cardiff | Intermediate | Sepr | | | | |
| 56077 | Mar | Donc. Wks | power earth fault | Mar | | | | |
| 56054 | Apr | Donc. Wks | Light | Jun | | | | |
| 56044 | May | Cardiff | Light | Jul | Jul | moved tyre | Jul | |
| 56086 | May | Donc. Wks | Unclassified | Jul | | | | |
| 56118 | May | Donc. Wks | Intermediate | Jul | | | | |
| 56102 | Jun | Donc. Wks | Unclassified | Jul | | | | |
| 56040 | Jul | Donc. Wks | Intermediate | Aug | | | | 16/8/95 - 6G37 xxxx Doncaster-Tyne test train |
| 56076 | Jul | Donc. Wks | Light | Oct | | | | 28/9/95 - 6G37 1400 Doncaster-Tyne test train |
| 56102 | Aug | Brush | Intermediate | early '96 | | | | |
| 56111 | Aug | Donc. Wks | Intermediate | Sep | | | | |
| 56010 | Sep | Donc. Wks | Intermediate | Nov | | | | |
| 56024 | Sep | Donc. Wks | Intermediate | Nov | | | | |
| 56100 | Sep | Donc. Wks | Intermediate | Nov | | | | |
| 56021 | Oct | Donc. Wks | Intermediate | Nov | | | | |
| 56033 | Oct | Donc. Wks | Light | Dec | | | | |
| 56056 | Oct | Cardiff | Light | early '96 | | | | |
| 56075 | Oct | Brush | Unclassified | early '96 | | | | |
| 56041 | Nov | Brush | Intermediate | early '96 | | | | |
| 56068 | Nov | Brush | Intermediate | early '96 | | | | |
| 56090 | Nov | Donc. Wks | Intermediate | early '96 | | | | |
| 56007 | Dec | Donc. Wks | Light | early '96 | | | | |

*Above:* 56032 heads Pathfinder's 'Rooster Booster' railtour past the Hodge Hill garden centre at Kidderminster. This loco passed through Transrail ownership without any change to its livery whatever. *Photo: Martin Loader*

between Slateford and Edinburgh during an engineering possession.

The third calendar year of Trainload private company operation began with an increase in imported coal through Avonmouth docks. In January 1996, the 19.09 Bescot-Avonmouth, 01.00 Avonmouth-Bescot and 12.40 Bescot-Avonmouth became regular 56 turns. 56018, 022, 037, 064, 070, 073, 093, 127 & 133 all appeared on these workings. Additionally, 56125 worked an 11.07 Avonmouth-Ironbridge MGR on 8th February.

North of the the border, availability was poor, hence the movement on 20th January of Cardiff's 56113 & 119 to Motherwell to join 56064 for a loan spell as cover for the depleted LGAM pool. Of Motherwell's official fleet, 56096 was in Doncaster works, while 56103 & 121 were undergoing engine repairs at Canton and not expected to be released until April 1st.

Meanwhile, in the final months before the takeover of all three companies by EWS, Brush's Loughborough works out-shopped 56041 & 068 in grey undercoat, pending the announcement of EWS's opening livery. Brush also dealt with 56044 & 056 in the early part of 1996, but they were the last before the three separate parts of the freight business became one again.

*Above:* On 8th February 1996, only weeks before the EWS takeover, 56125 climbs Brentry Bank with a train of imported coal from Avonmouth to Ironbridge power station. *Photo: Mike Goodfield*

# 8. THE EARLY EWS YEARS

*Above:* The launch of EWS took place at London's Marylebone station, with examples of locos from each of the three Trainload operators to show what EWS was taking on. 56102 represented Loadhaul at the event. *Photo: Paul Furtek*

Despite the expense of setting up three separate companies with three separate management structures, Loadhaul, Transrail and Mainline Freight were all sold to a single purchaser on 24th February 1996. The government had hoped that three independent buyers could be found, thereby creating the competitive situation promised (however misleadingly) by all privatisations of state assets. However, the prospect of having to compete obviously proved a major disincentive. Only two potential buyers emerged and both adopted the attitude that it was all three or nothing.

The more serious bidder was the American Wisconsin Central Transportation Corporation, whose interest the government embraced enthusiastically, despite the pitifully low price tag of £225.15 million it had attached to its bid. Wisconsin proposed a single operating company provisionally named North & South Railways, but this was changed to English, Welsh and Scottish Railway before the official handover at Marylebone station. At the same time, EWS also acquired Rail Express Systems (which included Special Trains, the former InterCity charter unit) and, within a year, National Power's railfreight operation along with its Class 59/2 fleet and dedicated wagon sets. EWS wrapped up the purchase of the entire freight network, with the notable exceptions of Freightliner and the nuclear traffic, by November 1996 when it also took over Railfreight Distribution. The railway's freight customers would have to wait a while longer for the beneficial effects of 'competition'.

The handover ceremony at London's Marylebone station produced 56102 in Loadhaul livery, 58050 in Mainline Freight blue and 60055 adorned with Transrail sticker. Apparently 56035, 58023 and 60084, all in similar liveries, were stabled nearby at Acton in case anything went wrong.

Whatever the politics of privatisation, the new era produced many highs and lows for all classes of locomotive, particularly when the private owner began to put new policies into practice. At the time the EWS purchase was announced, many locos were in works undergoing Intermediate overhauls. As mentioned in the previous chapter, three 56s (041, 068 & 096) were released prior to the announcement in white/grey primer and ran around in ghostly guise for several weeks (or more than a year in one case) until the new colours were unveiled.

A livery based on the Wisconsin Central house colours was eventually adopted. Much to the annoyance of the fat cat design consultants usually paid to develop corporate image, the logo was designed by way of a competition in *Rail* magazine. Appropriately, the winning entry depicted an English Lion, a Welsh Dragon and a Scottish Stag and inevitably became known as The Three Beasties.

In return for its £225 million, EWS inherited the majority of assets belonging to Loadhaul, Mainline and Transrail, including the best examples of the Class 47 fleet (Freightliner had been allocated the worst). The operational Class 56 fleet stood at 116, with another eight in store. After initial comments by Wisconsin's President, Ed Burkhardt, about the reliability of the 914 "life-expired" locomotives his company had inherited, it came as no surprise when an order for 250 new locomotives from General Motors was announced. The Class 66 was to be based on the successful SD series design which had formed the basis of Class 59. Despite the huge question mark this placed over 'classic locomotives', the feeling at the time was that the newer Class 58s and Class 60s would probably have a long and secure future.

To its credit, EWS did not adopt a 'slash and burn' approach (at least, not to begin with), preferring instead to watch and learn before taking drastic action. Of course, the company had a pretty good idea of its inheritance before agreeing to purchase but, even so, regular management reports on locomotive performance crossed the President's desk in the early years. Those relating to Class 56 make interesting reading today. Here are three of the subjects covered in summary:

*i) The Class 56 has a tendency to catch fire. In fact, a Health and Safety report listed the class as the third most frequent locomotive type to catch fire, with 33 instances in the 3-year period from 1992-1994. This represented 18% of all train fires.*

The usual causes were starter motors, traction motors and oil being carried over from the turbocharger into the silencer during long periods spent idling. For example, in March 1996 56004 suffered a traction motor fire while working a Silverwood-Bescot MGR train

*Above:* While a final decision on EWS's opening livery was pending, 56096 was out-shopped from Doncaster in all-over grey undercoat. The loco stands outside the paint shop in May 1996. *Photo: Derek Porter*

and went to Cardiff for attention. 56011 suffered serious fire damage in January 1997 and spent a considerable period on decision at Toton. (Incidentally, as part of the mini mods programme undertaken by Brush Traction, an air feed was fitted to the turbo-charger oil seals to provide back pressure, with the aim of reducing the amount of passing oil.) To reduce the instances of fires, EWS routinely investigated each case to determine the cause and, where relevant, compliance with its 'no idling' policy.

*ii) The use of the class in new areas occasionally results in 56s in the ballast as their bulk puts strain on track in sidings more used to Class 31 and 37. The class often seems to tilt over at 45 degrees following a derailment, which makes re-railing a more complicated task.*

The fact that train crew weren't familiar with the class also resulted in minor incidents. As examples, on 4th October 1996, 56110 derailed in the fuel road at Ipswich, while 56022 derailed after running through trap points in Healey Mills yard on 26th October.

*iii) The class is not easy to work on and the seemingly endless reorganisations brought about by sectorisation, the three freight companies and finally EWS, has left its mark.*

Many maintenance depots closed and many of the skilled men who understood the workings of Class 56 left railway service. In a ten year period, the changes had resulted in the class's entire concentration at Toton in 1987 but, within that decade, a similar concentration at Immingham, with allocations to numerous other depots in between. In addition, the heavy overhaul work previously dominated by Doncaster, and for a short spell Crewe, was spread around various EWS facilities at Toton and Cardiff, with other overhauls sub-contracted to Brush.

Despite their faults, as a high speed freight loco the 56s remained a useful resource and, because of numerical size, they continued to be an integral part of the EWS traction fleet. Replacing them could not happen overnight. Furthermore, the fact they had been used country-wide meant that crews were trained on them from Exeter and Kent right through to Aberdeen and the west of Scotland. Previous owners had demonstrated that dedicated fleets, if maintained at small depots, could return availability figures higher than the fleet average of 77%. In addition, a large proportion of the fleet had been through works recently and the Brush 'mini mod' program was beginning to produce improved reliability. A final plus point was the locos' ability to replace a Class 60, either singly or in multiple, depending on the route. A common substitution occurred on the heavy Port Talbot-Llanwern iron ore workings.

After gaining initial operating experience, EWS determined that while the class was acceptable in the short term, something better was required in the longer term.

The first of EWS's GM order arrived in April 1998. Despite this, the 20-year-old Class 56 fleet continued to receive works overhauls until such time as enough 66s were available to take over their duties. The plan then was to cease all overhaul work, run the survivors into the ground and discard them. In the interim, EWS devoted much effort to keeping the fleet in service; for example, forming its remaining 113 locos into a 'super pool' at Immingham in September 1997.

Many things had changed for the locos since their early days as dedicated coal machines, not least the kind of maintenance carried out. The class was running longer distances at higher speeds than before and the Enterprise trains proved perfect for the 56s' 80 mph capability. Intensive use at weekends was another dramatic change from the days when a visit to the north of England, Yorkshire, Nottinghamshire and South Wales stabling points could find over a hundred 56s standing idle. Of course, many depots previously carried out maintenance at weekends and the loss of this window for the bigger exams led to the introduction of the 'balanced B' - effectively spreading some of the work content of 'C', 'D' & 'E' exams over thirty, more detailed, three-monthly inspections during a 90-month cycle. As each exam had a similar hours content, depot workload could be better planned. For example, if an individual loco was late for a B14 at Immingham, another could be brought in early for its B19. Previously, a larger exam had filled up a maintenance bay for much longer. Furthermore, the new system was able

*Above:* 56041 heads through Lincoln with the Ripple Lane-Immingham newsprint empties on 10th May 1996. *Photo: Adrian Tibble*

to focus on areas in which longer distances and higher speed running had made maintenance more critical.

In considering all this, we should not forget that under British Rail and BREL heavy works attention was scheduled every four years and equated to 6,000-7,000 TOPS hours. The new EWS system aimed to stretch the period between main works attention to approximately seven-and-a-half years - equivalent to a TOPS accumulation of more than 10,000 hours.

To set the scene for future operations, the initial dispersal of Class 56 under EWS in February 1996 is shown in the table below.

Although the works overhaul programme continued, there were increasing instances of locos stopped for routine repairs undergoing assessment to determine if the repairs were economic. This practice became gradually more commonplace as additional Class 66s entered traffic and the need for 56s reduced. Often a loco refused repairs would simply be put into a storage pool and dumped on a depot's 'scrap' line, although some were liable to be rescued if a classmate failed and needed repairs of higher cost. This 'least cost' approach resulted in some locos going into and and out of store many times before they were finally reinstated or finally condemned.

Given Ed Burkhardt's comments about unreliable traction, the class needed to show a good performance more than ever before. Although BR and, later, RfD had hired in 56s for Freightliner work, it is interesting to note that EWS encouraged such use to a far greater extent than previous regimes. Main duties involved the 16.04 Felixstowe-Trafford Park, 17.31 Felixstowe-Wilton and 20.34 Felixstowe-Trafford Park. On 29th February these were worked by 56063, 027 & 055 respectively. Further north, 56031 from Thornaby's FMBY pool worked the 21.00 Basford Hall-Trafford Park. From 6th March 1996, the class was diagrammed to 4M92 19.10 Felixstowe-Landor Street and 4L69 01.53 Landor St-Felixstowe return. As before, the Wilton Freightliner service was used to moved 56s to and from Thornaby for maintenance.

To facilitate the system-wide use of the class, EWS continued to organise crew training, covering such diverse locations as Beverley on the Hull-Bridlington line. 56075 appeared on 9th March, followed by 003 & 039.

In another new departure, 56s took over the newsprint trains between Immingham and the industry's plants on the River Thames. The paper arrived at the docks in jumbo reels from Stora Enso's mill in Sweden. The trains operated in much the same way as the Deanside petfood workings, with one train each way each weekday, departing from Immingham at 06.50 and returning north empty from Ripple Lane at 10.08.

Although the official changeover date was April 1996 (replacing former-Loadhaul 37s), 56090 jumped the gun on 27th March with the southbound train, closely followed by 097 heading north the next day.

After the change, a little extra variety occurred on 18th April when 58049 topped white-liveried 56041. Another undercoated loco, 56068, appeared unaccompanied two days later. 56s became well-established on these trains and, despite the occasional glitch, developed a reputation for running to time on both workings.

Unusual reports from Scotland included the appearance of 56s at Glasgow Shields Road for tyre turning. 097 was present on 30th March 1996, leaving on April 2nd. These occasional visits continued until 1998.

On 22nd April 1996, 56109 made a rare appearance at Jarrow with an oil train from Humber. These trains had become increasingly heavy and Class 60s dominated for many years. Previously, the last reported 56 at Jarrow was in July 1994 and that was only because the 60 had failed in Jarrow terminal.

Three days after the Jarrow surprise, the final 56s were rostered on Port Talbot-Llanwern iron ore traffic. 56032 & 073 had worked on the penultimate day and 56119 & 052 handled the final turn before hired-in Mendip Rail Class 59s, and ultimately EWS Class 60s, took over.

An interesting few days concluded with 56021 hauling 6V14 Saltend-Baglan Bay with a trailing load of 1,013 tonnes. Usually a Class 37 duty, the gradual increase in train weight called for something more powerful.

Like Loadhaul in 1995, EWS also approached Brush about overhauling 56s. As part of a feasibility study, 009 was despatched to Loughborough on 7th May. The intention was to strip the loco of parts and use it merely as a power unit test bed. While at Brush, it even received a new powder blue livery and a new number - 56201. The loco was officially withdrawn from operational stock on 29th August 1996.

Unusual workings in the first few months of EWS ownership included 56092 & 099 on an Enterprise trip working from Dee Marsh to Warrington, conveying a solitary OTA timber wagon, 56045 hauling the Harwich International-Felixstowe leg of the 'Lost Horizon railtour on 18th May, 56132's rare appearance at Euston with an engineer's train seven days later, and 56112's visit to the Ipswich Open Day on 15th June.

The operational fleet declined by a further three early in June when 56018, 032 & 037

---

**Initial pools when EWS took over in February 1996.**

**Thornaby (26)**
*FMBY pool (26)*
56003 56006 56031 56035 56039 56045 56046 56048 56050 56061 56062 56063 56065 56069 56081 56084 56095 56097 56098 56108 56110 56112 56117 56120 56130 56134

**Cardiff (43)**
*LNBK main pool (19)*
56010 56032 56038 56040 56044 56052 56053 56060 56064 56066 56073 56076 56096 56103 56113 56114 56115 56119 56121

*LWBK - Springs Branch pool (25)*
56004 56007 56009 56018 56019 56022 56025 56029 56033 56036 56037 56047 56049 56059 56070 56071 56086 56092 56093 56099 56105 56125 56127 56132 56133

**Immingham (35)**
*FDBI main pool (12)*
56021 56041 56055 56068 56090 56100 56102 56106 56107 56109 56111 56118

*FDBK Knottingley pool (22)*
56011 56027 56034 56043 56051 56067 56074 56075 56077 56078 56080 56082 56083 56085 56087 56088 56089 56091 56094 56116 56126 56131

*FDKI contingency pool (1)*
56135

**Motherwell (11)**
*LGAM pool (11)*
56056 56057 56058 56072 56079 56101 56104 56123 56124 56128 56129

Stored locos in the legacy pools created by the 3 freight companies.

*LCWX Transrail stored (5)*
56001 56016 56020 56028 56030

*ENZX Mainline for withdrawal (2)*
56013 56023

*FDZX Loadhaul withdrawn (1)*
56015

*Above:* 56068 retained its 'ghost' livery for more than a year. The loco approaches Barnetby on 6th May 1997 with an Immingham-Scunthorpe MGR. *Photo: John Hooson*

were placed in store. However, all three were eventually overhauled in 1998 - the Romanian loco at Brush, the other two at their Doncaster birthplace.

56057 was named *British Fuels* on 27th June 1996 and became something of a celebrity. It was also the first repaint into EWS colours carried out at Motherwell. Just before naming, the loco worked the Grangemouth-Dalston fuel tanks on the 24th, followed by a Ravenstruther-Longannet MGR immediately after the ceremony. 057 was in the news again on 14th July when it became the first 56 carrying the new livery to work a passenger train, after 87007 failed before departure from Carlisle. The 56 worked 1A68 14.37 to Euston as far as Preston.

On 16th July, 56025 was employed on crew training at Whitehaven; the next day 56065 worked on 0Z88 Knottingley-Carlisle route learner in place of the rostered Class 58. In the same month, Worksop depot received a 56 for familiarisation, bringing to an end a long absence since the Mainline Freight era, during which 58s and 60s were the dominant traction.

As well as occasional turns on chemicals trains brought about by the non-availability of other traction types, petroleum traffic provided 56s with more than their fair share of multiple workings, usually as a means of shifting locomotives to or from appointments with the fitters. For example, on 10th August 56063, 069 &107 worked the Rectory Junction-Lindsey refinery empties - wholly excessive power for such a light train.

In August, 56036 returned to traffic after many months out of use at Canton with wheelset problems. At the same location, 56114 obviously received a poor assessment as 56101, which had spent many months side-lined with power unit problems, came out of store for less-expensive repairs than those required by 114. The latter went into store, presumably to await a worse 'least cost' failure than itself, but went to Brush a year later for a full overhaul.

Imported coal traffic continued much as before, through Avonmouth, Hull, Immingham, Redcar, Tyne, Gladstone Dock and Seaforth. The Gladstone-Fiddler's Ferry trains were doubled-headed. 56004 & 047 appeared on 7th August, followed the next day by 007 & 036. 60005 was also working the circuit, but full 56 domination resumed on August 20th when the pairs of 071 & 133 and 086 & 082 were in sole charge.

The subject of fuel deliveries to locomotive depots reared its head again in the summer of 1996. Workings to the more isolated locations, like Penzance and Holyhead, had always been vulnerable to replacement by road transport on grounds of cost; so, it was no surprise when 56099 worked the final rail delivery of fuel from Stanlow to Holyhead on 19th August.

As a result of the same operational review, some movements of rail vehicles to works or scrap yards also transferred to road, and there was a reduction in the once-common sight of departmental trains conveying rails, sleepers and ballast as much of this traffic had been accommodated in the Enterprise network.

Long-time Cardiff scrap line residents 56001 and 56016 were withdrawn during September 1996. However, scrap line sharer and non-Romanian 56038 was reinstated to traffic a month later.

On 12th September 56086 made the first recorded appearance for the class on 7V52 Bescot-Bridgwater flask train and 7M53 return. 56004 appeared on a similar nuclear duty on 31st October, hauling three flask wagons bound for Sellafield. However, EWS's involvement with this traffic, and therefore Class 56's, was short-lived. Direct Rail Services, a wholly-owned subsidiary of British Nuclear Fuels, itself owned by the government, had been set up in 1995 with the intention of placing all nuclear traffic under the control of a dedicated specialist company. DRS ran its first trains in September 1996 and, by the end of 1998, had taken over every flow to and from the ten nuclear power stations. Whether or not it was the government's main intention, the effect was to insulate essential nuclear movements from possible 'rationalisation' on the grounds of cost-saving.

By the end of 1996, the thrice-weekly 6M87 Sheerness-Willesden Enterprise had become a focus of interest for enthusiasts because of the wide variety of traction it threw up. The working had once been a solid LWBK pool Class 56 working, but a snapshot of traction employed in the week commencing 25th November shows how different things had become under EWS:

25/11  37194 & 676
27/11  56105
29/11  33202

Two weeks earlier, 60012 had been sighted on the train.

In case it be thought that Class 56 had ceased to be a coal machine through so many

*Above:* EWS finally adopted a red and gold colour scheme with a 'three-beasties' logo on the cabsides. 56115 shows off the new concoction at Gobowen on 7th September 1999 while working 6F71 Chirk-Walton Yard wood empties. *Photo: John Hooson*

other developments, movements of the black stuff continued to dominate the locos' working life in the EWS era. Extra flows had arisen in this former sector too, either from new opencast sites or resurrected collieries. On 4th December, the first train in five years worked away from Knockshinnoch, bound for Longannet power station behind EWS-liveried 56058, and work to clear the stockpiles at various other sites continued apace.

Works overhauls in 1996 can be summarised as follows:

Doncaster - 56007/041/058/089/096/112
Brush      - 56051/068/088/105/120

Despite reservations about the quality of its inherited traction, EWS still regarded Class 56 as front-line motive power as 1996 drew to a close. Even the former hard-hearted attitude towards the Romanian build appears to have softened. 56011 provides evidence of this. The loco suffered a serious fire at the end of 1996 and spent months afterwards 'on decision' at Toton. Eventually, Unclassified repairs at Brush were authorised, and therein lies the clue. Unclassified means unplanned and therefore unbudgeted, as opposed to Classified repairs which are pre-planned to take place on a fixed date under an annual financial plan. So, adding to the maintenance bill by repairing a seriously-damaged 'original' at this time of cost-saving suggests either a different approach . . . or that somebody mis-read the number on the damage assessment.

1997 began with another flurry of Class 56 activity in the Felixstowe area. An increase in traffic volume through the port produced additional workings, such as 56097 on 4Z81 Wilton-Ipswich on January 13th. Twelve days later, it was 56114 on 4Z20 Ipswich-Tees additional liner, the same day that 56110 worked 4S88 Felixstowe-Coatbridge.

The new year also threw up the first non-railtour appearance of a 56 at Inverness, when 56072 rolled in with 6Z71 Thislington to Fearn (on the Far North line). However, the Type 5 came off the train at Inverness and returned south light engine immediately. And the previous railtour working? 56104 on 6th August 1994.

56s also began to appear more often at Dalzell steelworks near Motherwell at this time, although only when reduced loads made a Class 60 a little too heavy on the power. In the early months of 1997, 56046, 071, 072, 077, 112 & 129 were all reported at the works.

The surviving steelworks at Dalzell, Workington, Lackenby, Scunthorpe, Shelton, Shotton, Ebbw Vale, Trostre, Llanwern, Port Talbot, Corby, Tremorfa, Aldwarke, Stocksbridge and Sheerness continued to generate traffic for the class, consisting either of inter-site slab and coil for further processing or finished product to terminals such as Wolverhampton, Round Oak, Blackburn and Wakefield. Although the newly-introduced 6E41 12.05 Blackburn-Lackenby Enterprise was meant to convey a variety of commodities, the load was often mostly steel.

As well as the increased 56 activity at Motherwell, the class's fairly frequent visits to Aberdeen became almost a daily occurrence in the spring of 1997. Although 56s were not the booked traction on Enterprise workings from Mossend, the following gives a flavour of their appearances:

1st April    Loadhaul-liveried 56100 worked 6A37 15.54 Mossend-Aberdeen and 6D05 22.05 return.
2nd April   56104 ditto.

Eventually, this became a regular duty for the class and explains why the soon-to-be introduced 56-hauled trip from Inverness to Aberdeen sometimes worked back north with a different loco.

Other one-off workings north of the border at this time included:

7th March - 56104 on 6Z52 Millerhill-Inverness Millburn Yard additional lime hoppers (HEAs)
21st March - 56118 ditto
Late March - 56079 & 118 working as a pair into Millburn (unconfirmed)
19th March - 56031 on the weekly Grangemouth-Prestwick aviation fuel tanks in place of the usual Class 60
9th April - 56132 on 6S71 Thrislington-Montrose lime train.

Other Class 56 appearances on 6S71 occurred, until it stopped running as a separate train and the wagons were attached to the tail of the Tyne-Aberdeen Enterprise instead.

13th April - 56124 worked a ballast on the Kincardine branch prior to a new MGR flow
15th May - 56104 Kincardine-Longannet empty MGRs
22nd May - 56058 ditto

Aviation fuel from Grangemouth for the RAF base at Leuchars was delivered to Linkswood depot by 56062 on 28th April

Pipe traffic was also flowing from Scotland. On 26th May, 56067 worked 6Z36 Bathgate-Peterborough pipes. 56101 shifted a similar load the next day.

56083, working 6S82 Tyne-Aberdeen Enterprise on 1st July, was handily placed to push 47769 clear of the main line at Linlithgow when the 47 failed with 1S25 Euston-Inverness sleeper.

Rounding off Scotland for the time being, the transfer of Loadhaul-liveried 56050 from Thornaby to Motherwell in late May marked

*Above:* 56123 *Drax Power Station* moves slowly through the unloading bunker at Cockenzie power station on 23rd July 1996. The train had originated from the nearby Blindwells opencast mine. *Photo: Martin Loader*

the official appearance of the livery in the area . . . a little late, as it was by then officially redundant. Even so, it is worth recording as this was the first time a Loadhaul-liveried loco had been allocated anywhere except Immingham or Thornaby.

Despite all this activity, a rumour persisted that Class 56s would be moved out of Scotland altogether, but 050's transfer and their continued use on Enterprise workings suggests the proposal had been put on ice. A paper transfer finally happened the following September, but nothing changed on the ground. 56s continued to operate from Motherwell depot.

Several hundred miles south, another London terminus had experienced the sound of a Grid on February 8th, when 56100 arrived at King's Cross during weekend engineering work. On the same day, 56066 & 099 were at either end of a permanent way train at Finsbury Park.

Numerically, Class 56 reduced by one early in May when 56020 was cut up at Booth's of Rotherham. However, its withdrawal date is shown as 16th June because of a delay in processing the paperwork. Parts of 56020 lived on; the agreement with Booth's called for the bogies to be returned to EWS for further use.

The next to disappear was 56016, cut up on site at Cardiff by the end of June and, presumably, also donating its wheelsets to the survivors. By then, 56001 (withdrawn in September 1996) had become the target of a preservation bid, but the proposal was rejected because of the acute shortage of spare bogies.

On 30th May, 56011 came out of store at Toton into the Immingham FDBI pool. 56061 went into store in its place.

Past associations were renewed on 10th June when 56101 ran light to West Ealing (with 31434 & 37710) and then travelled on to Hither Green for crew training between there and Acton Yard.

In mid-June 56134 worked a train of imported paper pulp from Sunderland Docks to the Iggesund Paper board works at Workington, but this was very much a one-off, probably linked to some problem with the pulping equipment at the Cumbrian paper mill.

Meanwhile, scrap traffic was increasing and workings to Stocksbridge steelworks at Deepcar brought a 56 onto part of the truncated Woodhead route on 24th June when 56003 worked 6J51 Aldwarke-Deepcar trip and 6J52 return. Three months later, 56130 worked the first train of scrap from Liverpool's Alexandra Dock to Handsworth.

The quirky Ketton operation continued to consume vast quantities of the high quality coal mentioned in an earlier chapter. The delivery trains still had to run past the cement works to Leicester, so their locos could run round and gain access on the up line (not very efficient). Formerly in the hands of Mainline Freight 58s, this working began to experience 56 power in 1997 on the odd occasion, such as 56069 with 6M93 14.45 King's Cross-Ketton on 14th July. Although 58s remained the booked traction, their poor availability often provided pairs of Class 31s with turns on the Ketton coal as well.

*Above:* The remains of 56005 & 026 stand in Booth's Yard on 21st June 1996. *Photo: Kelvin Guest*

*Above:* 56046 passes Stockton Cut Junction with 6G40 Hartlepool-Immingham gas pipe train on 22nd July 1996. This was a short-term contract which ran during the summer of 1996. *Photo: Martin Loader*

Gypsum, a by-product of the flue gas de-sulpherisation process pioneered at Drax power station, continued to provide two-way workings for EWS traction, including the occasional Class 56. The limestone required for the process arrived in one direction, while the gypsum went to the British Gypsum site at Newbiggin where it was compressed into plasterboard. Both flows were booked for Class 60, but 56120 appeared on 17th July with 6D89 Drax-Newbiggin.

A year later, structural problems with the loading equipment at Drax temporarily deprived British Gypsum of its raw material. Supplies were imported through Hartlepool and Hunterston until the problem was resolved. 56113 worked 6Z93 17.40 Hartlepool Docks-Kirkby Thore on 27th April 1998, followed by 56096 on 6th May.

In July 1997 the Willesden-Sheerness Enterprise was revised to operate as a core service rather than a feeder and was re-coded as 6S75 11.10 Sheerness-Mossend. 56021 worked the train from Kent to Bescot on 30th July, emphasising the fact that traction changes could often take place en route, at either Willesden, Bescot or Warrington.

In August a new working was introduced for Cobra - the Wakefield-Mossend Superdrug Enterprise which was aimed at reducing road journeys. A 56 was often provided, such as 56120 hauling the empty flats from Tees to Wakefield on the 6th.

The same month produced a 56 on the aluminium ingots from Lynemouth-Pengam. 56100 worked as far as Basford Hall on the first day of the grouse shooting season - August 12th.

Individual locomotives in the news at this time included 56103, which was named *Stora* to mark the movement of the one-millionth tonne of newsprint carried in the six years of the Immingham-Ripple Lane contract.

56060 also received a boost in July when the heavily-stripped loco moved from Cardiff to Immingham for repair assessment. Eventually, a year later, it went to Brush for overhaul.

56068 remained a curiosity. It was still running around in undercoat in August, sixteen months after its 1996 overhaul.

In September Class 56s re-established themselves at Worksop, where their reported duties included 7A23 21.00 Bentinck-Radcliffe MGR (56064 on 3rd September), 7A08 04.51 Welbeck-Tatcliffe MGR (56050 on the 16th) and Worksop-Haworth empty MGR (56094 on the 29th, followed by a loaded working to West Burton).

Further Freightliner hirings also cropped up in September:

Sept. 12th - 56125 on 4M92 1910 Felixstowe-Lawley Street. 125 failed on arrival.

Sept. 13th - 56076 on the return 4L69 01.47 Toton-Felixstowe.

Sept. 16th - 56067 on 4Z23 23.29 Felixstowe-Leeds additional liner.

Sept. 19th - 56003 & 47292 on 4Z85 11.51 Leeds-Felixstowe additional, with both locos under power.

EWS implemented another of its new policies (actually an old policy) on September 26th with a number of transfers aimed at concentrating specific classes of locomotive at single maintenance depots. All serviceable Class 60s were moved from Thornaby, Cardiff and Immingham to form a system-wide Class 60 pool at Toton, alongside the Class 58 fleet.

The 56s were concentrated at Immingham, calling for the transfer of 56010, 018, 032, 037, 040, 044, 052, 053, 064, 073, 076, 103, 113, 115, 119 & 121 from Cardiff, and 56050, 056, 057, 058, 072, 079, 104, 123, 124, 128 & 129 from Motherwell. Of note, 56037 & 040 had been allocated to Cardiff since 1979 - two of the first 56s to be allocated to the Western Region. The resulting super pool at Immingham - designated FDBI - comprised all 113 surviving locos. Despite the paperwork, heavy maintenance would continue to be carried out at Thornaby, Motherwell, Toton and Cardiff, as well as Immingham. Facilities for 'B' exams would also be available at smaller depots such as Doncaster Carr, Knottingley and Tyne Yard.

The idea of concentrating an entire fleet at one maintenance depot was not new. Class 58s had always been allocated to and maintained at Toton and had regularly returned better availability figures than Class 56. Also, higher-than-average availability was achieved when Knottingley lost its 47/3s and 56s became the only locos maintained there.

This immediately raises again the thorny question of Foster Yeoman's request to British Rail for a dedicated fleet of 56s to be maintained at Merehead with dedicated facilities and staff. If this wish had been granted in 1983, could 90%-plus levels of availability have been achieved, as was claimed at the time? And if they had, would Yeoman have looked overseas for the Class

59 alternative? If the American power had never materialised, and proved its superiority, it is arguable that Class 66 may not have been introduced either. Given that scenario, how differently might the 56 story have ended?

Meanwhile back in the real world . . . on the day of the mass transfer, 82% (93 locos) of the 113-strong FDBI pool were either working or available for traffic. From then on, EWS's 'common user' policy meant that any Class 56 could be allocated to any 56 duty. As a result, former-Loadhaul and Transrail-liveried examples began to appear all over the system. In fact, the spread of the locos, with many still physically in Scotland and Wales despite their re-allocation to Immingham, makes fascinating reading (see table).

In October 1997 EWS set up a Component Recovery and Disposal Centre (CRDC) facility at the former Springs Branch TMD with the specific purpose of taking in scrap locos and recovering re-usable components. If Class 56s were no longer to receive overhauls at main works, it would be up to the maintenance depots to keep the surviving fleet in service for as long as necessary. The components would come from other locos sacrificed to keep the rest in traffic. Of course, this policy would inevitably lead to a diminishing operational fleet as more and more withdrawals became necessary to keep the parts supply flowing. However, as EWS had no long-term need for the class, such doom-mongering was of little consequence to anyone except rail enthusiasts.

Notable workings as 1997 drew to a close included:

Nov. 5th - 56072 & 111 on 6M39 Grangemouth-Dalston tanks which had loaded to 18 bogies, necessitating the extra 56 (14 was the limit for a single unit).

Nov. 5th - 56068 on 6M12 10.37 Bishop's Stortford-Croft aggregates, normally a 100% solid Class 58 turn.

Nov. 8th - 56101, 134, 132 & 011 appeared on 6Z31 15.40 Immingham-Healey Mills, but with only 101 under power.

Nov. 8th - 56121 & 051 working in multiple on Margam-Dee Marsh steel, despite the diagramming of Class 60s from early October

Nov. 17th - 56133 on 6C65 13.35 Didcot-Avonmouth empty MGR in place of the usual Class 60.

Nov. 17th - 56045 on 06.25 Peak Forest-Ashburys MEA train. At this time the class was making regular appearances in the Peak Forest area.

Nov. 18th - 56032 on 6Z92 05.40 Humber-Spondon acid tanks, *vice* Class 37.

Nov. 19th - 56097 on 6Y41 10.35 March-Barham Stone train, instead of the usual 58.

December 1997 continued to provide the followers of the survivors with comparatively good news. 56027 returned to traffic after receiving repairs to bodyside damage, 56078 went back to work after alternator repairs at Crewe, and 56061 emerged from store . . . but only because 56078 had been side-lined. 56062 arrived in Aberdeen for crew training, but was replaced by 007 on 19th December. 007 also earned some revenue while in Scotland. On the 29th it ran light engine from Aberdeen to Inverness to collect 6A08 and then returned with 6H54. Maintenance beckoned on 6th January and 56088 took its place on the Aberdeen training run.

*Above:* 56103 *Stora* passes Fletton Junction on 20th March 1998. *Photo: Adrian Tibble*

**Status of Immingham's FDBI pool on 26th September 1997**

*In traffic:*
56003, 56067, 56116 and 56131 were on Freightliner trains to and from Felixstowe
56007, 56021, 56066, 56072, 56074, 56111 were on Anglo-Scottish MGR trains on the ECML
56027 was on Hunterston-Falkland imported coal duties
56062, 56106, 56113, 56118 were on steel services
56038 was on the Scunthorpe MGR circuit
56083 on the Hardendale-Margam limestone and 56117 on Westbury-Margam MGR.
56011 Hallen Marsh chemical train to Warrington
56056 was on the Ripple Lane-Immingham paper train
56082 on the northbound petfood train while 56084 had charge of the southbound train
56079 was on the Boulby branch
56120 was on the Bredbury-Roxby waste train
56133 Millerhill-Oxwellmains cement train
56124 handled the Mossend-Warrington Enterprise

| | |
|---|---|
| Millerhill | 56004 56034 56035 56065 56070 56090 56130 56132 |
| Motherwell | 56036 56054 56058 56061 56063 56101 56105 56114 |
| Ayr TMD | 56057 56094 56100 56112 |
| Killoch Colliery | 56010 |
| Tyne Yard | 56086 56097 |
| Thornaby | 56033 56041 56048 56076 56099 56107 56126 56128 |
| Tees Yard | 56093 |
| Immingham | 56006 56008(S) 56012(S) 56014(S) 56022 56025 56039 56050 56051 56071 56087 56092 56104 56108 56110 |
| Knottingley | 56019(S) 56043 56109 |
| Healey Mills | 56121 |
| Doncaster Decoy Yard | 56069 |
| Doncaster Carr Loco | 56073 56075 56127 56129 |
| Aldwarke Yard | 56135 |
| Rotherham Steel Term. | 56049 |
| Scunthorpe Yard | 56055 56085 56091 |
| Peak Forest SP | 56098 |
| Hope Sidings | 56088 |
| Bescot TMD | 56029 |
| Crewe | 56078 (engine repairs) |
| Warrington Arpley | 56095 56133 |
| Carlisle | 56080 |
| Worksop | 56081 |
| Leicester | 56032 56134 |
| Cardiff Canton TMD | 56018 56031 56040 56046 56089 56115 56125 |
| Margam | 56044 56052 56053 56102 56103 |
| Aberthaw PS | 56077 |
| Old Oak Common | 56045 |
| Ipswich | 56059 |
| Brush Loughborough | 56037 56047 56068 56119 |

*Withdrawn locos:*
| | |
|---|---|
| Brush | 56009 |
| Booth's | 56020 |
| Margam | 56028 56030 |
| Toton | 56013 56023 56122 |

*Above: 56056 runs along the north shore of the Firth of Forth at Culross with a loaded MGR for Longannet power station on 20th March 1997. Photo: John Hooson*

56083 had a passenger turn, of sorts, on December 3rd when it was called forward to push 1D44 17.05 King's Cross-Leeds out of the way while working 4D56 15.15 Biggleswade-Heck empties. 91007 had failed south of Grantham.

Two days before Christmas, 56118 worked a trial between Tower Colliery and Aberthaw - a Red Letter day for the local miners. This was the first train to bring coal out of Tower since they'd bought the pit four years earlier.

The importance of coal to EWS is demonstrated by the 1997 revenue figures. Of the company's £534 million turnover, 26% was generated by this traffic. Like previous years, the growth areas were long-distance imported flows and the re-opening of older collieries to rail traffic.

Unlike previous years, Doncaster carried out no Classified overhauls on Class 56s in 1997, although Brush turned out ten - 56032, 037, 059, 065, 067, 087, 103, 114, 117 & 119. Interestingly, 56087 had originally been booked to receive its Intermediate at Thornaby. This would have been a first for the Teeside depot, but it wasn't to be; Brush picked up the work instead.

Also of note, bearing in mind the operational reports to Ed Burkhardt, is that no fewer than four locos suffered fire damage between October and December. 56063 was repaired at Cardiff, but 56053 had to go to Brush for attention. 56039 was initially assessed at Toton but also went to Brush. When 56091 burst into flames, repairs were carried out locally at Thornaby.

Further traffic growth for EWS meant that Type 5s were even more in demand in January 1998. A partial solution was to reinstate three Class 47s (47315, 331 & 981) for drawback duties in the Scunthorpe yards which, in turn, released Class 56s from such mundane work.

As well as coping with traffic expansion, 56s continued to be called upon at short notice to replace other types of unavailable power. As one example, the Middleton Towers (near King's Lynn) to Barnby Dun (near Worksop) sand train (6E84) was usually a Class 58 working, but 56087 appeared on 5th January.

In a slightly ironic twist, Mendip Rail's 59005 was unavailable on January 22nd, a situation which brought 56021 & 134, working in multiple, onto the Llanwern-Port Talbot ore workings. On the same day in the same area, 6M86 10.59 Margam-Dee Marsh steel and 6V90 19.50 return produced another multi working, this time 56066 & 081 in place of the booked Class 60.

At least EWS wouldn't have to worry about supplying power to nuclear trains for much longer as DRS would complete its takeover of every flow within the year. Even so, 56033 appeared on the Bridgwater flasks again on 8th January.

Even more unusual, 56054 appeared at Ebbw Vale on 23rd January with 6B09 08.26 Llanwern-Ebbw Vale and 6B38 return.

Further pipe exports through Leith docks began on January the 9th, and 56035 was called out to work the 6E38 03.40 empties back to Hartlepool. 56107 worked a loaded train (6Z95) northbound three days later.

56049 had a slightly less successful January. It ran into a Salmon wagon in Warrington yard and suffered a badly-crushed no. 2 end. The loco was placed 'on decision' but was finally repaired at Brush, with Deltic 16 for company in an adjoining bay. During the year, 56011 and 56071 would also suffer collision damage but, again, would be repaired - a further indication that EWS wasn't yet ready to throw away its Type 5 inheritance.

As in previous years, 56s continued to have the occasional turn on the Ketton traffic (6D85 Peterborough-King's Cross, then 6M93 KX-Ketton). 58s were still the booked traction, but a period of poor availability (which is completely at odds with earlier claims about dedicated types at dedicated maintenance depots) meant that pairs of 31s continued to be rostered. The 23rd of February, however, produced 56134 on the 6M93 leg, standing in for a pair of 31s . . . standing in for a Class 58. You couldn't make it up!

Another unscheduled Inverness appearance transpired on February 26th when 56062 arrived after working 6H45 06.45 Enterprise from Mossend throughout. Very unusual.

Despite the emergence of DRS, 56s continued to take up the slack when other types were unavailable on the remaining EWS flask workings. 56135 on the Warrington-Sellafield train on 7th March, instead of the usual Class 37, and 56007 on 7V52 Sellafield-Bridgwater on April 13th are only two examples.

Little, if any, relief in Type 5 traction demand resulted from the cessation of oil workings between Stanlow and Jarrow. A 56 worked the last two trains out of Stanlow before it shut as a rail despatch terminal - 56004 with 6E48 07.09 Stanlow-Jarrow on 13th March and the 6E15 23.24 departure four days later. Jarrow, of course, continued to receive oil deliveries, but thereafter they originated from the Humber refinery. A single working, 6N04, departed at 13.24 and the load of 16 bogie tanks often resulted in the rostering of a 56.

The trend towards heavier but less-frequent trains almost reached breaking point on 29th March. 6E58 00.03 Cardiff Tidal-Wakefield needed assistance after the 2,000 tonne train came to a stand at the foot of the 1 in 37 Lickey incline. 56135 was the train engine, with 47365 & 37379 assisting at the front. The 11,000 available horsepower which failed to re-start the train was completed by 56070 shoving at the back - a dire situation by any yardstick.

In the absence of anything else, EWS had to stick with its available Type 5 fleet for the time being - a dedication confirmed by 56130's visit to the Midland Railway Centre for fuel tank repairs in mid-March because there was no spare maintenance capacity at nearby Toton.

*Above:* 56135 passes Whitwood Junction near Castleford with an empty shale train from Wellbeck on 15th May 1997. *Photo: Neil Harvey*

Staff in the operations department must therefore have been counting down the days until the arrival of the first Class 66. Almost two years after the order for 250 locomotives was placed, 66001 was ready for despatch across the Atlantic. Its arrival at Immingham on 18th April signalled the start of the GM revolution proper - very good news for EWS, less so for aficianodos of the much-loved but highly skittish Grid.

*Above:* On 6th March 1997, 56048 eases away from Eggborough power station at Whitley Bridge Junction, with a rake of empties for Gascoigne Wood. *Photo: Neil Harvey*

79

# 9. THE CANADIANS ARE COMING

*Above:* The arrival of the Class 66s had a significant effect on the Class 56 fleet. With only eighteen months left in traffic, 56093 heads away from Sudforth sidings. It went into store in July 1999. *Photo: Neil Harvey*

The title of this chapter can be read in two ways. The arrival at Immingham of 66001 signified the start of the first trans-Atlantic event to have a significant effect on the future of Class 56. Three years on, the takeover of EWS by Canadian National finished off what the first had begun. So, it might be said that 250 Canadian-built locos prompted a slow, lingering death for the class, leaving the later Canadian management to handle both the burial and the resurrection . . . but more of that later.

The arrival of 'proper' motive power was eagerly awaited by EWS, and no sooner had 66001's wheels touched down on the dockside track than 56028 & 030 were moved from store at Margam to Crewe Works for component recovery and scrapping. Although this happened within days of the Immingham arrival, it is probably one for the conspiracy theorists rather than the result of deliberate intent. It just looked like indecent haste at the time.

In reality, EWS operations were a long way from the Promised Land of 90%-plus reliability delivered by a modern, standardised fleet. Although the rapid rate of production delivered 44 of the new locos to Britain by the end of 1998, the summer of 1999 would roll around before the Canadian imports became numerically superior to Class 56. And because they replaced other classes too, even that is a misleading comparison.

So, the dear old 56s kept chugging away on much the same work as in the previous decade as well as picking up new work. In April 1998, for instance, 56032 worked 33 hoppers to the recently re-activated Gwaun-Cae-Gurwen branch in West Glamorgan (6G75 05.45 empties from Swansea Burrows) and returned with a loaded 6B71. Similarly, 56124 worked 6Z95 09.00 Britton Ferry-Jersey Marine, formed of 35 PGAs on 29th April, the same day that 56046 hauled an additional steel train from Ebbw Vale to Immingham, running as 6Z45.

Slightly more surprisingly, 56006 & 082 worked in multiple over the Highland Main Line earlier in the month with an MoD special. The 56s had originally rescued 87101, which had slipped to a stand on Beattock while working the train from London. The 87 was removed at Mossend and the 56s despatched north as the armoured vehicles aboard the train were urgently needed for army exercises. The Type 5s returned south with the 6D46 13.30 Enterprise to Mossend, which included the two inspection saloons attached to the northbound special.

For the return working on May 11th after the exercises had taken place, the train was split, with a 56 on each portion. 56033 worked the first (6D45 13.30 ex-Inverness) with 56112 close behind on the 6Z45 15.40 departure. The two portions re-combined at Mossend for the onward journey south.

Mossend was making good use of any 56s it found available. As one example, 56081 turned out on 6G10 06.05 Mossend-Cameron Bridge on April 22nd, replacing the booked 37. 56121 twice had charge of the same train either side of the last weekend of April.

As so often happened, a new traffic flow was preceded by engineering work to improve the track. The Rylstone branch received the treatment on Sunday 16th April when 56098 and 37380 appeared on engineer's trains, followed a week later by 56054 and 60033.

Slightly ominous news rounded off the month when Brush bought several Class 56 alternators from EWS for the Freightliner Class 57 project, leading to speculation that the conversion programme might create more casualties than merely the 47s donating their bodies. Fortunately for the 56 spares situation, the later 57/3 conversions used a slightly different design of alternator manufactured from new.

On 5th May, a heavy freight was diverted over the Central Wales Line following a derailment at Cardiff. 56022 & 076 worked 6Z80 Margam-Llanwern instead of the booked Class 60 because of the steep grades involved. The locos ran round at Craven Arms and worked to Llanwern via the Welsh Marches route, a diversion which added 155 miles to the normal 45-mile trip along the South Wales main line. Most other freight was cancelled until the derailment was cleared, but Llanwern's constant need for raw materials justified the extra mileage. The only previous

*Above:* 56035 at Reading with 1M79 to Liverpool on 20th May 1998. The Grid had worked in with 1V96 Edinburgh-Reading after taking over the train at Birmingham New Street. *Photo: Paul Furtek*

visit of a 56 to Craven Arms was thought to have been that of 114 with a railtour on 2nd September 1995.

By 1998, of course, all passengers services had been privatised too. Virgin had taken over the former InterCity cross-country network as, not surprisingly, Virgin CrossCountry or VXC, and a lengthy period of occasional Class 56 appearances began on these workings. In fact, almost every type of locomotive was substituted at one time or another as the Class 47/8s struggled to maintain the service with any degree of efficiency. The situation only improved when VXC loco haulage came to an end in 2002.

Mid-May 1998 was a particularly bad time for the 47/8s. One diagram which became a regular candidate for substitution was the infamous 1V96 Edinburgh-Reading and 1M79 Reading-Liverpool, which was often worked by other types (or non-heat 47s) between Birmingham and Reading because there was nothing else available at Saltley when the AC-hauled portion arrived from Edinburgh. As only two examples amongst many, 56004 hauled 1V96 south from New Street on May 15th and 56035 on the 20th. Both returned to Birmingham with 1M79. Obviously D9000 wasn't available on either of those two days.

As new work emerged from the shortcomings of the passenger network, other long-standing commitments came to an end. The last diagrammed 56 haulage of Felixstowe Freightliners took place on 22nd/23rd May, with 096 sighted on 4M93 and 4L69, 56018 on 6E60 22.35 to Wilton, 56054 on 4L79 16.13 from Wilton, and 56101 on 4M73 21.52 to Garston. The next day 56003 stood spare at Ipswich, as 56054 left with 4M56 00.42 to Trafford Park. Sadly, they failed and were replaced by 47270, one of the Freightliner pool of 47s set up to take over the workings. Meanwhile, 56096 was busy with the Ipswich-Felixstowe trips and, at the end of the day, 56054 & 101 departed light engine. 003 remained spare at Ipswich . . . just in case. Thereafter, 56s only appeared following failures or as substitutes on additionals, such as 075 on 6th June with 4Z70 06.13 Ipswich-Wilton which should have been a Class 47 working.

The heavy bulk of the class also came in useful for testing the hydraulic buffer stops at Glasgow Central - hardly a long-term career move. 56099 & 117 suffered this ignomiy on 24th May, followed by 56039 on 26th July. 039 had been released from Brush in May after repairs to fire damage. Still carrying Loadhaul colours, the loco had worked straight to Boston Docks to collect a steel train bound for Round Oak.

In a partial repeat of 56130's visit to the Midland Railway Centre, 011 arrived at Swanwick in early June for the removal of graffiti. It was eventually repainted in EWS livery although, unlike its classmates in the new colours, it had not received an overhaul.

Also of note in June was 56025's appearance at Newcastle Central, acting as the ECML Thunderbird after 47767 had failed with flat batteries.

3rd July gave a hint of things to come. 56057 paused en route at Burton with 6V67 1526 Wakefield-Cardiff Tidal to collect 66001 and tow it to Cardiff. After the mandatory test runs and staff familiarisation at Toton, the pilot loco had been allocated to crew and maintenance training in South Wales, indicating the area would be one of the first targeted for Class 66 takeover. 001 finally received full type approval on 14th August, by which time three more completed locos were about to begin their voyage across the Atlantic.

In the meantime, life continued much as before. 56s even enjoyed more outings on the rubbish trains in the first two weeks of July. It began with 56117 rescuing 59004 and 6V18 12.06 Hither Green-Whatley stone empties on July 3rd. Both Type 5s were removed from the train at Westbury in favour of 37707 & 711, allowing the 56 to dash back to the London area to work 6A54 23.45 Brentford-Appleford bins and 6A55 return in the early hours of the 4th. In a series of copycat workings, 56053 worked the Calvert Bins on the 8th and the Cricklewood-Forders the next day. 053 obviously liked rubbish; twenty-fours hours later it worked the Acton-Brentford bins and returned for another Cricklewood-Forders on the 13th. The attraction must soon have palled; the next day 053 assisted 47330 on 4O25 13.32 Ripple Lane-Southampton liner.

With so many 56 workings in Scotland, it was no surprise when they were called out to rescue failed passenger trains. On 14th July , for instance, 56118 picked up 1Y11 05.05 Edinburgh-Fort William sleepers after the failure of 37409. It worked the train, and the dead 37, as far as Cowlairs Junction where it was replaced by 37413. There was no choice but to remove the Type 5; its Route Availability 7 exceeded the West Highland Line's RA5 limit.

On 10th August, 56100 reached Inverness with Georgemas Junction-bound pipes. The train had originated on Teeside and was a trial working for a new flow which would bring several more 56s to Inverness in the coming months.

Other one-off workings at this time included 56131 on 6Z17 1600 Theale-Roberston Tanks on 19th July, another of the occasional 56 visits to the refineries of Pembrokeshire, and 56039 at London Bridge with a ballast train from Hoo

*Above:* 56110 at Allandale with the Fridays-only 6D16 Grangemouth-Motherwell fuel oil tanks on 23rd July 1999. *Photo: Martin Loader*

Junction the same day. Although 56s were regular visitors to St. Pancras and Paddington during their time working off Leicester and Westbury, London Bridge was nowhere near the top of anyone's Grid-spotting list.

One of the more unusual workings involved 56098 on 5th August, when it brought a load of large boulders to Hestle on the Yorkshire Coast for sea defence improvements. The train left Bardon Hill at 14.00 and ran as 7Z72.

Two weeks later, 56117 made a rare appearance on the 6M54 12.30 Thorney Mill-Bardon Hill stone working, shortly after 56133 arrived at Brush for collision damage repairs following yet another accident.

The 4th of September was a highly significant date. At the end of August 66003, 004 & 005 had landed at Newport Docks and 004 became the first to work a revenue-earning train solo that day - 6K63 and 6G12 Bescot-Longport Enterprise. Soon after, on the 15th, 66001 worked 6M84 05.50 Margam-Dee Marsh and 6V78 15.25 return after it was confirmed that 66s would replace 56s on these trains from late September.

The writing on the wall was becoming a little larger, but the significance of this event seems to have passed unnoticed at the other end of the country. 56 workings at Inverness were actually becoming more frequent. On September 5th, for example, 56131 worked 6H45 06.38 Mossend-Inverness instead of the rostered Res 47. The loco stabled in Milburn yard over the weekend and worked 7D46 13.30 back to Mossend on the Monday afternoon.

56114 repeated this pattern on the 19th, working in with 6H45 and returning with 7D46 on the Monday. Almost immediately, 56119 brought in 6X88 - another load of pipes bound for Georgemas Junction. 119 came off at Inverness, but the intensive crew training carried out in late 1997 was explained when it worked the next day's 6A08/6H54 trips to and from Aberdeen. It arrived back in Inverness in time to work the returning 6Z59 pipe empties to Teeside. 119 reappeared at Inverness the next day, confirming it had only worked the southbound train as far as Mossend. Both these diagrams produced frequent sightings of 56s at Inverness in the coming months.

New flows continued to arise too. One of them, steel from Humberside exported through Mostyn Docks on the North Wales coast, was later combined with the Mostyn to Saltend acid tanks, but retained a 56 as its traction. 025 was noted on 6E39, the westbound loaded steel train, on 18th September.

The new flow from Rylstone near Skipton commenced on 21st September. 56089 worked 6G80 09.30 departure for Dewsbury on the 22nd and this train became a regular 56 duty for a number of months.

The latest in a string of accidents occurred on 3rd November in spectacular fashion. 56094 derailed on the Boulby branch after it was pushed downhill by its train - 6F47 18.36 Lackenby-Skinningrove comprising 14 BBA wagons weighing 1,250 tonnes. 094 was towed to Thornaby for assessment by 56104 and the line remained shut for four days after the incident.

By the beginning of November 1998, 21 Class 66s had arrived at Newport and 20 of them were available for traffic on the 12th. The speed of entry into service, not to mention the rapid effect that increasing numbers had on older locomotive types, resulted partly from the new method of dockside commissioning. Readers with long memories will recall that earlier British locos, notably Class 92, had been subject to years of type approval trials before they could begin to recoup their investment. EWS Chairman Ed Burkhardt was having none of this and persuaded, some say bludgeoned, Railtrack into accepting this unprecedented system [*Route 66* by Ken Carr explains the dockside procedure in detail]. Not only did Class 66s enter service quickly, they almost instantly achieved high availability figures - 95% on 12th November and a higher-than-average 87% on 6th December (28 of 32 arrivals in traffic). Whether we liked it or not, Class 56's performance looked very poor when compared with these figures.

Even so, 56s continued to enjoy works overhauls, although an EWS spokesman confirmed that the company had such high hopes for its new motive power that it planned to withdraw significant numbers of British Type 5s in the near future. For reasons which defy explanation, the 56 super pool FDBI was re-named WGAN on 12th December but the locos remained based at Immingham . . . also on paper.

Notable workings as winter approached included 56067 & 039 tackling the weight of a single snow plough on the Perth-Inverness line. Running as 6A08, the pair first ran light from Thornton to Perth on 17th December.

A 56 reappeared on the rubbish on 15th December when 56088 worked 6A61/6C51 Cricklewood-Forders bins. 56067's outing the next day was slightly more up-market; the loco top & tailed with 47798 on the Royal Train when the Princess Royal visited Haverfordwest.

Works overhauls during 1998 can be summarised as follows:

Brush - 56018, 060, 069, 091 & 115
Cardiff - 56048, 063 & 073
Toton - 56071, 078, 094, 095 & 113

(although such was the need to get 56078 back into traffic that it left without the customary EWS repaint).

Additionally, Crewe took in 56110 for attention to its crankcase. Like 56127 a few years earlier, the visit was prolonged; 110 didn't leave until January 1999. Sadly, some repairs were carried out at the expense of the stored locos. 56006, for instance, received compressors and batteries recovered from 012 and 014 at Immingham. These two also had their fuel tanks removed for the spares pool.

The Toton overhaul operation was particularly interesting. Previously, the depot had operated as a 24-hour service centre for its own vast allocation as well as 'foreign' locos due for exams when they dropped in for fuel. Moderately heavy repairs like bogie swops had been carried out in BR days, mostly on the depot's Class 45 fleet, but the seriously heavy work was handled down the road at Derby Works. All that changed under EWS when a 40-tonne crane was installed in the roof of an extension to the main building, known as the Cathedral because of its extra height. The new crane was capable of lifting a complete power unit from a locomotive body - a necessary component in a full General overhaul or 'G' exam.

Unlike a main works, where every item requiring attention was once repaired and refurbished 'in house', the Toton operation had a modular element. Refurbished bogies came from Doncaster, replacement power units by road from Adtranz Crewe, while the mini mods package was installed by Brush electricians who travelled down the road from Loughborough. A pair of Class 37s were butchered to facilitate the engine swops. Their interiors were stripped out and their bodysides completely cut away between both cabs so they could act as cradles. As they were slightly lacking in power in this modified form, they were shunted in and out of the Cathedral by Class 08s, removing the old engine and manoeuvring the new one alongside the recipient loco. The newly-installed crane did the rest.

Like the first attempt at anything, the overhaul of 'pilot' loco 56094 took far longer than expected. Work on stripping it began in March 1998 with a planned schedule of six weeks. After a number of delays, *Eggborough Power Station* finally emerged, resplendent in EWS colours, on 4th August. To speed up the process, the repainting of No 2 end was completed by a video crew, so they could use the 'finished' loco as the closing shot in a railway programme about Toton. Their involvement may well have cursed it; 094 was the 56 involved in the unpleasantness on the Boulby branch a few months later.

The use of Toton as a mini-works for Class 56 was short-lived; after the five shown above, only two more went through the programme in 1999 before overhauls of the class were brought to an end. Even so, EWS saved considerably on the cost of sending the same locos to Brush and the Cathedral later repaid more of its investment by carrying out major overhauls on Freightliner Class 47s.

*Above:* 56094 before and after its Toton overhaul. This loco was the first of five to receive the equivalent of a General overhaul at the depot in 1998. Only two more were dealt with in 1999. The top photo shows 094 in March 1998, the one below on the day of completion - 4th August 1998. *Photos: Paul Furtek*

As 1998 drew to a close, the Class 56 'operational fleet' ( i.e those not officially condemned) still stood at 116 locos. Here is a reminder of the 19 withdrawn, in the order they departed:

1990  56042
1992  56002, 017, 012, 008, 122
1993  56013, 014, 023, 015, 028, 030
1996  56009, 005, 026, 001, 016, 024
1997  56020

None were withdrawn in 1998 itself.

1999 would be a year of significant change for the class as withdrawals began to take place at a much faster rate. EWS's Class 66 fleet, which stood at 44 locos at the start of the year, would increase to a staggering 189 by the end of it - a rate of delivery not seen on Britain's railways since the heyday of Class 47 production in the 1960s. For the Grid followers, the year began with a shock when the newest of the 56s, 135, was withdrawn in January along with 56123.

Despite the increased rate of withdrawal, the class's pattern of operation continued to resemble that of previous years, once again producing noteworthy workings such as 56105's visit to Rhymney with a steel working from Margam on January 8th. Even more remarkably, 56087 & 105 appeared on 7B52 11.02 Port Talbot-Llanwern iron ore on 11th January. EWS had hired in surplus Mendip Rail 59s to work these trains but, eventually, two of the former-National Power 59/2s took charge. The 56 working was probably a stop-gap during the changeover itself, although the ore traffic was again entrusted to 56s on 1st February, when 125 & 126 worked 7B40 07.54 Port Talbot-Llanwern and 6B60 14.40 return.

The 6A71/6A74 Northolt-Calvert bins also proved popular. Only a week before withdrawal, 56125 had charge of 6A71 12.59 Northolt-Calvert and 18.20 6A74 return on 27th January. 125 & 121 were both set aside in February.

56s enjoyed their very last moment on Felixstowe Freightliner traffic on 30th January. 57001 (with Class 56 alternator, let us not forget) failed at Leeds' Stourton terminal before it could work 4L83 to Felixstowe. Healey Mills provided 56039, which took the train as far as Ipswich and then returned light to Doncaster.

With talk of withdrawals and nothing else, observers were frequently surprised by one-off 56 workings, such as 56088's penetration of Scarborough with an engineer's train from Healey Mills on 1st February.

*Above: 56040 has just crossed Horsfall Viaduct with coal empties from Penyfford to Redcar on 18th June 1999. Photo: Neil Harvey*

Another one returned to old haunts two weeks later when Bescot provided 56069 for the 7V52 Bridgwater-Sellafield flasks and 7M53 14.27 return. By then, DRS should have taken over all the nuclear traffic, so this was clearly a last-minute and unplanned substitution.

The Calvert workings started to produce pairs in the middle of February. 56025 & 098 were noted on the 19th, 56007 & 025 on the 22nd, and 025 & 098 again a day later.

March's casualties were 56019, 035, 092 & 126. With the exception of 56035, which had been overhauled at Doncaster as recently as 1996 but had then suffered severe fire damage, all were a long time out of works and simply worn out. 56019, for example, hadn't seen the inside of a main workshop since 1988.

Pre-1999 withdrawals had centred on the Romanian locos, with the exceptions of 56042 (non-standard equipment) and 56122 (severe collision damage), but the random nature of the early 1999 withdrawals set the pattern for the next four or five years. From now on, not even Doncaster- and Crewe-built locos were safe.

To make matters worse, the Canadian factory had stepped up Class 66 production. Another 62 landed at Newport in the first four months of 1999 (including the wandering 66002). Although 105 Class 56s were still in traffic by the end of April, at this point overhauls of the class were officially stopped - the true watershed for the class. As they were supposed to go through works every four years or so, April 2004 became the theoretical date when even the most recently overhauled would be regarded as life-expired. Unless EWS changed its policy, the class was doomed.

Of course, EWS only cancelled the overhauls once it was certain the 66s were arriving on schedule and entering service without problems. Keeping the overhauls programme going from 1996 until April 1999 also ensured a degree of cover through the four-year cycle until individual locomotives withdrew themselves, either through major failure, unacceptable reliability, or by incurring costs disproportionate to their short life expectancy. Before the cancellation, Toton turned out 56062 & 081. The last to be overhauled, 56038, emerged from Brush in April.

In the months preceding the release of 56038, a number of others received repairs following collision damage or derailments. 56132 was at Toton for collision repairs in January, 56047 at Immingham for attention after a derailment. In February, 56071 had collision repairs at Thornaby. However, EWS's attitude towards such work would change drastically within twelve months, resulting in otherwise fit locos such as 56084 being instantly withdrawn with derailment damage only. In earlier years, rectification of 084's damage would have involved only a simple wheelset change or a visit to Thornaby for tyre turning. Not anymore.

The gloom amongst traditionalists deepened further when the arrival of each boatload of ten or so 66s every six weeks often resulted in a similar number of 56s going into store - hardly surprising when a brand-new fleet of 106 locos was showing a *minimum* availability of 89%. To put this into perspective, the surviving 105 Class 56s had 24 out of traffic (77% availability), the Class 58s could muster 41 out of 50 (82%) while Class 60 achieved 79 out of 100.

We should also consider the effect that politics and business practice had on events. Having glossed over the competitive advantages of privatising the network when that aspiration proved unachievable, the Conservative government had spoken at great length about creating a "business-led railway", whatever that meant. Of course, the Tories were out of office by 1997, yet EWS remained highly focussed on measuring performance and accurately assessing the nett revenue generated by each tonne transported. The Class 56 accounted for a substantial part of the costs of operating the longer-distance coal flows and clearly looked poor value when compared with the new, highly-efficient 66s. Hard-headed business decisions were therefore needed but, surprisingly, this worked in the 56s' favour when Class 58 became the sacrificial lamb.

The later BREL Type 5s were much easier to maintain and all fifty had been allocated since new to a dedicated facility at Toton. For much of the time, this combination yielded higher availability figures than Class 56 but still fell short of EWS's requirement for 90%-plus. On the down-side, the 58s were deemed to be non-standard because they were such a

### 56019 - An early celebrity

The Cult of Nineteen, if we can call it that, arose because the loco was the last to retain the popular Railfreight Redstripe livery. After storage at Wigan Springs Branch for many months, 019 was moved to Toton in April 1997 for assessment. Almost immediately it was assigned to the stored unserviceable pool (which is pretty much what it was in at Wigan) and looked a prime candidate for breaking for spares.

Against all the odds, 019 was reinstated to traffic on the following 10th October, operating from Knottingley as part of Immingham's FDBI common-user pool.

As it was the last in Redstripe, its movements were well-documented in the railway press, producing reports of otherwise mundane workings simply because 019 had worked them. However, a closer look at some of these reports shows how varied the class's duties had become under EWS ownership.

*Typical of the loco's work during 1997 / 1998 were:*

| | |
|---|---|
| 19th November 1997 - | 6Z82 1304 Milford-Killoch MGR empties |
| January 1998 – | 6V67 1535 Wakefield-Cardiff Tidal Yard and 6V78 15:30 Dee Marsh-Margam |
| 2nd April 1998 - | 6E52 0706 Holyhead-Humber coke train |
| 20th June 1998 - | 1V50 Preston-Birmingham N.S., 1O38 Birmingham N.S.-Bournemouth and returned with 1M81 1814 Bournemouth-Birmingham. |
| 30th June 1998 - | 7C71 1124 Hoo Junction-Grain empty ballast and 7T83 return |
| 2nd July 1998 - | 6Y59 2132 Cliffe-Purley as far as Hither Green |
| 5th July 1998 - | Ballast trips off Hoo Junction |

small fleet and they had a much smaller sphere of operation than Class 56. It may seem contradictory, but this goes some way to explaining the surprising decision to place all fifty in store by the year 2002 and to retain sixty or so Class 56s instead.

No matter how wonderful the Canadian imports, EWS knew it could not dispose of Class 56 entirely, let alone immediately, although an official statement had confirmed the intention to set aside a substantial number. However, the EWS rail freight business continued to grow (it still had little railway competition in the closing years of the old century) and this was the main reason Class 56 survived for so long after the arrival of the 66s. EWS had its concerns, though, not least about 56s operating over the West Coast, East Coast and Great Western main lines, where any delays caused by loco failure resulted in massive penalties from Railtrack. Somewhere within the organisation, a number-cruncher probably knew exactly how much each Grid cost the company in Railtrack fines!

Despite all the background noise in the first half of 1999, Class 56 continued to dominate the petfood workings (until a Class 66 was theoretically booked from March 2000) and regained the Immingham-Ripple Lane newsprint trains - an early takeover by imported power. A new flow from Mostyn Docks to Scunthorpe brought the class back to the North Wales coast, steel workings between Teeside/Lynemouth and Wolverhampton/South Wales continued, and there were regular visits to the Rotherham area on steel trains. Engineer's duties took the class to Carnforth, Chaddesden, Tallington and other unusual locations.

The depressing news kept coming, though. The arrival of thirteen more Class 66s in the second half of April prompted the withdrawal of 56003, 004, 052, 066, 080 & 082, followed by 56047 & 097 in May - all with high engine hours and at least four years out of works.

The shape of things to come revealed itself again on 1st June when 66s took over a number of duties previously dominated by Class 56, such as the Immingham-Stalybridge tanks and the Margam-Dee Marsh steel coil trains.

The Type 5 availability report for 18th June reveals a similar pattern as before:

| | |
|---|---|
| Class 66 | 97% (112 out of 116 available) |
| Class 56 | 76% (96 locos) |
| Class 58 | 90% (an usually high 45 locos) |
| Class 59/2 | 100% (no change there) |
| Class 60 | 88% |

June's casualties included 56021 with engine defects, 56045 going into store at Immingham, 56108 stored at Thornaby, 56124 stored at Knottingley, and 56130 at Toton with a camshaft defect and exhaust system problems. 56129 was assigned a B25 exam on June 29th, but the discovery of wheelset problems brought its withdrawal within a fortnight.

An unusual working in July 1999 featured 56011 on 1V64 14.06 Low Fell-Plymouth Res vans. The postal vehicles were usually moved from Low Fell to Tyne Yard for servicing by any loco Tyne had spare, often producing a 56, but it was exceptionally rare for one to work the post throughout.

That month, 56053, 057, 061 were noted at Toton, either stored or withdrawn, 56093 at Doncaster and 56128 at Immingham. On the 24th, 56006 & 118 were assigned to storage at Immingham. A week later, 56081 had a close call when it caught fire at Garsdale on the S&C. Thanks to the random nature of the fleet's management, repairs were authorised and the loco eventually returned to traffic. 56039 was not so lucky; the long-term, fire-damaged Thornaby resident was condemned in early August. In the same month, 56086 joined the Immingham storage collection after suffering a traction motor flashover. In mid-September, 56104 & 129 went to Immingham.

*Above:* The celebrity 56019 (*see previous page*) passes Culham, near Oxford, with 1M81 18.14 Bournemouth-Manchester Piccadilly on 20th June 1998. *Photo: Martin Loader*

56050's chances of survival went up in smoke on the first day of October when the loco caught fire at Dunfermline while working the 07.56 Hunterston-Longannet MGR. 050 was towed to Motherwell to await repair authorisation that never came. She was sent to Toton in November and donated her bogies to 56083.

Almost unnoticed in this time of so much change, the Wigan CRDC had continued to process withdrawn locos to keep the spares supply flowing. However, a stark reminder that EWS wasn't in business to satisfy anyone except its owners was communicated to would-be preservationists when Wigan adopted a new method of removing internal components which simply involved cutting away the locos' bodysides.

A rumour at the time insisted this method was not for the 'benefit' of preservationists at all, but to prevent operational motive power falling into the hands of potential freight competitors. There were certainly instances of indecent haste, and the mistaken cutting up of a Class 31 which *had* been secured for preservation. Following several complaints and an investigation, the Rail Regulator ordered EWS to cease and desist as the practice of destroying perfectly good locomotives was deemed to be "anti-competitive". The result was that many of EWS's discarded assets were put out to tender and either secured by preservationists and/or given a new lease of life by other freight companies.

On 18th October 56031 volunteered for early retirement with a collision at Redcar. The loco moved to Thornaby, but repairs were cancelled by the 28th and 031 stood idle at Thornaby until March the following year. 56075 failed at Immingham dock on the 24th and was assigned for movement into store at Immingham two days later.

031, of course, had been one of the famous Meldon pool allocated to Stewarts Lane. Even though the pool's locomotives had been dispersed across the network in 1994, their classmates continued to appear on the former Southern Region, notably at Eastleigh. On 28th October 1999, for instance, 56058 hauled an MoD train from there to Didcot; the same night 56025 turned up on the 20.30 Bescot-Eastleigh, then worked an Eastleigh-Hoo Junction-Three Bridges engineer's train before running light back to Eastleigh.

Other unusual sightings included 56029 on the Toton to Horbury leg of 8X99 on November 16th, moving London Underground stock to overhaul. The same loco took the return working, the 13.19 to Didcot, as far as Toton.

Despite this apparent widening of Class 56's sphere of activity, withdrawals and storage continued at the same steady pace in the final months of 1999. 56034, which had been on decision at Toton with bogie defects, and fire-damaged 56050 at Motherwell were both withdrawn, while 56072 was placed on decision at Toton. Blue-liveried 56010's 'OD' at Doncaster Carr resulted from nothing more serious than an oil leak, but repairs were not authorised and the loco was stored at Immingham on 28th November along with 56022. The latter had no reported faults and seems to have been side-lined purely for the 'crime' of being Romanian! Doncaster-built 56077 had been stored at Knottingley on 12th November.

In December 56029 went into store at Thornaby and 56079 at Toton, while the storage collection at other locations began to migrate to Toton to surrender parts. 56061 moved from Doncaster on the 4th, 56075 from Immingham four days later. Others were a little luckier; 56131, stored at Toton, went back to work after receiving the bogies from 56075 as a present on Christmas Eve.

And so, a new millennium dawned . . . which is not of the slightest relevance to the Class 56 story. The new decade may have seen their withdrawal from EWS service but, as that decade nears its end, a handful of the Type are still earning revenue on the British system. As for the other 990 years, the railway and the rest of us are unlikely to see much of them.

What did emerge in the year 2000 was the strength of EWS's determination to reduce its older Type 5 fleets as drastically as traffic demands allowed. The announcement that the Class 58 fleet would be reduced to only 20 examples by the following March only heightened speculation about which 56s, and how many, would shuffle off when the next batch of 66s berthed at Newport. In reality, the slashing of the 58s' numbers gave the 56s a temporary degree of protection against the foreign imports.

As explained previously, the fate of an individual locomotive was often determined by statistics - TOPS hours, cost of repairs, *et cetera* - but, sometimes, by mere circumstance. Under that heading comes luck, as in the case of 56043. This Construction-liveried loco remained in traffic for more than a month after its initial assignment to store at Crewe Diesel on 15th December. The assignment was issued again on 12th January and the loco allocated to 6M31 20.26 Doncaster to Warrington, after which it would run light to Crewe at 22.00. However, 043 was reprieved again; it never worked the Warrington-bound train but instead remained in traffic around the Doncaster and Immingham areas. A third assignment to Crewe was issued on 19th January, along with 56036, 064 & 109. 56036 arrived at Crewe the next day, 064 had reached Warrington, while 109 was working its way west on a Haworth-Fiddler's Ferry MGR; in fact, it remained on Fiddler's Ferry work for another week. The elusive 043, meanwhile, had also arrived at Warrington, from where it towed 064 & 113 to Crewe. 113 had caught fire at Speke on the 19th while working 6P97 Warrington-Seaforth and had been dumped at Warrington with a power unit full of foam. Although 043, 064 & 109 were all runners when they arrived at Crewe Diesel, 043's charmed life expired when its power unit was whipped out to resurrect the crippled 113.

Derailment damaged 56084 was stored as surplus to requirements on 11th January, but 56101, suffering oil contamination, had the problem attended to and went back into traffic.

At the end of January, 56049 went into store at Cardiff, 56072 at Toton. Three others were also assigned to store at the same time but were still in traffic - just. 56131 should have gone to Immingham after suffering a power earth fault at Hereford, but was repaired at Warrington and had its storage assignment cancelled. 56083 & 106 should also have gone to Cardiff but, along with 049 for good measure, were taken to Barry WRD on 11th February, sandwiched between 60056 & 075. On the last day of January, 56038 was stopped with faulty cylinder liners and seals at Doncaster Carr. However, while other locos with equally low hours were being withdrawn, 038 was repaired and back in traffic by the next day. Truly a lottery.

The only good news that month was that 56s had again resumed iron ore workings in South Wales after the hire arrangement for Mendip Rail Class 59s was terminated.

In the first week of February 56132 joined the storage collection, but the repaired 56113 was back in traffic by the 13th. Its donor, 56043, was moved to Chester wagon repair shops on 14th February along with 036, 064 & 109. On the 21st, 56116 was assigned for withdrawal the next day at Margam, while 56040 was briefly placed on decision at Immingham but returned to traffic within days. By this date 56025, 040, 055, 070, 074, 085 & 127 were all assigned to store and a number were reported to be heading for Chester. However, two (055 & 076) were removed from the list and remained in traffic. In the week commencing 28th February, 040 & 107 were taken out of traffic at Immingham, 56127 at Toton. Astonishingly, Redcar collision victim 56031 went back to work after 56035 donated both its cab rooves at Thornaby!

Mentions of Chester notwithstanding, 56025, 055, 070, 074 & 085 went into store at Cardiff in the second week of March. The once-reprieved 076 finally came out of traffic at Immingham at the same time, with 16,200

*Above:* 56088 hauls a rake of former-National Power hoppers at Burton Lane on 17th March 1999. *Photo: Neil Harvey*

*Above:* 56102 passes the 1886-built signal box at Medge Hall, between Scunthorpe and Doncaster, with 6M99 Immingham-Wolverhampton steel on 6th September 1999. During the mid '90s, 56102 was fitted with an adaptive tractive effort & automatic sanding modification which used wheelslip control techniques to increase its haulage capacity. There were hopes that a number of 56s would be similarly converted but like the unique 50/1 experiment it came to nothing. *Photo: Martin Loader*

TOPS hours on the clock. Under BR, the loco would have been into a main works twice while clocking up such service. Meanwhile, the withdrawal of 56025 and the storage of 56011 at Immingham had left only three Romanian locos in traffic - 007, 018 & 027.

In the early part of the month, EWS had announced the sale of 51 redundant locomotives, including 56008, 012 & 014 at Immingham and 013 at Toton. The three at Immingham were disposed of on-site by Raxstar during April, while 013 was bought for scrap by TJ Thompson.

Despite the number of withdrawals, the 'safe' storage at Chester and Barry was regarded as positive news. More locos moved to Barry on 14th March (025, 055 & 116 from Cardiff, top & tailed by 37404 & 414); three more followed in similar fashion the next day (070, 074 & 085). Within 24 hours, 56040 fired up at Immingham to haul 56011 & 107 to Crewe, where they joined 56077. All four were towed round to Chester by 47768 on 28th March.

Given this relentless decline, the last thing EWS needed was two locos catching fire within a week - first, 56044 at Tyne, then 56115 at Barnetby on 21st March while working 6V20 Humber-Baglan Bay. Repairs were authorised for both and they later returned to traffic. However, 56101 joined the storage batch on 28th March, 56098 on the 6th April.

The whole process slammed into reverse gear on 27th April when six locos were reinstated to cover increased traffic requirements at Thornaby - 56098, which received a bogie swop at Immingham, and five from those stored at either Chester or Barry. 56127 was soon pencilled in as the second of the six and repairs began at Doncaster Carr. 56011, 040, 055 & 074 were selected from the safe storage and despatched for B exams before reinstatement. 56011 went to Thornaby as it

*Above:* On 5th May 1999, only two months after withdrawal, 56126 rests on top of a wagon at EWS's Wigan CRDC, having already donated its bogies to a classmate. *Photo: Paul Furtek*

87

*Above: 56085 at Golcar on the Standedge route working 6M05 Roxby-Northenden on 16th June 1999. Photo: Neil Harvey*

needed tyre-turning, while 56040 travelled to Immingham and was delayed awaiting new batteries. 56055 & 074 moved from Barry to Cardiff and then on to Knottingley. 055 remained at Knottingley for its B exam while 074 went to nearby Ferrybridge. 56055 subsequently had to go to Thornaby for tyre turning too. When 56047 entered the frame by moving from Doncaster to Immingham for repairs on May 25th, it was assumed this was because 56127 was proving difficult to resurrect. However, when progress was made on 127, the late substitute became a bogie donor to 56098.

56040 was the first back in traffic on May 25th. 56055 followed two days later, 56074 on the 30th, 56011 on the 31st. 56098 didn't reappear until 15th June, when it was despatched from Immingham to take up MGR duties at Milford. Despite the optimism, 56127 encountered problems, and 56046 was returned to traffic on the 23rd June after standing idle at Toton for a month awaiting a fresh set of bogies.

As summer approached, many of the long-term stored locos were formally transferred into the WNXX component recovery pool. Picking up this code after the number usually meant a one-way trip to Wigan - hence bad news for 56019, 050, 066, 075 & 123 at the end of May.

Other 2000 transfers to WNXX included:

56034, 061, 080 & 132 (mid-July) and, 56010, 029, 039, 047, 057, 124 & 135 (September).

Slightly behind them in the oblivion queue, 56013 arrived at TJ Thomson's Stockton-on-Tees premises on 12th July. It survived for more than a year and was finally cut up by 24th September 2001.

Of the April reinstatements, 56074 appeared to be in trouble when called to Immingham for turbo repairs, but it was back in traffic by 3rd August. This loco was unusual in that it was one of six fitted with Brown Boveri turbo-chargers rather than the usual Napier units. Any terminal problem would have resulted in its withdrawal as there were unlikely to have been spare turbos in stock at this late stage in the locomotives' careers.

A second resurrection occurred early in September when a need for several Class 56s was identified as replacements for Class 37s transferring to seasonal Sandite duties. This time 56025, 072, 085, 106, 111, 118 & 127 were selected. By the 16th 56025, 085 & 116 had moved from Barry to Canton for attention, while Doncaster was preparing 56127, and Immingham had 56111 & 118. At Toton, 58042 and 58048 had somehow managed to sneak onto the list.

Before its return to traffic on 6th October, 56111 received the bogies from 56022. Meanwhile, 56118 had gone to Wabtec at Doncaster for engine repairs. It eventually received a power unit removed from 56097 at Wigan CRDC and was finally released to traffic at Immingham on the intensive Scunthorpe steelworks coal deliveries three days before Christmas.

56038 became the latest fire victim in early October at Ferrybridge, but its low hours and recent overhaul ensured, yet again, a return to traffic within a week.

By 9th October, Resurrection Two loco 56085 was working again off Newport, followed there two days later by 56025 & 116, working north on the 20.18 Newport-Lackenby steel. By then, 56085 had also travelled to Teeside. 56127 was released to traffic on Aire Valley MGRs after further attention at Ferrybridge, but only lasted until around 21st October. The loco failed and sat under repair at Immingham until 6th November, when it paired up with 56089 on 6D96 Wilton-Immingham. 56111 had been happily working MGR turns off Immingham since reinstatement, but a trip to the north-west found it side-lined with wheelset problems at Gobowen on 18th October. It arrived at Crewe Diesel depot for attention four days later.

After only five months back in traffic, 56040 was on decision again at Immingham on 27th October, reportedly for fumes in the cabs. The former *Oystermouth* was finally withdrawn four days later with 8,647 hours on the clock.

The low Class 60 availability became slightly lower when two of them collided at Llanwern on Bonfire Night, but the good news was another small increase in demand for Class 56. Even so, 56044 was withdrawn at Immingham on 15th December and by the end of 2000 the class had declined to 72 operational examples, concentrated on only two depots - Immingham and Thornaby.

There was another small slice of good news in January, with Doncaster's 'No. 2' under repair at Immingham and due to receive a fuel tank from 56019. 032's reinstatement followed a decision to withdraw 56100, with 10,000 TOPS hours, whenever its next 'B' exam fell due or when it failed in traffic.

Slice Two concerned 56111 which had been at Crewe Diesel under repair since October 22nd. It finally re-emerged on 20th January, working on drawback duties at Latchford - conveniently close to Crewe just in case.

On the downside, the recalcitrant 56127 was side-lined once more on 12th January with engine problems, this time at Bescot. It was booked to go to Thornaby for assessment five days later and, by the end of the month, had returned to traffic following repairs and a 'B' exam. At around the same time, 56069 went to Brush for repairs to its alternator and was released back to traffic in mid-March.

56032 returned to work on 6th February, operating from Immingham. Nine days later 56100 was assigned the TOPS code N/ONE at Ayr TMD. N/ONE identifies a loco pre-assigned a date and location for withdrawal owing to wear and tear. On 21st February the loco worked north on 4S84 Doncaster-Deanside and the next day handled 6R45 Grangemouth-Prestwick aviation fuel before running light back to Ayr. A brief stint as the depot's yard shunter ensued until it was formally transferred into the withdrawn pool on 1st March.

Before recording the fate of other Class 56s in 2001 and beyond, it is necessary to pause at this point and consider background events. EWS was about to enter a challenging period, not merely because of competition from emerging companies like GB Railfreight and the expansion of the Freightliner operation, but through the loss of major contracts like the Royal Mail traffic. Perversely, this difficult time ultimately proved beneficial to Class 56. The 'new' EWS began to look further afield for revenue and the search resulted in The French Connection, which not only ensured the remaining locos' survival until the present day but also raised the intriguing question - When is a withdrawal not a withdrawal?

# 10. UNDER NEW MANAGEMENT

*Above: 56038 at Burton Salmon with 6D95 Selby-Doncaster Belmont Yard Enterprise on 5th March 2001. Photo: Neil Harvey*

The takeover of EWS by Canadian National was a marriage of inconvenience. The new owner's sole interest was in securing the rights held by Wisconsin in North America, which would allow through running from Canada into the United States as far south as Chicago and Illinois (thanks to an earlier acquisition of Illinois Central). This 'filling in' of the existing gap made perfect commercial sense but, like Wisconsin's approach to buying the three British freight companies, the sale offer was for all of Wisconsin's assets, including its stake in EWS, on a 'whole lot or nothing' basis. CN had no interest in a short-distance, bitty operation 5,000 miles across the ocean, but reluctantly agreed to take on the subsidiary to secure the main prize.

Several attempts were made to sell off the EWS portion, but no other company was prepared to match the valuation placed on the British asset. Discussions with the French SNCF and the German Deutsche Bahn came to nothing, so CN had no choice but to continue, and so placed three of its representatives on the EWS board. The situation was further complicated by the fact that Wisconsin owned only 42% of EWS; 'sleeping partners' held the other 58% of the shares. Although negotiations began in January 2001, the takeover was not completed until the following September as the deal needed the approval of the US Surface Transportation Board.

It is also worth mentioning that the visionary Ed Burkhardt had left his post as President of Wisconsin by this date (we may never know the full circumstances of his sudden departure). His place as Chief Executive of EWS had been taken by Ian Braybrook, the former boss of Loadhaul. During this latter period, Engineering Director Jim Fisk returned to America, but his original 1996 plan for reducing and rationalising the EWS locomotive fleet remained in force. CN also inherited, albeit via a leasing company, the full fleet of 250 Class 66 locomotives. The last one had been unloaded at Newport on the 23rd of June, 2000.

In terms of the Class 56 story, therefore, the emergence of a third owner had little effect on the class's fortunes in the short-term. The pattern of withdrawals and storage, and the haphazard nature of repairs approvals, continued much as before. As one example amongst many, 56072 went into Toton in the middle of April for a 'B' exam, but its repair and return to traffic were put back so many times that it didn't re-emerge until September. In the meantime, it put in spells as the Toton yard pilot!

Also of concern at this time was the cluttering of many depots with stored locos, resulting in batches moving to new locations to clear space for the day-to-day work. Many of the stored Class 58s, for example, were moved from Stratford to Ipswich WRD.

The 20th of April 2001 was a bad day for the Grids. 56091 caught fire at Brighouse while working 6E14 Seaforth-Tinsley, and was later dumped at Scunthorpe; 56051 was stopped at Saltley needing derailment repairs; 56058 at Immingham with collision damage. Four days later, 56074 could be found at Worksop with fire damage. The Type 5 availability figure must have been terrible, which may be why all the above were repaired. 051 & 058 were both back in traffic by 24th April; 074, repaired at Toton, was back at work by the 27th; Immingham had restored 091 for further use by the 1st May.

In the same spring, 56004 & 006 were assigned to a new grouping known as the EWS Heritage pool, although the purpose of this move remained unclear.

One of many epithets applied to the new Class 66s by then was the nickname Ying-Yings. Given the frequency with which the surviving 56s went into and out of store, it is surprising they hadn't become known as Yo-Yos! Another six - 56025, 027, 073, 074, 112 & 116 - were earmarked on 20th May, all having accumulated high engine hours and with major repairs looming. Slightly luckier, 56112 was under repair at Thornaby, while Toton continued to work on 56072 & 130, although 075 had been returned to the dumping ground outside the depot.

Within weeks, however, prospects improved when the imminent requirement for 66s on the Channel Tunnel Rail Link prompted an EWS study to establish what was necessary to 'persuade' Class 56s to run up to 13,000 hours safely. The aim was simple; if a method were found, they could stand in temporarily for the absent 66s without undergoing the lengthy overhauls many of them needed.

The initial short-list comprised 53 locos, some of which were still in traffic. By the time

*Above:* 56037 passes Huntcliffe with 6F21 Boulby to Tees Dock on 16th August 2002. *Photo: Neil Harvey*

the CTRL locos were required, the earlier removal plan would have reduced Class 56 to only 33 examples, so the hasty inclusion of some of the recently-stored locos resulted. A detailed list was drafted, giving defects and estimated reinstatement cost for each one - a procedure which immediately eliminated several because they would have been too expensive to resurrect.

The successful candidates and their starting locations are shown in the accompanying table. Most were listed as 'runners', withdrawn solely because of high TOPS hours (up to and beyond the 10,000 limit in some cases), while others had the specific defects shown.

A handful of 58s were also included in the list but eventually dropped. Five of the 56s - 027, 073, 074, 085 & 116 - were immediately given 'B' exams and returned to traffic, while the rest were worked on during the coming months. 56130, at Toton, was excluded after an initial inspection revealed additional problems.

In fact, like all reinstatement programmes, locos that were not on the original list stepped up to fill the gap whenever one of the chosen was found to need more serious work. 56129, for example, seems to have taken the place of 56079 after the former was assigned a 'B' exam at Toton. 56100, the sole item on the Ayr list, also went to

Toton for a 'B' exam and further assessment, as did Barry's 56070 & 106.

56079 was not so lucky. Its assigned move to Toton from Immingham was cancelled. Instead, Doncaster dragged 56099 out of the wood yard and despatched it to Immingham in the 6D65 Enterprise behind 56065.

Four other locos with high hours were allocated special tests at Doncaster. Again, speculation became rife that this was the precursor to a major works overhaul programme, but it turned out to be exactly the opposite. It was merely another part of EWS's quest to find locos that could be safely run to 13,000 hours *without* works attention.

The next batch to move to Toton were Chester's 56077, 107 & 109. They arrived on August 20th behind 47773 and, following assessment, were given release dates between the 15th and 30th of September.

56100 & 129 re-entered traffic on September 13th. Six days later, 56033 moved from Doncaster to Thornaby for tyre-turning. The repaired 56109 worked a test train between Toton and Radcliffe (7A17) on the 19th and was released to traffic the next day. Its place at Toton was taken by Barry's 56049, which was unexpectedly joined at the end of the month by the 'heritage pool' of 56004 & 006. It was, thought, however, that 004 was more likely to donate parts to the reinstatement programme than to be part of it. So much for heritage.

In October, 56099 & 106 returned to traffic, working off Immingham, while 56070 joined them from Toton. By the end of the month, 56033 had moved from Thornaby to Immingham for its 'B' exam; it went back to work on 22nd November.

Wheelsets and bogies continued to be in short supply and many locos were effectively eliminated from a possible return to traffic by having their bogies removed for use underneath others. Quite often, the donor would simply be dumped on the scrap bogies, with no reconnection work. Such

### Class 56s identified for reinstatement - May 2001

*Chester*
56036  9,056 hours
56064  9,512 hours
56077  9,133 hours, wheelset change needed
56107  8,992 hours
56109  9,499 hours

*Toton*
56130  8,713 hours, camshaft defect
56133  8,860 hours, seized wheelset
56072  8,479 hours, starter motor fire

*Ayr*
56100  10,021 hours

*Barry*
56049  8,708 hours
56070  8,840 hours
56074  10,000+ hours
56083  9,388 hours
56085  10,000+ hours
56106  8,860 hours
56116  10,000+ hours

*Old Oak Common*
56004  9,010 hours, engine defects
56006  8,756 hours, worn centre castings

*Immingham*
56011  8,618 hours, 2 wheelset changes needed
56021  7,140 hours, engine defects
56076  8,654 hours, seized traction motor
56084  9,107 hours, derailment damage
56086  7,241 hours, traction motor flashover
56104  8,941 hours
56125  9,456 hours, wheelsets at scrap size
56128  8,837 hours, camshaft defects
56129  9,402 hours

*Doncaster*
56003  8,347 hours, worn centre castings
56033  9,988 hours
56093  8,972 hours
56099  8,271 hours

*Knottingley*
56124  8,000 hours

In *traffic*
56027  10,000 hours
56073  16,000 hours
56127  10,000 hours

locos often had bodyside jacking point covers left off and dampers and traction centres dumped in the cabs.

56027 was one of those assigned a bogie change at the start of October, but it was put back into traffic until a suitable donor could be found. By the end of the month, 56029 had been identified. The loco moved from Doncaster to Cardiff in readiness, but 14th November rolled around before 027 made it to Cardiff for the work to be carried out. Also in October, 56052 moved from Doncaster to Immingham where it donated its bogies to keep 56031 in traffic. At the same depot, a November swop involved 56021 surrendering its wheels to 56096. Meanwhile, and as expected, 004 surrendered both bogies at Toton to keep 56006 mobile. The heritage pool had suddenly become only one loco, but maybe that was always the intention.

The bogie challenge aside, it was also necessary to keep up the flow of other parts to the surviving locos. 56066 drew the short straw of a one-way ticket to the Wigan CRDC on 18th August and filled the space created by the destruction of 56092 a month earlier. In September, 56044 & 045 received similar bad news in their pay packets. They remained at Immingham for the time being, awaiting the call. 56036, once of Large Logo experimental repaint, was towed to the CRDC by 47635 on 14th December to donate much-needed wheelsets and other bits to the spares pool.

While the CRDC consumed locomotives at an alarming rate, there was some moderately good news. 56023, 080 & 097 were all purchased from an EWS tender list. Details of the buyers were a little vague at the time, but eventually it would be 56097 which rose from the ashes using parts from the other two.

By the end of November, it had become apparent which locos would *not* be making the trip to full reinstatement. One of them was 56003, which moved to Toton and gave up its bogies to fellow Romanian 007. At the same time 56104, an Immingham inclusion on the original list with 8,941 hours, returned to the scrapline. Not on anyone's radar throughout the process, 56112 was reinstated to traffic on 28th December after a bogie swop at Motherwell.

2002 was another year of gradual decline, with the same pattern of swops, storage and repairs only when they became absolutely essential. As the year began, 56049 (wheelsets) and 56007 (bogie change) returned to traffic but 56089, stopped at Thornaby with frame problems, would go into store within a month. Similarly, local work on 56077 failed to solve its wheelset problems and the loco was towed to Doncaster for specialist attention. By February it had moved on, so that Crewe could have a crack at the problem. That attempt failed too and the loco was assigned to store on 21st February.

Meanwhile 56127, another successful reinstatement originally, had been stopped at Thornaby and was also assigned to store, again, in February.

Making their first appearance during this period, 56043 & 064 were towed from Chester to Doncaster and then on to Immingham, possibly for reinstatement. One of Toton's nominations for the reinstatement programme (which seemed to be taking an *awfully* long time) finally returned to traffic on 12th February. However, 56133 immediately suffered a traction motor flashover but was released again on the 18th to make a test run on the Toton-Castleton CWR train.

Another 'low on the radar' example, 56048, returned to traffic on 2nd March, two days before the saved 56097 escaped from the CRDC for the first stage of its restoration at Cardiff Cathays. Its place in the endangered species park was taken by 56029 which arrived from Cardiff on 7th March, riding on the scrap bogies from 56027.

At the same time, a number of locos were stopped at Thornaby with various defects: 56059, 110 & 117 (all wheelsets), 56062 (camshafts), 56100 (turbo) and 56120 (dampers). Three - 059, 100 & 110 - were placed in store during April. The same fate befell 56025 at Immingham. Curiously, the abandoned 56077 still appeared in official records to be under repair at Crewe, as its 'Expected OK' dates were constantly updated on TOPS.

The Class 58 fleet continued to be decimated - eleven times if you apply the precise Latin meaning of the word. With no fewer than 36 in store, the 14 survivors had been concentrated in the Eastleigh, Hoo Junction and Didcot areas. In June and July 2002, a rumour persisted that the class would soon come out of service with EWS altogether. It is true that EWS looked into

*Above:* 56037 again, this time at South Bank, Middlesbrough, working 6F52 Boulby-Middlesbrough Goods. *Photo: Neil Harvey*

*Above:* 56088 restarts from Oakenshaw North Junction with 6D76 Doncaster-Monk Bretton Enterprise on 25th June 2001. *Photo: Neil Harvey*

allocating a small pool of 56s to Eastleigh to cover for the loss of the 58s in the south but, eventually, Class 56 reinstatements covered Class 66 duties nationwide when the Ying-Yings took over the former work of the Egg-Timers. Confused?

With the benefit of hindsight, Canadian National's takeover of EWS couldn't have happened at a more difficult time. The smaller companies had begun to flex their muscles and EWS was facing stiff competition for the first time since privatisation. DRS continued to add to its fleet with more Class 37s, even a couple of 47s and 33s. Freightliner, meanwhile, had begun to take delivery of its first Class 66s, having decided not to proceed with more Class 57/0 conversions.

To complicate the picture further, EWS had to cope with the inevitable changes in traffic patterns, not least the seasonal variations in the demand for coal. With the other companies bidding for this work too, gaining or losing a contract depended on how flexible the pool of operational locomotives could become in response to traffic requirements. Class 56 became the motive power of choice for the process of standing down and reinstatement to meet changing business demands. To this end, EWS created a new pool - WNTR, Withdrawn locos, Tactical Reserve - which contained a stock of power that could be re-activated quickly.

Along with three Class 37s, the four 56s stored on 9th April - 025, 059, 100 & 110 - became the first to be assigned to the new pool seven days later. 56110 was re-activated three days after that. Its place in the WNTR pool was quickly taken by 56055. This one worked into Tees with 6E62 from Carlisle soon after, demonstrating that WNTR pool locos could be returned to service in a matter of hours if necessary. The same pool also provided cover for locos out of service for repairs, and many of its members could often be found with their engines running at Thornaby to keep the air systems in good condition and the batteries charged. When 56100 began ticking over towards the end of May, it was no surprise that it re-entered traffic on the 28th, covering for 56059 which was undergoing wheelset repairs.

The formation and management of this pool was probably the single most significant factor in allowing EWS to keep the required numbers in traffic until the planned disposal in March 2004.

WNTR received 56041 & 054 at the end of May and both were located at Immingham. However, the introduction of buckeye-fitted hoppers on the intensive Scunthorpe-Immingham coal circuit was one traffic change which actually reduced the requirement for Class 56.

By the end of June, a number of locos were out of traffic in one reserve or another. 56006, 046, & 116 went into WNTR at Immingham, the location for 56063 & 134 re-assigned to WNSS (stored serviceable). Another WNSS member, 56077, stood at Crewe Diesel. The traditional storage pool WNXX acquired 56031, 073 & 131 at the same time. 56027, 105 & 111, however, were assigned for 'special tests', which usually meant they were to be assessed for further expenditure to keep them in traffic.

The benefits of the WNTR pool showed their worth when 56100, despite suffering wheelset problems, was brought back as cover for 56038 while the latter was under repair at Immingham in the last weeks of June. 038 had extremely low hours (5,312), making it an ideal candidate for WNTR when the repairs were completed. At that point, 56100 took its place in the WGAT Thornaby pool - a short-lived move as 56041 transferred to WGAT on 12th July, forcing 100 out of traffic. Two weeks later, 56058 was resurrected from WNTR to work engineer's trains but 56085, formerly of Barry and with more than 10,000 hours on the clock, went into store at Thornaby.

An extra advantage of WNTR was that its locos could be worked on without the normal, sometimes extreme pressure to get them back into traffic. All that was required was to have enough available in working order to meet demand when it arose. In another swop, 56048 was stood down on 4th August, having accumulated 14,165 hours. The low-hours 56038 transferred from WNTR to take its place in the Thornaby pool. Four days later, the discarded 56110 joined the WNSS stored collection.

The prospect of increased winter coal traffic created a requirement for six additional locos at the end of September. As expected, most were to come from WNTR - provisionally 56006, 025, 046, 054, 055 & 116. By October, 56025 had been dropped; it went into WNXX and was replaced by 56104, even though the latter had been out of traffic since September 1999. 56046 was also dropped and replaced by 56110.

56055 & 116 were the first of the latest reinstatements on 14th October. They were followed within five days by 56006, which was noted running light in Immingham docks before taking over 6C83 Scunthorpe coal. 006 had to return to the local depot for a traction motor change towards the end of the month - the same day that 56054 was reinstated.

It underwent a 'B' exam at Immingham and was quickly followed by 56104 in the maintenance shed. 104 re-entered traffic on 20th November after a 'B' exam and a bogie swop with 56063.

*Above:* 56091 at the junction of the Calder Valley and Diggle routes near Mirfield on 14th August 2003 with 6E33 10.57 Knowsley-Immingham. *Photo: John Hooson*

*Above:* 56049 departs from Healey Mills with 6E72 Stalybridge-Immingham tanks on 11th July 2002. *Photo: Neil Harvey*

The two locos bought at the same time as 56097 had moved to the MoD site at Ashchurch so the full restoration of 097 could begin. 56080 travelled by rail from the CRDC on October 10th; 56023 followed by road from Toton two days later.

CRDC stock was topped up on 6th December by the arrival of 56004, 034 & 132. Another from Toton was expected (075) along with four more from Immingham and two from Doncaster. The experimental engineering project known as 56077 was finally put out of its misery on 22nd October when it was withdrawn at Crewe. Whether the 'Expected OK' up-dates continued is lost in the mist of history.

Just to show that other classes were suffering too, 56103 hauled 86206 & 231 in the consist of 6D65 Doncaster-Immingham on 15th November for storage at the rail freight terminal. Less than a week later, 56087 tripped 86214, 244 & 256 from Carlisle Yard to MoD Longtown for storage.

By the end of the year, 56098 looked likely to be the next casualty. It was placed on decision at Immingham on 19th December and, with 11,833 engine hours, its repair was not expected to be sanctioned.

As 2003 began, two more high accumulators - 56041 (WGAT - 12,617 hours) and 56074 (WGAI - 12,768 hours) were transferred into WNTR but had to be reinstated twenty-fours hours later when 56032 and 56070 were assigned to storage at Cardiff and Toton respectively with wheelset problems. However, 56112 from WGAI (12,434 hours) enjoyed no such reprieve. The almost-invisible 56032 had repairs authorised so it would be available from WNTR if needed.

One of the recently-revived coal sextet ran into trouble on 24th January. 56116 suffered traction motor problems and was stopped at Immingham. With 12,244 hours on the clock, the loco went into WNSS on 3rd February, despite that pool's nominal status of 'serviceable'.

Although life was clearly continuing much as before as Class 56 entered the penultimate year of its first incarnation, 2003 threw up two more developments - one possible, one unavoidable. Stories began to emerge that EWS was considering major overhauls for between eight and ten of the stored 56s in the next financial year starting in April. Sadly, it all came to nothing when the accountants had other ideas.

The end of January was also the deadline for all locomotives to be fitted with the Train Protection & Warning System (TPWS) if they were to continue operating on the main network. So, another pressure arose; locos without the magic box were less likely to see active service again. Under that heading came the long-withdrawn 56039, which moved to Thompson's for scrap, 56003 at Toton and 56010 at Carr Loco. Those two made a one-way journey to Booth's in February.

The month continued to inflict casualties. The recently-reinstated 56041 was back on decision at Immingham and stored in WNSS and 56027 went into WNTR at Peterborough. 56104 was stored in the same pool at Doncaster Carr, but its life potentially improved when it was assigned for TPWS fitting. This became a standard pattern for locos re-assigned to WNTR. They could hardly be called Tactical or Reserve if the regulations prevented them from running, hence several visits to Doncaster Carr for the necessary work. With the usual symmetry, another WNTR member already fitted with TPWS would be reinstated as cover for the absent loco.

Wheelset casualty 56070 returned to traffic on 15th February, just as 56090 & 114 were going into WNSS at Thornaby. 56114 went into the shed for repairs, while 090 was towed to Immingham by 56109 for a bogie change.

WNTR's 56027 underwent brake repairs at Immingham and returned to traffic on 22nd February, while 56104 went back to work a few days later with the necessary black box. Immediately after release from Carr Loco, it worked 7H84 Doncaster-Peterborough engineer's trip. Its temporary replacement, 56074, went back into store at Immingham. By now, the management of WNTR had developed into something of an art form. EWS knew exactly how many 56s it needed in traffic at any one time and there were always substitutes on stand-by to cover availability issues with the core WGAT and WGAI fleet.

With wheelset repairs completed at Canton, 56032 went back into traffic. Predictably, 56027 returned to the tactical reserve. Similarly, when 56114 came off repairs at Thornaby on 18th March, 56055 (12,437 hours) was stopped at Knottingley and WNTR'd again. Despite the bogie transplant at Immingham, 56090 remained in the stored pool for the time being.

By the end of March, there were indications that up to twelve 56s could be stood down within days. Those with high engine hours were obviously vulnerable, as were any becoming due for major exams or repairs. 56106 was a

*Above:* 56104 took part in a Mid-Hants Railway diesel gala in May 2003. The loco arrives at Ropley shed on 17th May. *Photo: Carl Rayner*

prime contender for the chop as it was known to require camshaft attention.

The table at the bottom of this page lists the engine hours for the surviving fleet on 25th March 2003. No doubt somebody within EWS was studying a similar list while trying to decide which locos to dispense with. The listing of stored locos makes interesting reading, especially if you compare the number with *less* than 10,000 hours with the operational group.

As the new financial year dawned in April, the ratio of bad news to good continued to be poor. On the positive side, the return to traffic of 56090 on the 1st of the month proved that EWS hadn't put new bogies under it just for a laugh.

However, with the exception of 56068, 083 & 105, all locos with more than 11,500 hours went on decision on 2nd April. As we had come to expect, EWS changed its mind the next day; all allocations to store were revoked and 56102 was even allocated a 'B' exam at Immingham!

EWS managed to stick to the 'new' policy for a whole four days, but caved in on the 6th when five 56s were assigned to the N/ONE category. 56007, 033 & 111 were restricted to working the 'captive' Tees Dock-Boulby service, which at least ensured they wouldn't be requisitioned and end up in Aberdeen on the day they were due for withdrawal. 56067 & 100 (both WGAT) were assigned to N/ONE at Immingham. Within 24 hours, the five were joined by 56054 & 129 at Doncaster Carr and 56109 at Thornaby.

Not content with killing off eight members of the fleet, EWS put more into store the day after that:

56007 & 033 at Thornaby, stopped and transferred to WNTR
56067 & 100 at Immingham, ditto
56102 at Immingham, into WNSS while still undergoing a 'B' exam
56106 at Immingham, into WNSS but still authorised for camshaft repairs!

It's worth noting that two of these and one other WNTR loco - 56007, 033 & 056 - were in 'engine running' mode at Thornaby depot on April 24th and again on the 29th. On the second occasion they were joined by 56111. All four were actually fuelled and prepared for use on 2nd May but, despite hopes they would be used on weekend engineering trains, they stayed put at Thornaby waiting for their moment.

In a mind-boggling development, Freightliner hired in six of the highly flaky Class 47/8s from Porterbrook at this time. How this could happen when 56s, with a proven track record on Freightliner work, were being stood down is anyone's guess.

At least some were escaping the chop. With its 'B' exam completed, 56102 moved to Doncaster Carr in early May for TPWS fitting, suggesting it would not remain for much longer in WNSS.

Almost simultaneously, 56019, 022, 047, 123, 125 & 135, all standing at Immingham, found themselves transferred to the WNZX pool, making them likely candidates for an appearance on the next EWS tender list.

Bogie recipient 56090 was released back to traffic on May 9th, while 56067 & 106 were reinstated at Thornaby a week later and let loose from Immingham. 56104 also appeared at the Mid-Hants Railway's diesel gala on 16th May.

The confusion over whether 56129 was on N/ONE status or in store at Doncaster Carr was resolved the next day when the loco was reinstated to the WGAT pool.

Although nominally an operational loco, 56018 only received the mandatory TPWS equipment at the same depot at the end of May. On release on 5th June, it worked 6M67 Healey Mills-Carlisle with 66246.

Another Carr customer, 56100 (WNTR), was given an 'A' exam at Immingham on the 24th and was then hauled from Immingham to Doncaster for TPWS fitting. 56051 (also WNTR) arrived from Immingham for the same treatment on 7th June.

More special tests candidates were identified at Thornaby on the 27th. Both 56068 & 129 had high hours (12,442 and 12,490) and were due for B25 exams. Four more were expected to undergo similar tests when they reached the 12,500 hours mark - 56083 (12,011), 56090 (12,161), 56099 (12,238) and 56102 (12,104).

WGAT's 56068 & 129 had been authorised for 'B' exams, but they were replaced by 56054 & 100 from Doncaster Carr. The discovery of problems with 129's wheelsets probably didn't help. The reasons for 068's substitution remained unclear, although high hours combined with a 'B' exam falling due were probably enough. Both were stored in WNTR, 068 at Immingham, 129 at Thornaby.

On 28th July, the heritage pool's 56006 put in an appearance at the Wabtec Gala in Doncaster - a strange choice as it wasn't built there.

On the last day of the month 56094 & 103 (both WNTR) went into store at Thornaby, reportedly with wheelset problems. They were replaced by 56033, reinstated to WGAI from store at Thornaby in August, and 56051, which went into the WGAT pool from Immingham. However, the first two were expected to go back into traffic once replacement wheelsets had been sourced.

At this point, the Harry Needle Railroad Company entered the Class 56 story with an announcement that it had successfully acquired 56123 & 135 at Immingham for scrap. In the same round of tender bids, Fragonset bought 56022 & 125, while Sandbach Car & Commercial acquired 56047 and the 'celebrity' 56019. Both 019 and 047 were later sold on to HNRC which scrapped all four on-site at Immingham. 123 & 135 had disintegrated into piles of tangled metal by 20th August.

Between 8th and 11th August, 56054 & 105 at Immingham and 56100 & 106 at Thornaby were assigned to store, reducing the Class 56 fleet to only 39 operational locos.

### Engine Hours as at 25th March 2003

*Operational locos*
- 12,500+ 56111
- 12,000+ 56007, 033, 054, 056, 068, 100, 109, 129
- 11,500+ 56067, 083, 099, 102, 105
- 11,000+ 56072, 088, 096, 103, 106, 107, 118
- 10,500+ 56049, 051, 058, 065, 070, 114, 117, 120
- 10,000+ 56006, 059, 087, 119, 133
- 09,500+ 56060
- 09,000+ 56018, 032, 104
- 08,500+ 56037, 078
- 07,500+ 56069, 071, 091, 094, 095, 115
- 07,000+ 56062, 113
- 06,500+ 56081
- 06,000+ 56038

*Stored locos*
- 16,000+ 56073
- 15,000+ 56063
- 14,000+ 56031, 048, 131, 134
- 13,000+ 56019, 046, 074
- 12,000+ 56027, 041, 055, 085, 112, 116
- 11,000+ 56025, 090, 098, 110
- 10,000+ 56043, 052, 066, 132, 127
- 09,000+ 56004, 010, 029, 034, 036, 044, 047, 053, 057, 061, 064, 075, 077, 079, 082, 084, 089, 093, 123, 125, 135
- 08,000+ 56003, 011, 022, 040, 045, 050, 076, 108, 121, 124, 128, 130
- 07,000+ 56021, 039, 086
- 06,000+ 56101

Two derailments on the same day could therefore have been more bad news. On 14th August, 56067 came off at Scunthorpe within hours of 56090's derailment at the Redcar ore terminal. Although both had high hours (more than 12,200), they returned to traffic within days.

Not quite so minor was 56006's incident in Tees Yard on 28th August. The loco had just arrived at Tees with the 6N20 steel empties from Lackenby when 56107, working 6M57 Tees Dock-Carlisle, collided with the rear of 6N20 at about 20 mph. 006 sustained severe crushing to one side of the back cab in another 'wagon coming off better than the loco' incident.

Suggesting that the 'heritage' status meant something after all, Thornaby used parts from 56039 to repair 006 and return it to traffic within two weeks of the accident. The loco reappeared sporting oval buffers at No. 2 end rather than the round ones it had picked up during its 'retro-isation' process at Old Oak Common.

As August rolled into September, three WNTR locos - 56055, 056 & 109 - moved to Doncaster Carr for TPWS fitting. The reason became clear in the middle of the month with news of an EWS plan to increase the active Class 56 fleet to forty-three. Obviously, the three at Doncaster were on the list and they would be joined by 56094 & 113 once replacement wheelsets became available at Thornaby. Other locos in the depot's collection were also being assessed, such as 56100 & 106 & 111, all of which were noted running and on test.

It was during this period that a number of stored Class 37s and 58s at Eastleigh were being examined before the start of an infrastructure contract in France and Spain - a diversification of EWS's business that would later provide Class 56 with a new experience.

It had been known for some time that March 2004 was the date pencilled in for the class's withdrawal, by the simple expedient of counting forward four years from the emergence of the last one from major overhaul. Even so, it came as something of a shock to hear rumours that EWS planned to stick to this date, despite the usual disclaimers about timescales and the mysterious phenomenon known as 'events'. The realists accepted immediately that EWS was indeed serious about eliminating the Class 47 and 56 fleets, as well as down-sizing the 37s and making some reduction in Class 90. The impressive availability of the 'new' 66s was cited as one factor allowing the company to implement this policy of standardisation, which was rather curious when the fleet was clearly stretched to handle the core business and seasonal traffic requirements such as the Sandite work. Whatever the arithmetic of the remaining fleet size, a deadline was a deadline. And so, the countdown of Class 56's last seven months in normal traffic began.

The repainting of 56078 at Toton in the middle of September was therefore something of a surprise, especially as none had been re-liveried since the overhauls stopped, except for 56011. That one only received EWS colours 'out of course' after a serious vandal attack.

Surprise doubled when 078 emerged from Toton on 25th September in Large Logo blue - a scheme it had never carried before. 078 had been in shabby triple-grey. It also received the name *Doncaster Enterprise*, formerly carried by the LNER apple green-liveried 47522. With a major open day looming at Doncaster Works, 47635 had been chosen for the Large Logo/re-naming treatment as a special exhibit at the event. 56078 was the fall-back plan in case problems arose with the 47, but it was deliberately chosen above other 56s because of its low engine hours and the fact it was the only 56 not repainted into EWS livery during its last overhaul.

The list of locos tempting fate lengthened on 9th September when the high hours 56114 (WGAI) suffered a minor fire while working 4D56 Biggleswade-Heck. The loco was placed on decision at Peterborough, but repairs were authorised at Immingham and it returned to traffic on the 30th.

To cover for Class 37s needed for the imminent Sandite season, a number of 56s returned to traffic at the end of the month. Immingham's 56054 was the first, along with 56100 & 106 from the Thornaby stock. Within a week, they were joined by 56103, 056 & 109, but 56037, 088 & 102 were stored in exchange. 102 needed two replacement wheelsets and the plan was to carry out the work before swopping it back with 103. However, multiple faults were discovered when the loco was inspected at Thornaby and, drained of fluids, it went in store.

*Above:* The EWS Heritage pool's 56006 stands at Bewdley on the Severn Valley Railway on 29th September 2000 after its retro repaint into rail blue at Old Oak Common. Greatly loved by many, it remains less so by the selection committee for the National Collection, who have failed to snap up Britain's first Type 5 freight locomotive. *Photo: Paul Furtek*

Slightly off the beaten track, 56067 arrived at Eastleigh on 1st October with six HST vehicles in tow as 5Z50 from Derby works. Proving that 56s are like buses, another one appeared only a few days later. 56081 worked in with 6C42 from Newport ADJ and lingered a while in the south. On the 11th, it visited Machen Quarry with 6B80 and 6C80 return; the next day it was 6W33 Exeter Riverside-Westbury. The loco was still dabbling in the unusual on 21st October when it worked 5Z45 Oxley-Wembley with seven redundant Virgin coaches ultimately heading for store at Shoeburyness.

Despite the established pattern of storage and reinstatement, it appeared that EWS planned to mothball up to 15 of the remaining fleet by the end of the November. The remaining 25 or so would be concentrated in the north-east, but with the WNTR pool available for short-term replacement as necessary. Of course, when a fleet is reduced in size and concentrated on a relatively small geographical area, it is important that train crew maintain traction knowledge over the routes concerned. Because of earlier changes, many drivers in former 56 areas no longer 'signed' the class - another contributing factor to their confinement to an ever-decreasing

*Above:* 56119 at Hambleton West Junction with a spoil train from Selby on 5th February 2003. *Photo: Neil Harvey*

95

*Above: 56027 at Over on 26th April 2002 with one of the more unusual duties in the past few years - 4Z93 Cardiff-Crewe which the 56 worked as far as Birmingham. Photo: Duncan Jennings*

area. The Grid was viewed with much affection by a large number of drivers and there were instances of crews actively swopping duties towards the end so they could enjoy one final fling on the locos. They may have felt differently if they'd had to maintain them.

A new twist on the 'when is a withdrawal not a withdrawal?' conundrum became apparent when sixteen of the Class 58s stored in late 2002 were officially listed for the overseas work in France, suggesting that a class could be withdrawn en masse and still have a role in the EWS plan. Encouraged by this news, many Grid enthusiast suggested that March 2004 might not be the end of life as we had known it after all. In the end, they were proved right, but it was no more than inspired guesswork at the time.

Further proof of Class 56's haulage capability came on 30th October when 90022 failed in the Oxenholme area with the Euston-Glasgow sleeper, loaded to around 16 vehicles. Fortunately, 56095 was following with 6X77 Wembley-Mossend and was called forward to assist. The 56 pushed the failure into the loops at Oxenholme where, astonishingly, 56072 appeared to take the beds forward. The chances of getting two Grids on a service train were slim enough when there were 135 in service; to get two when there were only 40 left was something of a scoop . . . except for those who slept through it all.

On 3rd November, 56003 in the Toton Training Compound (an impressive name for a gigantic scrap line) and 56010 at Doncaster Carr transferred to the WNZX 'for disposal' pool. They were later joined by 56029 standing at the CRDC.

Eight days later, having spent the previous two weeks ticking over on the depot, 56007 was reinstated at Thornaby, temporarily boosting the fleet to 43 in number. It didn't last; in the same week, 56114 suffered wheelset problems and, with more than 12,000 hours on the clock, was placed on decision at Immingham.

Three locos suffered problems after taking part in the 'Lounge Lizard' railtour that month - 56096 with a coolant leak, 56099 with traction motor defects, and 56058 with wheelset issues. 096 & 099 were moved from Peterborough to Toton by 56069 for attention. 56099 subsequently transferred to Immingham, but was placed on decision on 26th November after working 6E87 Brierly Hill-Scunthorpe two days earlier. One up the list, 56100 needed tyre turning on arrival at Canton and was also placed on decision.

A dozen or more locos were expected to go by the end of November, with 56099, 100 & 114 looking like the first ones. 56007 also became a candidate when its 'B' exam at Immingham was cancelled.

As ever, the choice rested on many factors, but engine hours was the prime statistic. A quick count revealed that some eighteen of the survivors had clocked up more than 12,000 hours, while only ten could claim less than 10,000. Of course, the fleet had run for so long past the traditional limit that it was easy to fall into the trap of regarding a 9,500 hours loco as a low example. How relative such judgements were is revealed by 56038. Although the last out of main works in April 1999, it had already clocked up 7,600 hours. Under the old regime, a BR shopping controller would have identified this loco some 500 hours earlier and restricted it to local working off a depot like Knottingley, awaiting the call to Doncaster. Those days, sadly, were gone, and we can only speculate on the same controller's reaction to a loco like 56073 which somehow accumulated 16,000 hours before going into store!

On the first day of December, eight locos were stood down and all but two of the remainder transferred to Immingham's WGAI pool. The stored locos were:

56099 into WNSS at Immingham
And these seven moved into WNTR
56006 Immingham (power earth fault)
56007 Immingham (B exam due)
56103 Immingham (oil leak)
56114 Immingham (wheelsets & hours)
56100 Cardiff Canton (due for tyre turning)
56113 Doncaster Carr (fire protection equipment)
56118 Crewe Diesel (brakes).

WGAI acquired 56018, 051, 054, 056, 058, 059, 060, 065, 067, 070, 071, 083, 095, 106, 117, 119 & 133, leaving Thornaby with only 56038 & 049.

This round of changes left the fleet standing at 35, but not for long. The next day 56090 was pre-assigned to store at Crewe Diesel and the last two Thornaby locos were effectively stored in the WNTR pool, thus rendering WGAT pool extinct.

Thornaby's 56038, however, was thrown a lifeline when it was assigned for TPWS fitting at Carr Loco. At Doncaster it joined 56049, 055 & 113 and all were regarded as possible candidates for a quick return to service if necessary.

By December 5th, 56117 had also been assigned to store at Crewe, where 56090 arrived on the 8th. As expected, 56049 & 113 returned to traffic to balance the storage of those two in WNTR. 117 still hadn't made it from Doncaster at this point, but it had reached Warrington behind 56067.

Within a day, 067 was also pre-assigned to storage at the soon-to-close Crewe diesel depot. When EWS decided to store four more on 16th December - 56054, 083, 109 & 120 - the storage location changed to Ferrybridge. Five of the above were switched off in the WNTR pool by 22nd December, but 56067 & 083 lingered in traffic at Knottingley. They avoided Ferrybridge until 29th December.

56038 returned to traffic after TPWS fitting, increasing the WGAI fleet to 34, although five were still facing the chop. On the physical chopping front, 56003 & 010 arrived at Booth's by the end of the year, but 003 would later escape into preservation in an exchange deal which consigned 56080 and 37904 to Booth's.

N/ONE status was applied to three locos on 28th December - 56058 at Bescot, 56096 at Immingham and 56106 at Healey Mills. 106 had failed on a railtour a few days earlier. All three were stored in the WNSS pool by 5th January. 56087 was also stored, requiring attention to its fire protection equipment, but went into WNTR.

So, at the start of 2004, all these changes left EWS with only 25 active Class 56s - three more than the surviving Class 47 fleet and 25 more than Class 73. The unique electro-diesels had already been eliminated.

There was hardly time to absorb the impact of these losses before the announcement of a reduction in Class 56 diagrams to only 17, for which EWS optimistically calculated it would need a pool of 21 locos.

By this time, interest in the sole surviving Romanian was obviously high, but 56018 set hearts a-flutter when it went into WNTR on 20th January because an exam had fallen due. To everyone's great relief, it returned to traffic four days later. 56087 also came back from a short period in store, following a bogie swop at Immingham with 56131. Thornaby, meanwhile, was considering whether to send 56094 back to work. The thinking was simple; if EWS returned those three, it could take out three locos with much higher hours, as well as

*Above:* 56078 emerged from Toton in Large logo blue on 25th September 2003, carrying the name *Doncaster Enterprise* before the celebrations soon to be held at Doncaster Works. *Photo: Paul Furtek*

the four casualties resulting from the diagrams reduction.

In fact, five went initially:

56032 on 23rd Jan. - into WNTR at Immingham, after standing out-of-use with a serious oil leak

56107 on 27th Jan. - into WNSS at Ferrybridge. This one was approaching a new 13,000 hours limit, apparently imposed by EWS's insurance company!

56095 - into WNTR at Thornaby

56049 on 3rd Feb. - into WNTR at Thornaby from WGAI, the last loco in Dutch livery

56104 on 3rd Feb. - into WNTR at Immingham from WGAI, the last to carry Freight Grey with Coal Sector branding.

At the same time, 56087 at Immingham was reinstated to WGAI, producing the desired number of 21 operational locomotives. 56094 also returned to traffic at Thornaby on 9th February, but this was off-set by 56072 going into WNTR at Doncaster Carr.

As ever, the 'final position' of 21 locos lasted about five minutes. Seven more went into WNTR store at Healey Mills on 14th February - 56038, 051, 056, 065, 069, 070 & 133. At this rate of attrition, many began to wonder if Class 56 would last long enough to see the March deadline - a date EWS was no longer denying. The writing on the wall became large enough for even the most myopic when Pathfinder announced details of the final railtour to be run on 31st March.

However, a beacon of hope for the future emerged on 14th February when 56078 operated a demonstration engineer's train at Eastleigh for a delegation from France, who had travelled across to see a Class 56 in action. A deafening silence accompanied 078's return north four days later in the consist of 6M28, but many remained hopeful that March was not the great chasm of oblivion that it appeared.

Apart from 56088 going into WNSS at Thornaby, there was more silence for several days towards the end of February. Then 56062 arrived at Cardiff Canton with fire damage, its chances of survival obviously rated as poor. They were; it found itself consigned to WNSS two days later. The future also looked bleak for 56059 & 119, both of which were due for 'B' exams.

With the vultures visibly circling, a degree of excitement broke out when 56049, 088 & 095 were spotted idling at Thornaby Depot on February 29th. 56119 was also on the fuel point that day, having been restricted to local working pending withdrawal. However, it did manage one final Awayday to Trafford Park and back before the clock wound down.

Surprisingly, 56059 *was* given its 'B' exam but 56113 went into store instead. One of 113's last workings was in multiple with 56078 on the Doncaster-Castleton rail train before the pair returned light to Healey Mills. 56113 & 119 nominally went into WNTR on 1st March, although both were still in traffic. 113 soon arrived at Knottingley, but 56119 remained on various duties around Thornaby on the 2nd. A glance at the workings that day reveals 81% availability, although when the pool comprises only 11 locos, the loss of one drops the figure by 9%! Anything can be proved with numbers. Here's a summary of WGAI's activity on 2nd March:

| | |
|---|---|
| 56018 | Doncaster Carr on transfer from Peterborough to Immingham |
| 56059 | Immingham 'B' exam |
| 56060 | 7M18 Doncaster-Toton, 7E20 return, 7H84 Doncaster-Peterborough |
| 56071 | 6D78 Healey Mills-Neville Hill, 6D79 Neville Hill-Healey Mills |
| 56078 | 7B71 Worksop-West Burton |
| 56081 | 6D88 Goole-Doncaster |
| 56087 | Warrington |
| 56091 | 7G21 Bescot-Washwood Heath, 7G22 Washwood Heath-Bescot |
| 56094 | 6D51 Doncaster-Hull, 6D54 Hull-Doncaster |
| 56115 | 6G50 Bescot-Wolverhampton, 6E00 Wolverhampton-Scunthorpe |
| 56119 | WNTR hired to WGAI: 4E54 Trafford Park-Tees Dock, 6N48 Tees Dock-Tees Yard |

The availability took a dive when 56059 was in trouble soon after release from its 'B' exam, which may well have been the last carried out on the class during Incarnation No. 1.

The loco had been deployed on shunting duties at Immingham after release as a means of keeping an eye open in case problems arose. They did; 059 caught fire but the damage was slight and Immingham returned it to traffic the next day, 4th March.

The loaned-in 56119 returned to WNTR store at Knottingley, reducing the WGAI fleet (therefore operational Class 56) to 10. That number was maintained on March 18th despite 56018's move into the WNSS pool. 56095 took its place in WGAI, but had to be removed from a South Wales-bound service near Thirsk after suffering a fire. The loco was taken to Thornaby for attention, but the damage must have been slight as it worked into Rotherham steel terminal on the 23rd.

On 20th March, Dutch/Transrail-liveried 56049 had been noted at Thornaby with white buffer surrounds, painted pipework and repainted cab ends. It was idling on the depot with 56088, leading to speculation that 049 might be reinstated for the final railtour eleven days later. More hopeless optimism.

The inevitable news broke on 25th March: All ten remaining locos were pre-assigned for storage on the 29th March, apart from 56078. This one had been given 1st April as its withdrawal date so it could work the final railtour. Somebody from Pathfinder must have reminded EWS that the tour spec called for two locos - hence the magical amendment of 56115 to 1st April.

Not surprisingly, little had changed by Sunday the 28th, although a couple of locos were on engineering trains despite their impending withdrawal the next day. Here are their final positions:

56059 Peterborough
56060 Healey Mills
56071 Doncaster area (engineer's workings)
56078 Peterborough
56081 Thornaby OOU

97

*Above:* 56033 & 109 head through Garsdale with 6C02 Crewe-Carlisle slinger train on 19th March 2003. *Photo: John Hooson*

56087 Scunthorpe OOU
56091 Rotherham steel terminal
56094 Doncaster area (engineer's workings)
56095 Old Oak Common
56115 Rotherham steel terminal

Over the next few days, the eight locos not involved in the railtour began to make their way to Knottingley and Healey Mills. The two survivors remained active on 30th March, 56078 working around the Doncaster area and 56115 hauling a steel train to South Wales so it would be in position for the charter the next morning.

On 31st March, 56115 set off from Bristol with the 'Twilight Grid' as far as York, where 56078 took over for a run across the Pennines to the east Manchester suburbs before returning to York. Back at York, the pair were 'multied up' for the return to Bristol but, being 56s, they didn't want to work in multiple. The solution was to swop them around, which is how 56115 came to lead off at 17.43 with the final Class 56 passenger train.

The scenes at Bristol were redolent of many class farewells in the past, although the playing of The Last Post by the Secretary of the Class 56 Group was a new innovation. As the pair were uncoupled and their tail lamps faded into the night, many wondered if they were indeed heading for oblivion or simply off to pack their suitcases. We didn't have to wait long for the answer.

On the day after the railtour, 56078 & 115 ran back north but only made it as far as Saltley. The depot staff couldn't resist and 078 was coupled up to 4G05 06.08 Hams Hall-Daventry, despite its new status in the WNTR pool. The loco returned light to Saltley, rejoined its partner and continued north towards the date with the de-fuelling man at Knottingley.

Further north, the other survivors of WGAI continued to gather. 56071 & 059 moved on from Doncaster Carr, 56091 from Rotherham steel terminal and 56095 from Wembley to Healey Mills. At the same time, 56060 & 094 ran from Healey Mills to Knottingley for de-fuelling. Over the next few days, the rest would also visit Knottingley for this procedure before returning to Healey Mills yard. The only straggler was 56087, which had extracted itself from Scunthorpe steelworks but had then run off in the wrong direction to Immingham - a little comedy to lighten the gloom of a very sad week.

*Above:* The End . . . well, for the time being anyway. 56115 & 078 after arrival at Bristol Temple Meads with the farewell railtour on 31st March 2004. In fact, 56078 managed a sneaky extra run with a Hams Hall-Daventry service the next day when it should have been en route to Knottingley for de-fuelling. *Photo: Duncan Jennings*

**GRIDS**

# 11. LIFE AFTER DEATH

*Above:* 31st March 2004 wasn't the end after all. Thirty of the class were temporarily exported to France to work ballast trains during a high-speed line construction project. 56059 and partner arrive back at Pagny yard after a day's ballasting on 22nd May 2006. *Photo: Pauline McKenna*

As everyone had hoped, 31st March 2004 was not the last of Class 56 as main line motive power. EWS's hire of thirty locos to the Fertis company for a French infrastructure project, and the emergence of Fastline Freight and Hanson Traction would ensure, in one way or another, the survival of the majority of those that made it to the official 'last day'. Not surprisingly, there were also a number of developments on the preservation front in the ensuing five years.

To keep Grid followers up-to-date, there was no shortage of information on the internet, particularly Ian Furness's End of the Line site (www.wnxx.com), providing day-to-day news of where the survivors were located.

Despite the rumour of the French contract, EWS put a number of 56s up for sale. While a number were secured for preservation, the majority on this list were heavily stripped of parts - so much so, that some could only be moved by road thereafter.

Movements by rail continued. Four days after the final working, 56090, 117 & 118 were towed from Crewe Diesel to Barton Hill by 66101. This OZ56 convoy arrived on April 8th after a lay-over at Newport. Within days, 56090 was noted idling outside the Bristol depot.

On the 10th, 56078 & 115 moved to Knottingley via York and Milford, while 56090, 094 & 115 returned to Healey Mills after de-fuelling at Knottingley. Five days later, 56053, 055 & 072 were cleared out of Carr Loco; they also moved to Healey Mills. Meanwhile, 56006 returned to Old Oak Common to be prepared for an appearance at the NRM's York Railfest, amid more speculation that the loco would become part of the national collection. This had already been dealt with; although 006 was technically Britain's first Type 5 freight locomotive, it had been turned down by the selection committee on grounds of birth. After the Railfest event, 006 moved to Barrow Hill, where it has mostly remained ever since.

Disposals continued too. 56125, bought from the tender list by Fragonset the previous summer, moved to the Derby site of FM Rail on 21st April (FM had been formed by the merger of Fragonset and Merlin Rail). Two days later, 56004, 034, 036, 121 & 132, all standing at the CRDC, were offered for sale on a new list. Four earlier candidates - 56029, 050, 075 & 130 - were all moved to Booth's for scrap by 9th May. Another sale from 2003, that of 56057 to Sandbach Car and Commercial Dismantlers, resulted in the loco's movement on 23rd June. However, this one was not scrapped but sold on to Neil Boden, who would later base it at the Nene Valley Railway. The preserved 56003 moved from Booth's to MoD Ashchurch on 23rd June. Both of these would appear again as the Class 56 story moved on to a new chapter, as would 56045 and 56124. Those two were sold briefly into preservation via HNRC in the middle of July, but eventually would become the first two locos of a small fleet returning triumphantly to main line work.

Of far greater significance at the time, 'reserve celebrity' 56078 moved from Knottingley to Toton on 26th May for another repaint, and this time emerged in the colours of Fertis in readiness for a visit by officials of the French infrastructure company. Fertis had a contract to operate ballasting trains for the LGV Est high-speed line project between Paris and Strasbourg and was also considering Class 37s and 58s for this work.

By the end of June, the contract appeared to be gathering momentum when twelve Class 56s were allocated to a new pool - WZGF - for locos in preparation for overseas work. Ten Class 58s also joined this pool. The 56s were 038 & 049 at Thornaby, 117 & 118 at Barton Hill and 051, 059, 060, 065, 069, 078, 081 & 087 at Healey Mills. By early July, EWS had announced an adjustment of the numbers to 24 Class 56s and 14 Class 58s. Ultimately, 30 of one type and 19 of the other made the trip.

The preparatory work involved a huge number of maintenance staff at the four depots, as EWS raced the clock to have enough locos ready in time. Items given particular attention included:

i) Bogies and tyre profiles, with tyre turning if required
ii) Ultrasonic axle tests, to ensure there were no hairline cracks
iii) The air system, with meticulous attention to the air tanks and brake detail
iv) Re-certification of items like the air tanks
v) Engine testing on the load bank
vi) Carrying out each loco's next due 'balanced B' exam
vii) Additional heavier component replacement where necessary

*Above:* 56051 obliterates partner 56031 at Tramery on 21st March 2006 as it sets off for the yard at Ocquere. 56051 was one of six Class 56s fitted with Brown Boveri turbochargers which were smaller than the Napier version fitted to the rest of the fleet. The other locos fitted were 56038, 074, 078, 094, 110. *Photo: Anthony Sayer*

viii) Provision of new batteries
ix) Fitting a Q-tron 'black box (to monitor performance and investigate any accidents which might occur)
x) Attention to rusty bodywork, and
xi) A full repaint into Fertis livery.

Only Toton had a purpose-built paint plant employing the latest 'two-pack' spray-painting technique. Eastleigh, Old Oak Common and Barton Hill used the more traditional method of hand-painting with a brush.

When 56078 was inspected by the French delegation at Toton, they were said to "very impressed" by the locomotive's condition. In fact, very little work had been required apart from the repaint, as 078 was one of the last two that survived until the very end in April 2004.

The exception to the general rule was 56049, which had its preparation work carried out at Thornaby in early July. In the following weeks several of the Healey Mills collection and others from Thornaby, made their way to Eastleigh for preparation, often via Carlisle or Warrington and then forward in the consist of 6O12 Mossend-Eastleigh.

Others, such as 56038, 060 & 065, were called to Toton for special tests before joining the project. Soon after, 56046, 073 &128 were moved to Toton to donate spares.

At one point, it looked as if Three Bridges depot would join the other four. On 22nd June, 56081 was hauled to West Sussex from Eastleigh, closely followed by 56065, but hindsight reveals they had only gone there for short-term storage.

By 19th August, 56038, 060, 069 & 087 had all been on the Eastleigh load bank, while Toton continued to make good locos out of what it had available. After stripping for parts, 56073 & 128 moved from the shed to the training compound in early August, while 56069 arrived from Eastleigh for a spell in the paint shop. Meanwhile, 56117 & 118 were being prepared for painting at Barton Hill. 56090 had originally arrived in Bristol at the same time as 117 & 118, and was eventually added to the WZGF pool and given the new colours. Pilot loco 56078, as it had become, moved from Toton to Bescot on 3rd September with 58046 in the consist of 6V19 Immingham-Margam. Both had moved on to Wembley yard by the 6th and then Dollands Moor, to await their movement to France. The pair went through the tunnel on the 9th in service 4404, hauled by 92028 & 043.

Seven days later, repainted but unbranded, 56117 & 118 moved to Toton for load bank testing. By then, 56046 had been separated from all of its re-usable parts and had joined 073 & 128 in the scrapline.

On 28th September, 56069 & 118 moved to Wembley to join 58007. All three went through the tunnel on 1st October, followed five days later by 56087 & 117. Others heading down the hole in the next three weeks were:

56038 & 58015 - Oct. 7th
56059 & 56060 - Oct. 12th
56090 & 58032 - Oct. 20th

Elsewhere, the impending closure of another depot closely associated with Class 56 was imminent. Appropriately, 56100 was started up to shunt the stored locos out of Cardiff Canton before they were dispersed to other locations. 56062, which had arrived on shed with fire damage in February, only weeks before the final day, was moved to Margam along with 56100. They remain there in October 2009.

On 17th November, 56097 moved from Cardiff Cathays to Brush for a bogie change and the fitting of an overhauled power unit originally from 56047. By 4th December, 56065 & 081 had come out of storage at Three Bridges and returned to Eastleigh, joining 56049 & 051. By Christmas, 56049 & 065 had been attended to and load-banked; they arrived at Barton Hill for painting on the 30th.

Four more locos were added to WZGF that month - 56096, 099, 105 & 106. They were towed from Immingham to Toton by 60044 on 1st January 2005. The assessment of others continued; 56007, for example, was moved from Immingham to Old Oak Common for special tests.

The rest of the 2005 temporary exports, in the order they went, were as follows:

| | |
|---|---|
| May | 56096, 105, 018, 106, 032, 049, 065 |
| June | 56058, 051, 091, 031 |
| July | 56081, 095, 094 |
| August | 56071 |
| September | 56007, 074 |
| October | 56104 |
| November | 56103, 113, 115 |

The 30th and final locomotive, 56115, joined the French pool on 4th November.

All the 56s going abroad had very high engine hours (by then, there was no such thing as a low hours Grid) and there were no published figures for how many extra hours they clocked up while in France. Even now, TOPS reports show the hours accumulated by each one as at 31st March 2004. Of course, none of the exports received major overhauls, so it is remarkable that they proved so reliable, given that they were maintained so far from home. It is safe to assume that some of the power units were close to the 14,000 hours mark by the end of the project, yet there were no reports of major failures and certainly no 'legs out of bed' - a common problem with Class 60s once EWS began running them way past their hours limit.

Two returned prematurely, such as 56118. It came home in June 2006 after suffering a fire the previous November, barely two months after it began work. 56091 returned with a camshaft defect in April 2006, but was repaired at Old Oak and given a bogie swop with 56112. It returned to France as a replacement for 56118 in early May.

Work on the track-laying and ballasting contracts for TGV Est began at the end of 2004. The former work was entrusted to SECO and TSO, both of whom also hired in Class 58s from EWS. Fertis supplied its own drivers for the Class 56s & 58s in its care. These drivers had been instructed in fault-finding techniques by their British counterparts, and maintenance was supervised by EWS engineers seconded for the duration.

The British locos operated from three bases in all: Work first began from a temporary depot at St. Hilaire, between Reims and Châlons-en-Champagne. Although this site stood roughly in the centre of the LGV route, it was more convenient, and quicker, for trains to begin laying track in both easterly and westerly directions simultaneously. The second base at Ocquerre (near Meaux on the eastern side of Paris) began work in the middle of 2005, striking out eastwards towards the section completed from St. Hilaire. Pagny-sur-Moselle depot opened a few months later. At its height, track-laying was estimated to be progressing by as much as 600 metres each day.

The Type 5s immediately proved their worth on the 1,800 tonne ballast trains, although double-heading or top & tailing was commonplace because of the severe gradients involved (as steep as 1 in 28 in some places). This was a major factor in choosing Type 5s rather than the Class 37s used earlier on the Sud-Est high-speed project; they had run into occasional difficulty with the combination of train weight and gradient. Incidentally, there is a wealth of background detail on all the British locomotives that have worked on European infrastructure projects in *Brits Abroad* by Ken Carr & David Maxey, also published by Visions.

As St. Hilaire ran out of route, its staff and locomotives moved to the other two bases. The first depot was slowly run down as the stretches of track laid by all three began to connect up. By the end of 2006, LGV Est was in its final stages of testing. As the number of engineering trains declined, the Fertis 56s and

*Above:* 56031 & 060 drop their ballast at Vrignes on 20th March 2006. Alongside is 58034 with another ballast train. Both had worked to the site from Ocquere. *Photo: Anthony Sayer*

*Above:* 56018 & 078 lead a rake of ballast wagons, and 56038 & 58004, out of Pagny-sur-Moselle on 23rd March 2006. *Photo: Anthony Sayer*

*Above:* 56302 (formerly 56124) heads a Fastline test train from Doncaster Belmont Yard to Barrow Hill at Old Denaby on 17th April 2006. *Photo: Martin Loader*

58s slowly made their way back to Britain through the tunnel. The entire fleet returned to store; the 56s originally gathered at Wembley yard and Old Oak Common; almost all the 58s ended up back at Eastleigh.

Despite fears that some might not return, 56065, 095 & 117 were the first home on 9th October. The rest followed steadily, and all except 56078 & 106 were back on British track by the end of January 2007. Unlike a couple of unfortunate Class 37s, which suffered collision damage while on a similar contract in Spain and were abandoned as scrap, no 56s were left abroad. 56078 was away the longest; the first to leave in October 2004, it was the second last to return in May 2007. The recovery of 56106 on 24th June completed the French adventure. Nothing similar has arisen since - at least not for Class 56 - but the retention of the French locos suggests that someone within EWS/DB Schenker is at least hopeful they may be hired again.

If the use of thirty Grids in a foreign country was remarkable, the return of a small number of others to the main line in Britain has truly been the icing on the cake. However, we should not become over-excited. Only five have been involved, and some of those are currently moth-balled until rail traffic picks up when the recession finally ends.

It began with an announcement at the end of 2004 that the Jarvis company was entering the locomotive hire business. Initial indications were that this would involve infrastructure trains, but this turned out to be incorrect. What Jarvis had in mind was the rapidly-expanding container traffic, hence the setting up of a new company called Fastline Freight.

Most surprising of all, Fastline planned to work its containers with a number of Class 56s which had already been bought by preservationists from EWS.

The locos acquired by the company moved to Brush's Loughborough works for major attention before entering service. The programme of work was devised by Fastline's chief engineer Wilson Walshe, who later had one of the locomotives named after him in recognition of his efforts.

56045 and 56124 were the two chosen, and they emerged from Brush as 56301 and 56302. The most noticeable difference, apart from the striking yellow livery, was the removal of the buffer beam skirts on 301. Purely by chance, the closure of the Wigan CRDC had been announced around this time. After some long-standing transport access problems, a ten-week window was established for the clearance of all locos from the site - hence the movement in mid-August 2005 of 56029 and 56034 to Brush to support the Fastline overhauls.

56045 (301) was already in works, having arrived from Immingham that month. 56124 (302) arrived in early September, after moving by rail from Healey Mills to Doncaster and then by road to Loughborough.

Other Wigan clear-outs included 56004, 036, 121 & 132, all of which moved to Booth's in July and August. The four were inspected by interested parties, with a view to preservation, but were found to have been heavily robbed - both officially and unofficially - during their Wigan vacation. To seal their unsuitability for further consideration, all the copper cable had mysteriously vanished. After donating what few usable spares remained, to keep preserved 56s in service, all four were cut up.

Soon after, EWS offered another eight 56s for sale. It was hoped these would be in better condition as the majority had been stored at Immingham - 56011, 021, 040, 044, 063 & 098, and 56131 & 128 at Toton. Two of these - 56040 and 56098 - were bought by Edward Stevenson, who later sold 040 to the Class 56 Group. He then purchased 56044, 063 & 131 from Booth's. These three had originally been earmarked for the Fastline fleet as 56304-306, but the Grid project was abandoned when Fastline opted to buy brand-new Class 66s for its growing business. All three spent a considerable time at Brush before moving to Booth's.

Meanwhile, the other Stevenson machine, 56098, moved from Immingham to its new home on the Northampton and Lamport Railway on 15th November 2005, from where, after a camshaft replacement, the loco set off on its lengthy tour of the private railways. Less concerned with preservation, FM Rail bought 56011 and 56021, while HNRC acquired 56128. One of FM's other 56s, 125, was worked on at RVEL Derby, including fitting the mini mod equipment and roof filters recovered from one of the withdrawn locos. 56125 would eventually be hired to Fastline as 56303. FM's 56061 remained at Barrow Hill, while 56066 was recovered from the CRDC on 1st November 2005. The bogie-less loco went to RVEL for component recovery before despatch to Ron Hull's Rotherham yard for breaking.

After some delay, FM Rail finally picked up 56011 & 021 from Immingham, almost the last from the July 2005 tender list to be collected. The Class 56 Group's 56040 left Immingham only two days before the FM pair, but for a good reason. The loco had been waiting for a slot in the depot's busy work schedule to have the traction centres refitted. It became the last 56 to be lifted in the bogie shop at Immingham.

The two Fastline locos were released from Brush in April 2006. Soon after, 56125 moved from Derby to Barrow Hill for repainting into similar colours. 56302 worked a trial run in what would become the path of the Doncaster-Grain service on 8th May. Both 301 & 302 ran from Roberts Road to Scunthorpe the next day to test the multiple-working equipment.

On 20th May 2006, 56302 became the first Class 56 to provide main line passenger action since the farewell railtour at the end of March 2004. The loco was scrambled from Doncaster to rescue a northbound tour headed by FM Rail's 33103 & 202 which had come to a stand at Newark. 302 took the train forward to Doncaster where the K&WVR-bound charter was terminated.

On 23rd June FM Rail sent 33103 & 31190, with a rake of coaches to provide brake force, to collect 56011 & 56021 from Immingham. Unfortunately, the inbound locos passed a signal at danger in the depot area. The author, making a progress call to check on preparations for the imminent departure of 56040, was told by the depot manager that it was chaos, the job was stopped, the FM train was impounded and he had transport police running all over his depot! Needless to say, it was a very short phone call. After 56011 & 021 were finally collected successfully and taken to Derby, they moved on to Coalville for storage, prompting rumours that FM was about to establish a base there. It didn't.

At the end of June 2006, 56040 arrived at the Mid-Norfolk Railway. Meanwhile, 56003 continued its tour of the country, performing at both the Churnet Valley and the East Lancs Railway that year.

*Above:* 56303 at Wychnor Junction with Fastline's 4E90 10.51 Doncaster-Grain on 3rd July 2008. *Photo: Anthony Sayer*

In July 2006 FM Rail operated a trial coal train using Class 31s, prompting speculation that the five 56s it owned would be returned to traffic for a big coal contract. More wishful thinking.

The Fastline trio soon settled down, initially working between Doncaster and the container port at Grain on the Kent coast, and later from Birch Coppice to Grain. Despite poor loadings to begin with, the service soon became very busy. The principal workings were 4O90 10.51 Doncaster-Grain and 4E90 00.07 Grain-Doncaster, and 4M90 23.53 Grain-Birch Coppice and 4E90 11.00 return. The same 56 would often power the trains day after day, not only because of the nature of the duty but also because Fastline went through several lengthy periods with only one serviceable 56/3. By the

*Above:* 56302 was the first Class 56 to work a railtour since the 'farewell' in March 2004. On 20th May 2006 it came to the rescue of 33103 & 202, which had failed at Newark with a charter to the Keighley & Worth Valley Railway. 302 took the train forward to Doncaster where the tour was terminated. *Photo: Pauline McKenna*

*103*

*Above:* 56057 at Wansford on the Nene Valley Railway on 10th October 2004. The loco had originally been sold to a scrap merchant by EWS, but it was saved by Neil Boden. 057 later received a repaint into Large Logo blue. However, it was sold on again to Hanson Traction and is now back on the main line as 56311. *Photo: Duncan Jennings*

end of 2006, 56302 was performing most of the Fastline duties as 301 & 303 spent much of the time out of traffic at the Roberts Road base in Doncaster. However, 301 was noted trundling around the yards at Doncaster on 6th January 2007. By the 26th, 303 had gone back to RVEL Derby for minor repairs, but returned to work 4E90 on 1st February. The return of 303 allowed 302 to tow 301 to Derby for attention the next day!

For a time, 303 dominated the container traffic. It even managed to squeeze in a trip to Whitemoor Yard on 13th February to deliver an autoballaster and bring back a train of recovered track panels.

In February 2007, 302 and 303 shared the duties, leaving the surplus loco available for route learning trips to Crewe via Derby and Nuneaton. On 16th March, 303 worked a route learner over the S&C, followed by a trip to Ditton on the 29th, running via Sheffield, Derby, Tamworth, Stafford and Runcorn.

Unfortunately, 303 became increasingly unreliable. It failed with 4O90 on 12th April and was in trouble again with an exhaust defect on the 29th. During that month, 302 had the lion's share of the container traffic, while 303 was relegated to route learners. Meanwhile, 301 was still at Derby for what had become extensive repairs.

There was little good news on the Grid front generally. By the end of 2006, FM Rail had found itself in financial difficulties and would soon be placed in administration.

Meanwhile, further south, the dumping ground at Old Oak Common was looking increasingly depressing. By then, the depot held French returnees 56032, 049, 051, 059, 060, 071, 074, 090, 103, 113 & 118, as well as 56037 & 133 which hadn't been anywhere. A number were moved to the carriage sidings to free up space on what was becoming a very crowded depot. By 1st January 2007, 56065, 094, & 115 had moved north from Dollands Moor and had reached Wembley yard.

The depression lifted a little in the spring of 2007 when 56011, 021, & 022 were sold to Ealing Community Transport. All three were re-allocated to a new pool - MRLS Nemesis Rail. 56011 & 021 later moved to Coalville, while 022 eventually went to the Weardale Railway in September 2008.

On 26th May, 56057 worked its last train in preservation for the foreseeable future before it left the Nene Valley for the RVEL workshops at Derby, where it would be renumbered as 56311 and certificated for main line running on behalf of its new owners, Hanson Traction. Around this time, 56128 was offered for sale by HNRC, but nobody made a bid.

By now, the plan for further Fastline 56/3s had been consigned to the waste bin. The company announced it was leasing five Class 66s from General Motors. This effectively signed the death warrant for 56044, 063 & 131, which had been earmarked to become 56304-306.

56/3 spares donor 56034 was moved to Booths in May 2007, along with 56044, 063 & 131. All had been reduced to scrap by the end of the year. Once again, Booth's allowed preservationists to recover parts from these locomotives.

On the 1st October 2007, 56302 was named *Wilson Walshe* at the NRM York.

*Above:* 56003 & 098 approach Wansford on 3rd March 2007. At the time, 56003 was owned by Steve Benniston, but he later sold it to Hanson Traction who returned it to the main line as 56312 *Artemis* or, if you prefer, **ARTEMIS** (sorry to shout). 56098 is owned by Ed Stevenson and, at the time of publishing, the loco was undergoing attention at Barrow Hill and a repaint into Loadhaul colours. *Photo: Adrian Tibble*

*Above:* Hanson Traction's 56312 & 56311 head north at Shilton with a Dollands Moor-Hams Hall intermodal for Norfolk Line in September 2009. *Photo: Scott Borthwick*

Sadly, the architect of the Jarvis /Fastline 56 project had passed away before the small fleet entered service.

Further changes lay ahead for some of the surviving 56s. The Fastline business had expanded to cover coal trains from Daw Mill and Hatfield collieries to Ratcliffe-on-Soar power station, as well as Daw Mill to Cottam and Immingham to Ironbridge. The plan was to begin these workings with the soon-to-be-delivered fleet of 66s and ninety-four 102-tonne hoppers. The prospect of Grids reappearing on coal trains immediately diminished as the hoppers had buckeye couplers (shades of Immingham-Scunthorpe). Four 66s were needed for the coal turns - an availability of 80% - so even if it proved possible to couple the wagons to a 56, it seemed unlikely they would be needed as standby locos for a type whose availability rarely dropped *below* 80%. The 56s did contribute by providing route learning trips to Immingham, but the only stand-in was 56303's rescue of 66305 on the 6th August 2008 after the 66 ran out of fuel on its way to Ratcliffe with a loaded coal working.

In the autumn of 2007, EWS, owner of a huge collection of redundant 56s, was rumoured to be the subject of a takeover bid by DB Schenker, a subsidiary of Deutsche Bahn which, you'll recall, was one of the companies to whom EWS had been offered by Canadian National, without success, in 2001. Naturally, talk of another new owner prompted more idle chatter about all 80 locos on the company's asset register being brought back into service. In fact, their greatest value was as scrap; metals prices were very high at that point.

Despite its ownership, one loco which did seem to have a reasonably secure future was 56006. The blue Romanian had been a regular at open days and special events since it was placed in the EWS Heritage pool. It was now based at Barrow Hill, where it was kept in working order and often used as the yard shunter. One of its appearances was at a staff open day held at Ratcliffe power station on 21st September. It was towed there via Worksop by 66220 as it no longer had main line certification under its own power.

By the end of 2007, the number of Class 56s preserved (in the traditional sense) remained pitifully low, and many began to realise that even those were in a volatile position because of demand from emergent freight operators. 56057 had already gone to Hanson but it still came as a shock when Steve Benniston, co-owner of 56003, sold the loco to the same company for possible main line use. Hanson also bought 56128, although it remains unclear whether that one was simply intended as a spares donor.

Fastline had a rare good day on 7th November, when 56301 was on the Birch Coppice containers, 302 was returning to its home depot from Sheffield and 303 was out on route learning duties. By 22nd December 56302 was in trouble again, with loss of power and dragging brakes on the northbound Grain service and had to be rescued by 66055 at Bescot. It was back out on a route learning trip on the 29th, when it turned up at Crewe. The same day, 56301 returned to RVEL and had moved on to Brush by the middle of January. 56303 appeared at Trafford Park via Crewe on the 14th, while 302 needed the fitters' attention during its Derby stop with 4E90.

On 16th January 2008, Hanson's newly-acquired 56128 moved by road from Toton to RVEL Derby. 56003 had already been there for TPWS fitting, as the main line beckoned once more.

It was around this time that Fastline decided enough was enough and hired 66415 from DRS. The GM's first duty on 23rd January was to take 56302 back to Brush, where it joined 56301 for what were reported variously as "minor modifications" or "repairs under warranty". 56303 also went to Brush for modifications and was back in traffic soon afterwards. 56301 didn't leave until 8th February but seemed to perform well, taking 56303 to RVEL for a 'B' exam on the 24th. 301 came back under its own power.

The route learning trips to Trafford Park were explained when Fastline launched a new service between the Manchester container terminal and Grain. The duty involved a 56 running light from Roberts Road on a Monday to work 4O60 15.36 train to Grain, arriving there at 22.55. It returned as 03.57 Grain-Trafford Park. The same loco repeated this pattern until Friday when, after bringing the northbound train into Trafford Park at 12.11, it took the unloaded wagons to Longsight for stabling before running light to Doncaster. The first of these ran on 27th February, starting from Doncaster and running to Grain to get the wagons in position for the northbound 4M60.

*105*

*Above:* The Class 56 Group's 56040 starts up during the Mid-Norfolk's September 2008 diesel gala. Photo: Ian Parish

On 15th March, Pathfinder ran another railtour, the 'Choppington Changer', which featured 56303 from Doncaster Royal Mail Terminal to the Blyth and Tyne network in the north-east.

Meanwhile, the owners of 56011, 021 & 022 were rumoured to be ready to sell them. HNRC eventually took over 56011 & 021, but only after the copper fairies had topped up their supply at Coaville where the locos were stored. The radiator elements and all the traction cables went missing on that occasion.

News then emerged that the Hanson 'fleet' would also be numbered in the 56/3 series - hence 56057 became 56311 and 56003 became 56312. The next number along was assigned to 56128.

56311 was out on test from Derby on 2nd May, running as far as Leicester with a Class 31 as insurance. By then, it was in a new livery scheme of wrap-around yellow cabs with grey bodysides, but 312 was the one that raised eyebrows when it appeared with purple bodysides, beautifully offset later by *green* vinyls spelling out the name ARTEMIS.

On the depleted preservation front, the Class 56 Group's 56040 had moved from Immingham to a new home at Dereham on the Mid-Norfolk Railway, where its power unit was started up on 4th May 2008 for the first time since October 2000.

That same year, the government announced the Crossrail project for the thirteenth time in living memory, insisting it really would be built on this occasion. As the ancient Old Oak Common depot stood on the proposed route from the West London suburbs, the site's closure was announced for April 2009. The Class 56s dumped there would have to be dumped somewhere else. 56007 saw its chance to escape early and volunteered to be the test bed for the GSM-R cab-to-shore communications equipment, which had to be fitted and proven on any traction type authorised to operate on the network. After a 'fitness to run' exam, 007 moved north to Warrington on August 4th in the consist of 6X77 from Wembley. 66166 recovered it at Warrington and towed it back to Crewe for the equipment to be fitted.

Railtour fans were disappointed in May when Fastline was unable to provide a 56 for the 'Settle for Carlisle' charter. Increasing demand for its available 56s meant that one couldn't be spared on the day. One of the trio was receiving planned maintenance at Derby but, although it would be completed in time, Network Rail's requirement for a hundred hours of trouble-free running before it was allowed to haul a passenger train produced the ludicrous situation of the 56 running just ahead of the tour from Doncaster to Carlisle. Many passengers speculated that it might wait at Carlisle and either take over there or wait to haul the return journey. It must have been little bit hard to take when the loco hurtled past southbound, horns blaring merrily as it continued its acceptance testing!

Meanwhile, Fastline had to hire in a 66 from DRS again - 66430 this time - although 56302 was collected from Brush around the 6th of May. Eight days later, Hanson's 56311 ventured out on further test runs which, over the next three days, took it to Derby, Duddeston and Daw Mill.

Fastline had to keep the 66 as 56303 went to RVEL on May 19th; by the 23rd, 301 was the only one of the three 56s still in service. Things deteriorated by another 33% on 2nd June when all three were at RVEL - 301 for a 'B' exam and turbo repairs, 302 awaiting alternator attention, and 303 with low power. 301 was released to traffic on June 3rd, but was topped by 56311 on 4O90. The next day the pair worked 4M60 Grain-Trafford Park. Many began to think 311 belonged to Fastline. In fact, one character phoned the company's HQ to complain about the awful livery on it. When the reply came "It's not ours, we're only borrowing it", the line went very quiet apparently.

56311 continued to assist Fastline in an arrangement obviously beneficial to both parties. Fastline got the use of a 56 that worked, while Hanson enjoyed test facilities without having to arrange special runs which would have to be paid for.

By 5th June 2008, 56311 was allowed out alone and worked the positioning move for the Trafford Park service from Hexthorpe to Grain. Fortunately 303 became available around the 16th and joined 311 in providing the backbone of the container service. 301 & 302 were still at RVEL. 302 eventually came good towards the end of the month and worked its first train since mid-January. Once Fastline were happy with it, 311 was released and sent back to Derby on the 24th. With motive power available once more, Fastline continued route learning trips in the Bristol area, which took its 56/3s to Portbury on runs originating from Chaddesen sidings.

*Above:* 56040 returns to action. The loco approaches Dereham on the Mid-Norfolk Railway on 27th March 2009. Photo: Ian Parish

*Above:* Not an everyday sighting at Fleet services on the M3 motorway. 56098 was stranded there in July 2009 during its transfer from the Mid-Hants Railway to Barrow Hill when the transporter was found to have strayed from its approved route. The body was separated from the bogies and the constituent parts made their way north as two loads rather than one . . . but not before the body had decorated the lorry park for a fortnight. *Photo: Ian Parish*

A whole three months passed before 37423 towed 301 & 302 from Derby to Brush for attention. The same day, 22nd September, evidence of the downturn in traffic levels became apparent when 56311 was spotted on Oscar 90 with a single KFA wagon. The return trip, Echo 90, was a little better but not much; although it comprised a full rake of KFAs, there was only a solitary container aboard the train.

*Déjà vu* resurfaced on 9th October when 56303 was again the only working example. The same day, 56311 was moved from RVEL to Wansford on the Nene Valley by road. By the 29th, 301 was still at Brush, although 302 was spotted in action at Chaddesden sidings. As usual, 303 was on 4O90 Birch Coppice to Grain.

By October 2008 the takeover of EWS by DB Schenker was complete. One of the new owner's first actions was to put a number of Class 56s up for sale. All were sitting at Immingham and had to be moved as the depot was about to close and much of the land redeveloped. Despite some professional interest in the twelve locos, which had benefited from years in store at probably one of the most secure locations on the railway, more were bought for preservation than would eventually end up with main line operators.

A small group of Class 56 Group members secured 56101 and the loco would eventually move by rail to its new home at Barrow Hill. Booth's initially bought 56086, but Edward Stevenson stepped in again and arranged for the loco to move to the Battlefield Line at Shackerstone.

Hanson also bought two more - 56027 & 114 - although it transpired that 027 was only of interest for its wheelsets, which would go under 56114. The latter remained in the Hanson Fleet, 027 joined the other eight on DBS's tender list at Booth's, where they were all cut up between January and March 2009. So, farewell, then, 56025, 043, 052, 064, 076, 082, 084 & 089. As ever, none were wholly wasted. Many spares were recovered by preservationists for future use inside 56040, 56086, 56097, 56098 & 56101.

Booth's collection increased by one with the arrival of 56011 from Long Marston, after the loco had given up its bogies for re-use under 56098. The late arrival was cut up during March.

Within a month of issuing its first tender list, DBS had another crack at its Type 5 fleet by clearing all the 56s out of Wembley. The reasons are unclear, although it is rumoured that a senior manager spotted the collection parked outside the windows of his new office and went ballistic. 56031 & 065 were the first to depart on 3rd November, first to

*Above:* 56101, bought by members of the Class 56 Group, was returned to working order in August 2009 and repainted into Large Logo blue. *Photo: Gareth Broughton*

*Above:* 56303 re-entered service in September 2009 . . . painted green! The loco approaches Wychnor Junction with the Colas steel working from Boston Docks to Washwood Heath. *Photo: Scott Borthwick*

Warrington, then to Crewe. The same day 56115 & 117 went to Eastleigh, prompting hopes that another foreign contract would see them put to good use again.

Over the next six months, both Wembley and Old Oak were completely cleared. Many of the locos ended up at Crewe Diesel. Another two went in the Eastleigh direction, although 56059 & 095 ended up in the yard rather than the nice, warm TMD where 56091, 115 & 117 were stored.

56018 was the last one out of Wembley but, at the time of writing, it is still at Warrington Arpley after its tripping to Crewe ran into difficulties when the train loco couldn't release 018's brakes. The fact that it has stood at Warrington for so long probably says more about the urgency to get the 56s out of Wembley and Old Oak than the urgency to get them to Crewe or Eastleigh for further use. Maybe the questions raised about why they weren't earning revenue and how much they were worth for scrap were true after all.

The clear-out from Old Oak Common in 2009 included the movement of four by road on 29th April - 56070, 112, 118 & 133. Having donated so many parts to the Fertis programme, they were deemed unfit to move by rail. The road access to Crewe Diesel is difficult, so those four were taken to Crewe Electric where they could watch 56007 being fitted with the GSM-R equipment.

The rest of the Old Oak collection went to Crewe by rail via Warrington in two, lengthy convoys in May. 56077, already at Crewe, was joined by 56031, 032, 037, 038, 049, 051, 058, 065, 071, 074, 078, 081, 087, 090, 094, 096, 103, 104, 105, 106 & 113. Of this group, only 56037 had not been to France.

Hanson, meanwhile, had been using 56s to power trains for Colas from Immingham Nordic Terminal to Washwood Heath, conveying steel coils for the Honda plant at Swindon. The steel had originally been destined for other sites, but the economic crisis meant that car production was virtually stopped in some areas. To protect the coils, the train was formed of covered vans which 56311 & 312 had collected from Long Marston a few days before the service began on 18th November 2008. Both were used on the first day, but thereafter only the lead loco was under power. The train was much publicised on the web and many photographers made the effort to record such a colourful working. This traffic only ran until early 2009, but another Colas steel flow soon sprang up between Washwood Heath and Boston Docks.

*Above:* On 18th September 2009, the Class 56 Group's 56040 won the inaugural Visions-organised Carry on Clagging Cavalcade Cup, held at Shackerstone station on the Battlefield Line. *Top & Bottom Left:* The winning run. *Photos: Madeleine Carr. Right:* The ever-so-proud proud winning team: from left to right, driver Micky Doyle, Chairman (and author) Keith Bulmer and Technical Officer Gareth Broughton show off their prize. *Photo: John Hooson*

During this period, the Fastline locos appeared to have a better availability. Both 301 (Trafford service) & 302 (Doncaster train) were working on 30th January, for example, while 303 was at RVEL for maintenance. However, as the recession continued, Fastline was carrying less and less traffic and the company called time on its Grids on the 29th of March. After working into Birch Coppice, 56303 went off lease and back to RVEL. 56301 & 56302 were put into 'hot store' for about four weeks to see if traffic picked up, but were finally drained of fluids for what looked like a long period out of action at Roberts Road.

On the plus side, 56311 & 312 satisfied the number-scratchers when they worked in multiple on 4th May's 'Retro Avon Grid' railtour to Bristol and Bath, while 56101 was started up on 8th July at Barrow Hill for the first time since going into store at Immingham in March 2000. The loco made its first runs in preservation during the August diesel gala.

Less fortunate was 56098, which enjoyed an unscheduled holiday at Fleet Services on the M3 motorway in July 2009. The loco was heading for Barrow Hill from a Mid-Hants Railway gala when problem arose with the transporter. Enquiries by the Highways Agency revealed that the vehicle had strayed from its authorised route and had already travelled over one weak bridge on its way to Fleet. As there was another weak bridge before the next exit from the motorway, there was no alternative (allegedly) but to dismantle the locomotive and make two loads rather than one. The body of 56098 finally followed its bogies up the M3 some two weeks later!

In the same month there was another concentration at Crewe when some of the Ferrybridge stored locos moved west. 66090 hauled away 56054, 067, 083, 107, 109 & 120 (all WNXX) and took them via the Diggle route for old times' sake. A few days later, 56021 finally met its end at Thomson's in Stockton.

Elsewhere, Hanson 56s continued to operate spot flows, mainly for Colas Rail, such as those into Boston docks (6Z56 06.15 from Washwood Heath and 6Z57 07.00 return) to collect steel traffic, and a Dollands Moor-Hams Hall intermodal working for Norfolk Line. There have also been occasional trips to locations such as Ditton, Dagenham (Ford sidings) as well as the locos' regular use on stock transfers. As one example, 56311 was enlisted to move Class 87 locos from Long Marston on the first leg of their journey to a new life in Bulgaria.

The Hanson fleet actually expanded during August 2009. After wheelset changes and initial tests at the Nene Valley, 56114 was towed to the company's new facility at Washwood Heath by 56311 in mid-August.

RVEL's 56303 had done little since the end of the Fastline work, but it was reinstated in early September and emerged from Washwood Heath in what appeared to be all-over BR Brunswick green before operating a number of the Boston trips for Colas. Green Grids - whatever next?!

So, it's not all doom and gloom, although you have to look quite hard for the bright spots. Let us finish on a positive note by summarising the survivors as they stood on 15th October 2009.

Of the original 135 locomotives, 83 still exist in more-or-less one piece. Three are currently active on the main line and Hanson is preparing two more. The Fastline duo remain in reserve. Five have been preserved, but the bulk of the survivors - 71 locos - are in store. 68 are owned by DB Schenker, one each by HNRC, Mainline Rail and Brush Traction. A full summary of the class, loco by loco, appears at the end of the book.

The DBS locos can be found, with a good pair of binoculars, at the following locations:

| | |
|---|---|
| Crewe Diesel | 30 |
| Crewe Electric | 5 |
| Healey Mills | 15 |
| Thornaby | 7 |
| Eastleigh | 5 |
| Margam | 2 |
| Toton | 2 |
| Warrington | 1 |
| Barrow Hill | 1 |

The chances of any of those working again in the traditional sense are not good. They have such high engine hours, not to mention the number sitting on scrap or near-scrap bogies, that an investment of millions of pounds per loco would be needed to bring them back to the standard they once enjoyed under British Rail.

Eventually, DB Schenker will dispose of its collection, either piecemeal or in one, gigantic clear-out. If so, the number of preserved locos may well rise if the better examples appear on a tender list at a reasonable price. Rumours of future contracts notwithstanding, the most likely outcome is that the majority will go for scrap.

Predicting the modern railway is not an exact science, so it is equally possible that an announcement about their future will appear before the ink in this book is even dry. Like a railway operating company, and the entire Class 56, you will have to allow for 'events'.

*Above:* Ed Stevenson's 56086 returned to operational condition at the September 2009 gala on the Battlefield Line, looking superb in its new coat of Large Logo blue (sponsored by The Buffer Stop Shop). Here, 086 heads for Shenton with 56040 & 73114 during the Visions-sponsored event. *Photo: Martin Loader*

# THE CLASS 56s

| Loco | Batch | Built at | Works No. | Arr At Zeebrugge | To Service | Initial Depot | Last overhaul | | Withdrawal at | | TOPS Hours | Reason |
|---|---|---|---|---|---|---|---|---|---|---|---|---|
| 56001 | 1507 | Craiova | 750 | 04/08/76 | 28/02/77 | TI | Jan-89 | ZF | Sep-96 | CF | 5271 | robbed for spares |
| 56002 | 1507 | Craiova | 751 | 04/08/76 | 28/02/77 | TI | Mar-91 | ZF | May-92 | DR | 424 | collision damaged |
| 56003 | 1507 | Craiova | 752 | 13/08/76 | 28/02/77 | TI | Jan-95 | ZF | Apr-99 | DR | 8347 | centre castings worn |
| 56004 | 1507 | Craiova | 753 | 13/08/76 | 28/02/77 | TI | Mar-94 | ZF | Apr-99 | IM | 9010 | engine defects |
| 56005 | 1507 | Craiova | 754 | 09/09/76 | 14/03/77 | TI | Nov-94 | ZF | Jul-96 | ZF | 6186 | fire damage |
| 56006 | 1507 | Craiova | 755 | 08/09/76 | 25/02/77 | TI | Oct-94 | ZF | Dec-03 | IM | 11500 | power earth fault |
| 56007 | 1507 | Craiova | 756 | 08/09/76 | 13/04/77 | TI | Mar-96 | ZF | Dec-03 | IM | 12424 | surplus to requirements |
| 56008 | 1507 | Craiova | 757 | 15/09/76 | 13/04/77 | TI | Jun-87 | ZF | Oct-92 | IM | 7921 | engine defects |
| 56009 | 1507 | Craiova | 758 | 01/10/76 | 27/05/77 | TI | Apr-90 | ZF | Feb-96 | TO | 8500 | due works attention |
| 56010 | 1507 | Craiova | 759 | 01/10/76 | 28/07/77 | TI | Mar-95 | ZF | Nov-99 | DR | 9069 | oil leak |
| 56011 | 1507 | Craiova | 760 | 30/11/76 | 29/06/77 | TI | Jan-94 | TO | Feb-01 | IM | 8618 | wheelsets |
| 56012 | 1507 | Craiova | 761 | 23/12/76 | 18/04/77 | TI | May-87 | ZF | Jun-92 | IM | 7370 | engine defects |
| 56013 | 1507 | Craiova | 762 | 23/12/76 | 01/08/77 | TI | May-88 | ZF | Apr-93 | TO | 7610 | fire damage |
| 56014 | 1507 | Craiova | 763 | 03/01/77 | 28/03/77 | TI | May-88 | ZF | Jun-93 | IM | 7282 | engine defects |
| 56015 | 1507 | Craiova | 764 | 03/01/77 | 21/03/77 | TI | Jan-88 | ZF | Nov-93 | TO | 7152 | due works attention |
| 56016 | 1507 | Craiova | 765 | 06/01/77 | 27/05/77 | TI | Jul-86 | ZF | Sep-96 | CF | 9875 | due works attention |
| 56017 | 1507 | Craiova | 766 | 06/01/77 | 13/05/77 | TI | Nov-89 | ZF | May-92 | ZC | 3473 | collision damaged |
| 56018 | 1507 | Craiova | 767 | 14/01/77 | 23/08/77 | TI | Apr-98 | ZB | Mar-04 | IM | 10500 | surplus to requirements |
| 56019 | 1507 | Craiova | 768 | 14/01/77 | 13/04/77 | TI | May-88 | ZC | Mar-99 | IM | 13287 | due works attention |
| 56020 | 1507 | Craiova | 769 | 15/01/77 | 20/05/77 | TI | Jun-05 | ZF | Jun-97 | CF | 8163 | due works attention |
| 56021 | 1507 | Craiova | 770 | 09/03/77 | 17/06/77 | TI | Nov-95 | ZF | Jun-99 | DR | 7140 | engine defects |
| 56022 | 1507 | Craiova | 771 | 16/03/77 | 24/05/77 | TI | May-94 | ZF | Nov-99 | IM | 8996 | due works attention |
| 56023 | 1507 | Craiova | 772 | 30/03/77 | 11/07/77 | TI | Jun-88 | ZF | Jun-93 | TO | 8127 | due works attention |
| 56024 | 1507 | Craiova | 773 | 30/03/77 | 15/06/77 | TI | Nov-86 | ZC | Oct-96 | IM | 8000 | due works attention |
| 56025 | 1507 | Craiova | 774 | 18/04/77 | 05/07/77 | TI | Sep-94 | ZF | Apr-02 | IM | 11366 | surplus to requirements |
| 56026 | 1507 | Craiova | 775 | 18/04/77 | 15/07/77 | TI | Sep-94 | ZF | May-96 | TO | 7319 | due works attention |
| 56027 | 1507 | Craiova | 776 | 07/07/77 | 19/09/77 | TI | Feb-95 | ZF | Mar-03 | IM | 12563 | EWS hours limit |
| 56028 | 1507 | Craiova | 777 | 07/07/77 | 14/09/77 | TI | Apr-88 | ZF | Nov-93 | CF | 7338 | engine defects |
| 56029 | 1507 | Craiova | 778 | 07/07/77 | 12/09/77 | TI | Mar-94 | ZF | Dec-99 | TE | 9421 | on scrap bogies - ex 56027 |
| 56030 | 1507 | Craiova | 779 | 19/07/77 | 21/10/77 | TI | Sep-83 | ZF | Nov-93 | CF | 7824 | wheelset |
| 56031 | 1508 | Doncaster | | | 24/05/77 | TO | Mar-93 | ZF | Jul-02 | IM | 14541 | EWS hours limit |
| 56032 | 1508 | Doncaster | | | 19/07/77 | TO | Sep-97 | BR | Apr-04 | IM | 10700 | oil leak |
| 56033 | 1508 | Doncaster | | | 02/08/77 | TO | Dec-95 | ZF | Oct-03 | IM | 12500 | power earth fault |
| 56034 | 1508 | Doncaster | | | 25/08/77 | TO | Aug-94 | ZF | Nov-99 | TO | 9492 | bogies defective |
| 56035 | 1508 | Doncaster | | | 13/10/77 | TO | Feb-96 | ZF | Mar-00 | TE | 8000 | fire damage |
| 56036 | 1508 | Doncaster | | | 16/08/78 | TO | Feb-93 | ZF | Jan-00 | CD | 9056 | due works attention |
| 56037 | 1508 | Doncaster | | | 02/01/78 | TO | Nov-99 | ZB | Sep-03 | IM | 9500 | surplus to requirements |
| 56038 | 1508 | Doncaster | | | 19/02/78 | TO | Apr-99 | ZB | Feb-04 | HM | 7700 | surplus to requirements |
| 56039 | 1508 | Doncaster | | | 07/02/78 | TO | Jul-94 | ZF | Aug-99 | TE | 7973 | fire damage |
| 56040 | 1508 | Doncaster | | | 15/02/78 | TO | Aug-95 | ZF | Oct-00 | IM | 8647 | fumes in cabs |
| 56041 | 1508 | Doncaster | | | 15/02/78 | TO | Mar-96 | ZF | Feb-03 | IM | 12717 | surplus to requirements |
| 56042 | 1508 | Doncaster | | | 14/05/79 | TO | Jan-87 | ZF | Sep-90 | TO | 3135 | bogies defective |
| 56043 | 1508 | Doncaster | | | 31/03/78 | TO | Feb-94 | ZF | Jan-00 | CD | 10114 | surplus to requirements |
| 56044 | 1508 | Doncaster | | | 14/05/78 | TO | Jul-95 | CF | Dec-00 | IM | 9797 | due works attention |
| 56045 | 1508 | Doncaster | | | 01/06/78 | TO | Feb-95 | ZF | Jun-99 | IM | 8483 | due works attention |
| 56046 | 1508 | Doncaster | | | 18/07/78 | TO | Apr-93 | ZF | Jul-02 | IM | 13334 | EWS hours limit |
| 56047 | 1508 | Doncaster | | | 28/07/78 | TO | Jul-93 | ZF | Mar-99 | DR | 9030 | due works attention |
| 56048 | 1508 | Doncaster | | | 19/09/78 | TO | Nov-98 | CF | Aug-02 | IM | 14165 | due works attention |
| 56049 | 1508 | Doncaster | | | 11/10/78 | TO | Jan-93 | ZF | Feb-04 | TE | 12400 | wheelset |
| 56050 | 1508 | Doncaster | | | 25/10/78 | TO | Oct-94 | ZF | Nov-99 | ML | 8387 | fire damage |
| 56051 | 1508 | Doncaster | | | 04/11/78 | TO | Dec-96 | ZB | Feb-04 | HM | 11800 | surplus to requirements |
| 56052 | 1508 | Doncaster | | | 06/12/78 | TO | Apr-94 | CF | Apr-99 | DR | 10117 | overdue works |
| 56053 | 1508 | Doncaster | | | 29/12/78 | TO | May-94 | CF | Jul-99 | TO | 9654 | due works attention |
| 56054 | 1508 | Doncaster | | | 26/01/79 | TO | Jun-95 | ZF | Dec-03 | FB | 12332 | due works attention |
| 56055 | 1508 | Doncaster | | | 01/02/79 | TO | Jul-95 | ZF | Mar-03 | KY | 12442 | due works attention |
| 56056 | 1508 | Doncaster | | | 12/03/79 | TO | Jan-96 | CF | Feb-04 | HM | 12364 | surplus to requirements |
| 56057 | 1508 | Doncaster | | | 27/03/79 | TO | Jan-92 | ZF | Jul-99 | TO | 9685 | due works attention |
| 56058 | 1508 | Doncaster | | | 29/04/79 | TO | Jun-96 | ZF | Jan-04 | BS | 12400 | wheelset |
| 56059 | 1508 | Doncaster | | | 16/05/79 | TO | Apr-97 | BR | Mar-04 | PB | 11200 | surplus to requirements |
| 56060 | 1508 | Doncaster | | | 09/06/79 | TO | Feb-98 | BR | Mar-04 | HM | 11079 | surplus to requirements |
| 56061 | 1509 | Doncaster | | | 09/08/79 | TO | Jan-93 | ZF | Jul-99 | TO | 9429 | due works attention |
| 56062 | 1509 | Doncaster | | | 29/08/79 | TO | Feb-99 | TO | Feb-04 | CF | 8600 | fire damage |
| 56063 | 1509 | Doncaster | | | 06/09/79 | TO | Sep-98 | CF | Jul-03 | IM | 15577 | EWS hours limit |
| 56064 | 1509 | Doncaster | | | 17/09/79 | TO | Mar-95 | CF | Jan-00 | CD | 9515 | surplus to requirements |
| 56065 | 1509 | Doncaster | | | 17/10/79 | TO | Jun-97 | BR | Feb-04 | HM | 11700 | surplus to requirements |
| 56066 | 1509 | Doncaster | | | 11/12/79 | TO | Jun-89 | ZF | Apr-99 | CF | 10989 | power earth fault |
| 56067 | 1509 | Doncaster | | | 11/12/79 | TO | Mar-97 | BR | Dec-03 | FB | 13000 | EWS hours limit |
| 56068 | 1509 | Doncaster | | | 11/12/79 | TO | Apr-96 | BR | Jul-03 | IM | 12461 | hours & due B exam |
| 56069 | 1509 | Doncaster | | | 11/12/79 | TO | Jun-98 | BR | Feb-04 | HM | 9300 | surplus to requirements |
| 56070 | 1509 | Doncaster | | | 21/12/79 | TO | Nov-94 | ZF | Feb-04 | HM | 12261 | wheelset |
| 56071 | 1509 | Doncaster | | | 21/12/79 | TO | Dec-98 | TO | Mar-04 | DR | 8993 | surplus to requirements |
| 56072 | 1509 | Doncaster | | | 07/01/80 | TO | Nov-93 | TO | Feb-04 | DR | 13000 | surplus to requirements |
| 56073 | 1509 | Doncaster | | | 29/02/80 | TI | Nov-98 | CF | Jun-02 | IM | 16267 | EWS hours limit |
| 56074 | 1509 | Doncaster | | | 23/03/80 | TI | Aug-94 | ZF | Feb-03 | IM | 13007 | EWS hours limit |

| Loco | Status/Location as at 15/10/09 | Name & date named | Name Removed | Liveries | To & from France |
|---|---|---|---|---|---|
| 56001 | c/u May-97 at CF | Whatley - 29/10/87 | Oct-94 | B, FA | |
| 56002 | c/u Mar-94 at DR | | | B, FO, FC | |
| 56003 | HTLX HQ r/n 56312 | **Artemis** | | **B, FU, HP** | |
| 56004 | c/u Jul-06 at CFB | | | B | |
| 56005 | c/u Aug-96 at CFB | | | B, FO, FC | |
| **56006** | **WNXX BH** | **Ferrybridge C Power Station - 28/02/95** | | **B, FO, FC, LH, B** | |
| **56007** | **WZGF CE** | | | **B, FO, FC, TR, FE** | 01/09/05 05/11/06 |
| 56008 | c/u Apr-00 at IM | | | B | |
| 56009 | Stored Brush r/n 56201 | | | B, FO, FC, BS | |
| 56010 | c/u Apr-04 at CFB | | | B, TR | |
| 56011 | c/u Apr-09 at CFB | | | B, FR, FU, EW | |
| 56012 | c/u Apr-00 at IM | Matlby Colliery - 30/06/89 | May-92 | B, FC | |
| 56013 | c/u Sep-01 at TJT | | | B, FC | |
| 56014 | c/u Jan-00 at IM | | | B, FC | |
| 56015 | c/u Mar-96 at ZF | | | B, FR*, FC | |
| 56016 | c/u Apr-97 at CF | | | B, FO, FC | |
| 56017 | c/u May-94 at TO | | | B, FO, FC | |
| **56018** | **WZGF WA** | | | **B, FO, FC, TR, EW, FE** | 04/05/05 27/01/07 |
| 56019 | c/u Nov-03 at IM | | | B, FR | |
| 56020 | c/u Jan-98 at CFB | | | B | |
| **56021** | **MRLS LM** | | | **B, FC, LH** | |
| **56022** | **MRLS WO** | | | **B, TR, FU** | |
| 56023 | c/u Aug-04 at CFB | | | B, FC | |
| 56024 | c/u Aug-96 at CFB | | | B, FO | |
| 56025 | c/u Mar-09 at CFB | | | B, FC, TR | |
| 56026 | c/u Jun-96 at CFB | | | B | |
| 56027 | c/u May-09 at CFB | | | B, FC, LH | |
| 56028 | c/u Sep-98 at ZC | West Burton Power Station - 10/09/88 | Feb-93 | B, FC | |
| 56029 | c/u Apr-07 at EMR | | | B, FC, TR | |
| 56030 | c/u Sep-98 at ZC | Eggborough Power Station - 02/09/89 | Apr-93 | B, FC | |
| **56031** | **WZGF CD** | **Merehead - 16/09/83** | **May-96** | **B, FA, DC, FE** | 28/06/05 23/12/06 |
| **56032** | **WZGF CD** | **Sir De Morganwg/County of South Glamorgan -14/10/83** | **Jun-97** | **B, FA, FM, EW, FE** | 14/05/05 30/10/06 |
| **56033** | **WNXX HM** | **Shotton Paper Mill - 18/12/95** | **unknown** | **B, FO, FA, TR** | |
| 56034 | c/u Nov-07 at CFB | Castell Ogwr/Ogmore Castle - 05/06/85 | Sep-03 | B, FO, FA, LH | |
| 56035 | c/u Jun-00 at CRDC | Taff Merthyr - 09/11/81 | Jul-89 | B, FO, FA, LH | |
| 56036 | c/u Mar-06 at CFB | | | B, LL, FO, FP, DC, DT | |
| **56037** | **WZTS CD** | **Richard Trevithick - 23/07/81** | **Aug-97** | **B, FO, FA, TR, EW** | |
| **56038** | **WZGF CD** | **Western Mail - 02/06/81** | **unknown** | | |
| | | **Pathfinder Tours - 05/05/03** | **Apr-04** | **B, FO, TR, FE** | 07/10/04 27/12/06 |
| 56039 | c/u Mar-04 atTJT | ABP Port of Hull - 19/07/94 | Jul-97 | B, FO, FA, LO | |
| **56040** | **Preserved, at SN** | **Oystermouth - 25/03/82** | **Jun-05** | **B, FO, FM, TR, FO** | |
| **56041** | **WNXX HM** | | | **B, FO, FA, UC, EO** | |
| 56042 | c/u Apr-94 at TO | | | B, FU | |
| 56043 | c/u Feb-09 at CFB | | | B, FO, FA, FM | |
| 56044 | c/u Sep-07 at CFB | Cardiff Canton - 09/08/91 | Dec-92 | | |
| | | Cardif Canton - Quality Assured - 31/12/92 | | B, FR, FM, TR | |
| **56045** | **RCJA RR r/n 56301** | **British Steel Shelton - 30/01/97** | | **B, FO, FA, LH, FL** | |
| **56046** | **WNXX TO** | | | **B, FO, FA, DC** | |
| 56047 | c/u Dec-03 at IM | | | B, LL, FC, DC, DT | |
| **56048** | **WZTS HM** | | | **B, LL, FR, DC, DT** | |
| **56049** | **WZGF CD** | | | **B, LL, FR, DC, DT, FE** | 26/05/05 19/11/06 |
| 56050 | c/u Jun-04 at CFB | British Steel Teeside - 04/10/96 | | B, FO, FA, LH | |
| **56051** | **WZGF CD** | **Isle of Grain - 30/06/93** | **Jun-96** | **B, FO, FA, EO, FE** | 22/06/05 13/10/06 |
| 56052 | c/u Apr-09 at CFB | The Cardiff Rod Mill - 01/05/97 | Jun-05 | B, FR, FA, FU, TR | |
| **56053** | **WNXX HM** | **Sir De Morganwg/County of South Glamorgan -17/03/86** | **Jun-05** | **B, FO, FA, FU, TR** | |
| **56054** | **WNXX CD** | **British Steel Llanwern - 31/05/94** | | **B, FC, FM, TR, FU** | |
| **56055** | **WNXX HM** | | | **B, FO, FA, LH** | |
| **56056** | **WNXX HM** | | | **B, FO, FA, TR** | |
| **56057** | **HTLX HQ  r/n 56311** | **British Fuels - 27/06/96** | | **B, FO, FA, EO, HG** | |
| **56058** | **WZGF CD** | | | **B, FO, FA, FU, UC*, EO, FE** | 15/06/05 15/10/06 |
| **56059** | **WZGF EH** | | | **B, FO, FU, FA, EW, FE** | 12/10/04 03/11/06 |
| **56060** | **WZGF CD** | **The Cardiff Rod Mill - 01/12/92** | **Mar-97** | **B, FO, FA, TR, EW, FE** | 12/10/04 23/10/06 |
| 56061 | c/u at Dec-06 at TJT | | | B, FO, FA, FU, FM | |
| **56062** | **WNXX MG** | **Mountsorrel - 21/03/89** | | **B, FO, FA, FU, EW** | |
| 56063 | c/u Nov-07 at CFB | Bardon Hill - 06/10/86 | | B, FO, FA, FU | |
| 56064 | c/u Mar-09 at CFB | | | B, FO, FA, FM, TR | |
| **56065** | **WZGF CD** | | | **B, FO, FA, EW, FE** | 26/05/05 09/10/06 |
| 56066 | c/u Dec-05 at R HULL | | | B, FO, FC, TR | |
| **56067** | **WNXX CD** | | | **B, FR, FC, EW** | |
| **56068** | **WNXX HM** | | | **B, FR, UC, EW** | |
| **56069** | **WZGF CD** | **Thornaby TMD - 29/09/86** | **Jul-98** | | |
| | | **Wolverhampton Steel Terminal - 22/07/98** | | **B, FC, FM, EW, FE** | 30/09/04 11/01/07 |
| **56070** | **WNXX CD** | | | **B, FA, TR** | |
| **56071** | **WZGF CD** | | | **B, FC, TR, FE** | 24/08/05 03/11/06 |
| **56072** | **WNXX HM** | | | **B, FC, TR** | |
| **56073** | **WNXX TO** | **Tremorfa Steel Works - 14/03/93** | **Jun-05** | **B, FC, FM, TR** | |
| **56074** | **WZGF CD** | **Kellingley Colliery - 14/06/82** | **Oct-02** | **B, FC, LH, FE** | 06/09/05 25/10/06 |

| Loco | Batch | Built at | To Service | Initial Depot | Last overhaul | | Withdrawal at | | TOPS Hours | Reason |
|---|---|---|---|---|---|---|---|---|---|---|
| 56075 | 1509 | Doncaster | 06/04/80 | TI | Jan-94 | ZF | Oct-99 | IM | 9987 | failed in traffic |
| 56076 | 1509 | Doncaster | 14/04/80 | TI | Sep-95 | ZF | Mar-00 | IM | 8654 | traction motor siezed |
| 56077 | 1509 | Doncaster | 18/05/80 | TI | Dec-94 | ZF | Feb-02 | CD | 9341 | wheelset |
| 56078 | 1509 | Doncaster | 25/05/80 | TI | Jun-98 | TO | Apr-04 | KY | 9944 | surplus to requirements |
| 56079 | 1509 | Doncaster | 22/06/80 | TI | Mar-95 | ZF | Dec-99 | TO | 9456 | due works attention |
| 56080 | 1509 | Doncaster | 13/07/80 | TI | Feb-94 | TO | Apr-99 | IM | 9000 | overdue works |
| 56081 | 1509 | Doncaster | 24/08/80 | TI | Mar-99 | TO | Mar-04 | TE | 7861 | surplus to requirements |
| 56082 | 1509 | Doncaster | 24/08/80 | TI | Apr-94 | ZF | Apr-99 | IM | 9476 | overdue works |
| 56083 | 1509 | Doncaster | 07/09/80 | TI | Dec-94 | ZF | Dec-03 | FB | 13000 | EWS hours limit |
| 56084 | 1509 | Doncaster | 26/10/80 | TI | Apr-95 | CE | Nov-00 | IM | 9107 | derailment damage |
| 56085 | 1509 | Doncaster | 12/01/81 | TI | Apr-95 | CE | Jul-02 | TE | 12012 | wheelset |
| 56086 | 1509 | Doncaster | 07/12/80 | TI | Jul-95 | ZF | Aug-99 | IM | 7241 | traction motor flashover |
| 56087 | 1509 | Doncaster | 21/12/80 | TI | Aug-97 | BR | Mar-04 | IM | 11500 | surplus to requirements |
| 56088 | 1509 | Doncaster | 25/01/81 | TI | Oct-96 | BR | Feb-04 | TE | 13000 | EWS hours limit |
| 56089 | 1509 | Doncaster | 25/01/81 | TI | Jun-95 | ZF | Feb-02 | IM | 9884 | alternator defect |
| 56090 | 1509 | Doncaster | 08/03/81 | TI | Dec-95 | ZF | Dec-03 | CD | 13000 | EWS hours limit |
| 56091 | 1510 | Doncaster | 21/06/81 | TI | Aug-98 | BR | Mar-04 | TO | 9310 | surplus to requirements |
| 56092 | 1510 | Doncaster | 21/06/81 | TI | Sep-93 | TO | Mar-00 | SP | 9000 | due works attention |
| 56093 | 1510 | Doncaster | 28/06/81 | TI | Mar-94 | ZF | Jul-99 | DR | 9692 | due works attention |
| 56094 | 1510 | Doncaster | 09/08/81 | TI | Aug-98 | TO | Mar-04 | HM | 8488 | surplus to requirements |
| 56095 | 1510 | Doncaster | 16/08/81 | TI | Nov-98 | TO | Mar-04 | OC | 9370 | surplus to requirements |
| 56096 | 1510 | Doncaster | 13/09/81 | TI | Nov-96 | ZF | Jan-04 | IM | 12700 | surplus to requirements |
| 56097 | 1510 | Doncaster | 04/10/81 | TI | Apr-93 | ZF | Apr-99 | DR | 9000 | due works attention |
| 56098 | 1510 | Doncaster | 18/10/81 | TI | Nov-93 | ZF | Apr-00 | IM | 11833 | camshaft defect |
| 56099 | 1510 | Doncaster | 08/11/81 | TI | Oct-93 | TO | Nov-03 | IM | 12900 | flat batteries & EWS hours limit |
| 56100 | 1510 | Doncaster | 15/11/81 | TI | Nov-95 | ZF | Dec-03 | CF | 12384 | tyre turning required & EWS hours limit |
| 56101 | 1510 | Doncaster | 21/12/81 | TI | Jan-95 | CF | Mar-00 | IM | 6708 | multiple faults |
| 56102 | 1510 | Doncaster | 20/12/81 | TI | Jan-96 | BR | Sep-03 | TE | 13000 | EWS hours limit |
| 56103 | 1510 | Doncaster | 27/12/81 | TI | Jul-97 | BR | Dec-03 | IM | 11737 | oil leak |
| 56104 | 1510 | Doncaster | 21/02/82 | TI | Feb-93 | ZF | Feb-04 | IM | 10766 | surplus to requirements |
| 56105 | 1510 | Doncaster | 28/03/82 | TI | Nov-96 | BR | Aug-03 | IM | 12445 | EWS hours limit |
| 56106 | 1510 | Doncaster | 25/04/82 | TI | Mar-95 | ZF | Jan-04 | IM | 12005 | surplus to requirements |
| 56107 | 1510 | Doncaster | 16/05/82 | TI | Jun-95 | BR | Jan-04 | FB | 12827 | EWS hours limit |
| 56108 | 1510 | Doncaster | 20/06/82 | HM | Jan-94 | TO | Jun-99 | TE | 8962 | coolant leak |
| 56109 | 1510 | Doncaster | 15/08/82 | TI | Mar-95 | ZF | Dec-03 | FB | 12483 | EWS hours limit |
| 56110 | 1510 | Doncaster | 03/10/82 | HM | Jul-95 | CE | Jul-02 | IM | 11128 | wheelsets |
| 56111 | 1510 | Doncaster | 24/10/82 | HM | Sep-95 | ZF | Apr-03 | TE | 12843 | surplus to requirements |
| 56112 | 1510 | Doncaster | 21/11/82 | TI | Mar-96 | ZF | Jan-03 | TE | 12447 | surplus to requirements |
| 56113 | 1510 | Doncaster | 12/12/82 | TI | Oct-98 | TO | Mar-04 | KY | 8628 | fire protection equipment defective |
| 56114 | 1510 | Doncaster | 23/01/83 | TI | Jan-97 | BR | Dec-03 | IM | 12018 | defective centre axle bearings |
| 56115 | 1510 | Doncaster | 30/01/83 | TI | Dec-98 | BR | Apr-04 | KY | 9089 | surplus to requirements |
| 56116 | 1510 | Crewe | 13/03/83 | TI | May-95 | CE | Feb-03 | IM | 12244 | traction motor problems |
| 56117 | 1510 | Crewe | 13/03/83 | TI | May-97 | BR | Dec-03 | CD | 12000 | surplus to requirments |
| 56118 | 1510 | Crewe | 17/04/83 | TI | Jul-95 | ZF | Dec-03 | CD | 12400 | brake defects |
| 56119 | 1510 | Crewe | 15/05/83 | TI | Dec-97 | BR | Mar-04 | KY | 11800 | B-exam required |
| 56120 | 1510 | Crewe | 29/05/83 | TI | Sep-96 | BR | Nov-03 | FB | 12200 | camshaft defects |
| 56121 | 1510 | Crewe | 19/06/83 | TI | Feb-93 | ZF | Feb-00 | CF | 8527 | due works attention |
| 56122 | 1510 | Crewe | 03/07/83 | TI | Mar-88 | ZF | Oct-92 | TO | 6536 | collision damage |
| 56123 | 1510 | Crewe | 31/07/83 | TI | Jul-92 | ZF | Jan-00 | IM | 9000 | due works attention |
| 56124 | 1510 | Crewe | 25/09/83 | TI | May-93 | ZF | Jun-99 | KY | 8453 | due works attention |
| 56125 | 1510 | Crewe | 20/10/83 | TI | Oct-92 | ZF | Feb-00 | IM | 9456 | wheelsets |
| 56126 | 1510 | Crewe | 15/11/83 | TI | Oct-93 | ZF | Mar-99 | IM | 9000 | due works attention |
| 56127 | 1510 | Crewe | 13/12/83 | TI | Jun-99 | TO | Feb-02 | TO | 10209 | wheelsets |
| 56128 | 1510 | Crewe | 18/12/83 | TI | Nov-92 | ZF | Jul-99 | IM | 8837 | camshaft defect |
| 56129 | 1510 | Crewe | 08/01/84 | TI | Mar-93 | ZF | Jul-03 | TE | 12492 | wheelsets |
| 56130 | 1510 | Crewe | 01/04/84 | GD | Nov-94 | ZF | Jun-99 | TO | 8713 | camshaft defect |
| 56131 | 1510 | Crewe | 29/04/84 | GD | Feb-94 | ZF | Jul-02 | IM | 14484 | EWS hours limit |
| 56132 | 1510 | Crewe | 10/06/84 | GD | Nov-93 | ZF | Jan-00 | TO | 10375 | due works attention |
| 56133 | 1510 | Crewe | 29/07/84 | GD | Mar-94 | TO | Feb-04 | HM | 11646 | wheelset siezed |
| 56134 | 1510 | Crewe | 09/09/84 | GD | Aug-93 | ZF | Jul-02 | IM | 14886 | EWS hours limit |
| 56135 | 1510 | Crewe | 04/11/84 | TI | Aug-93 | TO | Jan-99 | IM | 9000 | due works attention |

NB - Only Romanian locos carried numbered worksplates, the rest carried a plate showing year and place of build only.

**KEY**

**Depots & Locations**

BH Barrow Hill
BR Bristol
BS Bescot
CD Crewe Diesel
CE Crewe Electric
CF Cardiff Canton
DR Doncaster
FB Ferrybridge
GC Great Central Ruddington
GD Gateshead
HM Healey Mills
IM Immingham
KY Knottingley
ML Motherwell
OC Old Oak Common
PB Peterborough
SN Shackerstone
SP Wigan Springs Branch
TE Thornaby
TI Tinsley
TO Toton
WO Wolsingham
ZB Brush, Loughborough
ZC Crewe Works
ZF Doncaster Works

**Pool codes**

HTLX Hanson Traction Locos
MRLS Mainline Rail Ltd Stored Locos
RCJA Fastline Freight Ltd Locos
WNXX DBS Stored Unserviceable
WZGF DBS Contract Hire locos
WZTS DBS Contract Hire Reserve

**Scrap Locations**

CATH Cardiff Cathays
FB C F Booth, Rotherham
CRDC Component Recovery & Distribution Centre, Wigan
EMR European Metal Recycling, Kingsbury
R HULL R Hull, Rotherham
TJT T J Thompson, Stockton on Tees

| Loco | Status/Location as at 15/10/09 | Name & date named | Name Removed | Liveries | To & from France |
|---|---|---|---|---|---|
| 56075 | c/u Jun-04 at CFB | West Yorkshire Enterprise - 09/07/85 | Oct-99 | B, FO, FC, FU | |
| 56076 | c/u Feb-09 at CFB | Blyth Power - 08/09/82 | Sep-86 | | |
| | | British Steel Trostre - 31/05/93 | Oct-95 | B, FR, FC, FM, TR | |
| 56077 | WNXX CD | Thorpe Marsh Power Station - 04/09/90 | Jun-05 | B, FO, FC, LH | |
| 56078 | WZGF CD | Doncaster Enterprise | | B, FA, FU, LL, FE | 09/09/04 05/05/07 |
| 56079 | WNXX HM | | | B, FO, FC, TR | |
| 56080 | c/u Dec-03 at CATH | Selby Coalfield - 30/10/89 | | B, FC, FU | |
| 56081 | WZGF CD | | | B, FC, FU, FE | 01/07/05 27/09/06 |
| 56082 | c/u Apr-09 at CFB | | | B, FC, FU | |
| 56083 | WNXX CD | | | B, FO, FC, LH | |
| 56084 | c/u Mar-09 at CFB | | | LL, FO, FC, LH | |
| 56085 | WNXX TE | | | LL, FO, FC, LH | |
| 56086 | Preserved, at SN | The Magistrates Association - 04/10/95 | | LL, FO, FC, TR, LL | |
| 56087 | WZGF CD | ABP Port of Hull - 31/08/97 | | LL, FO, FC, FM, EW, FE | 05/10/04 25/01/07 |
| 56088 | WNXX TE | | | LL, FR, FC, EO | |
| 56089 | c/u Feb-09 at CFB | Ferrybridge C Power Station - 15/09/91 | Jan-95 | LL, FR, FC, EO | |
| 56090 | WZGF CD | | | LL, FR, FU, LH, FE | 19/10/04 23/10/06 |
| 56091 | WZGF EH | Castle Donnington Power Station - 18/06/89 | Aug-98 | | |
| | | Stanton - 29/08/98 | | LL, FC, FU, EW, FE | 23/06/05 27/12/06 |
| 56092 | c/u Jul-01 at CRDC | | | LL, FC, FU, TR | |
| 56093 | WNXX HM | The Institution of Mining Engineers - 29/11/89 | Jun-99 | LL, FC, FU, TR | |
| 56094 | WZGF CD | Eggborough Power Station - 30/04/93 | | LL, FC, EW, FE | 21/07/05 04/12/06 |
| 56095 | WZGF EH | Haworth Colliery - 29/10/87 | Nov-98 | LL, FC, FU, FE | 12/07/05 09/10/06 |
| 56096 | WZGF CD | | | LL, FO, FC, UC*, EW, FE | 27/04/05 2710/06 |
| 56097 | Preserved, GC | | | LL, FC, FM, FC | |
| 56098 | Preserved, BH | | | LL, FC, FU, FR | |
| 56099 | WNXX HM | Fiddlers Ferry Power Station - 15/07/89 | Jun-05 | LL, FC, FU, TR | |
| 56100 | WNXX MG | | | LL, FR, FC, LH | |
| 56101 | Preserved, BH | Mutual Improvement - 28/04/90 | | LL, FC, TR, LL | |
| 56102 | WNXX TE | Scunthorpe Steel Centenary - 19/03/90 | Sep-95 | LL, FC, FU, LH | |
| 56103 | WZGF CD | Stora - 18/07/97 | | LL, FA, TR, EW, FE | 03/11/05 17/11/06 |
| 56104 | WZGF CD | | | LL, FC, FE | 21/10/05 17/01/07 |
| 56105 | WZGF CD | | | LL, FA, EW, FE | 27/04/05 27/01/07 |
| 56106 | WZGF CD | | | LL, FC, LH, FE | 04/05/05 24/06/07 |
| 56107 | WNXX CD | | | LL, FR, FC, LH | |
| 56108 | WNXX TE | | | LL, FR, FU | |
| 56109 | WNXX CD | | | LL, FC, LH | |
| 56110 | WNXX HM | Croft - 09/06/92 | Jun-05 | LL, FA, LH | |
| 56111 | WNXX TE | | | LL, FC, LH | |
| 56112 | WNXX CE | Stainless Pioneer - 01/09/96 | | LL, FC, LH | |
| 56113 | WZGF CD | | | LL, FU, FC, TR, EW, FE | 03/11/05 15/10/06 |
| 56114 | HTLX HQ to be 56314 | Matlby Colliery - 1/7/97 | Jan-97 | LL, FC, TR, EO | |
| 56115 | WZGF EH | Bassetlaw - 30/06/01 | Dec-01 | | |
| | | Barry Needham - 21/01/02 | Apr-04 | LL, FU, FC, TR, EW, FE | 04/11/05 01/12/06 |
| 56116 | WNXX HM | | | LL, FC, LH | |
| 56117 | WZGF EH | Wilton Coalpower - 01/09/92 | Dec-98 | LL, FC, EW, FE | 05/10/04 09/10/06 |
| 56118 | WZGF CE | | | LL, FC, LH, FE | 30/09/04 07/06/06 |
| 56119 | WNXX HM | | | LL, FC, TR, EW | |
| 56120 | WNXX CD | | | LL, FC, EO | |
| 56121 | c/u Dec-05 at CFB | | | LL, FC, FU, FC, TR | |
| 56122 | c/u May-98 at CFB | Wilton Coalpower - 14/04/88 | Mar-92 | LL, FC | |
| 56123 | c/u Aug-03 at IM | Drax Power Station - 11/05/88 | | LL, FC, TR | |
| 56124 | RCJA RR r/n 56302 | Blue Circle Cement - 24/10/83 | Oct-89 | | |
| | | Wilson Walshe - 01/10/07 | | LL, FC, TR, FL | |
| 56125 | RCJA DF r/n 56303 | | | LL, FC, TR, FL, GR | |
| 56126 | c/u Apr-01 at CRDC | | | LL, FC | |
| 56127 | WNXX TE | | | LL, FC, FU, TR | |
| 56128 | Hanson to be 56313 | West Burton Power Station - 28/02/93 | Jan-95 | LL, FC, TR | |
| 56129 | WNXX TE | | | LL, FU, FC, TR | |
| 56130 | c/u Oct-04 at CFB | Wardley Opencast - 06/11/90 | | LL, FC, LH | |
| 56131 | c/u Dec-07 at CFB | Ellington Colliery - 20/08/87 | | LL, FC, FU | |
| 56132 | c/u May-06 at CFB | Fina Energy - 01/10/86 | Mar-89 | LL, FC, TR | |
| 56133 | WZTS CE | Crewe Locomotive Works - 02/06/84 | | LL, FC, FU, TR | |
| 56134 | WZTS HM | Blyth Power - 31/10/86 | | LL, FC | |
| 56135 | c/u Aug-03 at IM | Port of Tyne Authority - 29/10/85 | Jun-05 | FO, FC, FU | |

*Liveries*

| | | | |
|---|---|---|---|
| B | Standard rail blue | FR* | Railfreight red stripe, carried in Crewe Works only |
| DC | Yellow & grey (Dutch) | FU | Triple grey, No branding |
| DT | Transrail yellow & grey | GR | Green |
| EO | Original EWS red & gold | HG | Hanson grey |
| EW | Revised EWS red & gold | HP | Hanson purple |
| FA | Triple grey, Construction branding | LH | Loadhaul black & orange revised |
| FC | Triple grey, Coal branding | LL | Large logo blue |
| FE | Fertis white | LO | Loadhaul black & orange original |
| FL | Fastline black & grey | TR | Transrail triple grey |
| FM | Triple grey, Metals branding | UC | Light grey undercoat |
| FO | Railfreight grey | UC* | Light grey undercoat, carried on test train only |
| FP | Triple grey, Petroleum branding | | |
| FR | Railfreight red stripe | | |

# PASSENGER TRAINS

This is a complete listing in chronological order of every known Class 56 passenger working. Service trains appear in black type, charters/railtours in green and private trains in red. This has been compiled from an original listing created by Roger Elliott.

| Date | Grid | Train Details | Grid Worked Train From / To | Notes |
|---|---|---|---|---|
| 22-Jun-77 | 56004 | 1020 Penzance - Leeds | Wincobank - Leeds | |
| 24-Jul-77 | 56008 | "Melton Mowbray Pieman" railtour | Barnsley - Melton Mowbray & rtn | BR (Sheffield) railtour |
| 21-Jan-78 | 56004 | "Class 44 Farewell" railtour | Barnsley - Dodworth | BR railtour, assisted from back, 44009 leading |
| 14-May-79 | 56053 | 1330 Birmingham NS - Euston | Birmingham NS - Nuneaton | Drag |
| 28-Nov-79 | 56064 | 0835 Birmingham NS - Paddington | ? - Paddington | |
| 17-Dec-79 | 56065 | 0935 Euston - Inverness | Winsford - Mossend Yd | Drag |
| 18-Jan-80 | 56069 | 1122 Liverpool LS - Paddington | nr Leamington Spa - ? | 50008 failed |
| 9-Mar-80 | 56066 | 2030 Wolverhampton - Euston | Birmingham NS - Nuneaton | Drag 87014 |
| | 56066 | 2035 Euston - Manchester Piccadilly | Nuneaton - Birmingham NS | Drag 87010 |
| 14-Mar-80 | 56059 | 1153 St Pancras - Sheffield | Westhouses - Sheffield | 45110 failed |
| | 56059 | 1600 Sheffield - St Pancras | Sheffield - Derby | 45110 failed |
| 10-Apr-80 | 56066 | 0950 Edinburgh Waverley - Plymouth | Washwood Heath - Birmingham NS | 50014 failed |
| 11-May-80 | 56061 | 1000 Wolverhampton - Euston | Wolverhampton - Nuneaton | Drag |
| | 56061 | 0940 Euston - Wolverhampton | Nuneaton - Wolverhampton | Drag |
| | 56061 | 1300 Wolverhampton - Euston | Wolverhampton - Nuneaton | Drag |
| | 56061 | 1240 London - Wolverhampton | Nuneaton - Wolverhampton | Drag |
| 26-May-80 | 56042 | 1135 Poole - Newcastle | Reading - Birmingham NS | |
| 13-Jul-80 | 56067 | 0800 Wolverhampton - Euston | Wolverhampton - Nuneaton | Drag |
| | 56067 | 0740 Euston - Wolverhampton | Nuneaton - Wolverhampton | Drag |
| | 56067 | 1200 Wolverhampton - Euston | Wolverhampton - Nuneaton | Drag |
| | 56067 | 1140 London - Wolverhampton | Nuneaton - Wolverhampton | Drag |
| 20-Jul-80 | 56051 | 1000 Wolverhampton - Euston | Wolverhampton - Birmingham NS | Drag |
| 3-Aug-80 | 56052 | 1100 Wolverhampton - Euston | Wolverhampton - Nuneaton | Drag 87004 |
| | 56052 | 1040 Euston - Wolverhampton | Nuneaton - Wolverhampton | Drag 87101 |
| | 56062 | 1500 Wolverhampton - Euston | Wolverhampton - Nuneaton | Drag 86213 |
| 31-Aug-80 | 56058 | 1340 Euston - Birmingham NS | Nuneaton - Birmingham NS | Drag 86254 |
| 5-Oct-80 | 56063 | 1340 Euston - Shrewsbury | Nuneaton - Shrewsbury | Drag |
| 4-Jan-81 | 56056 | 0900 Wolverhampton - Euston | Birmingham NS - Nuneaton | Drag |
| 10-May-81 | 56076 | 1200 Wolverhampton - Euston | Birmingham NS - Nuneaton | Drag 87019 |
| | 56078 | 1400 Wolverhampton - Euston | Birmingham NS - Nuneaton | Drag 87013 |
| | 56078 | 1340 Wolverhampton - Shrewsbury | Nuneaton - Birmingham NS | Drag |
| | *56071* | *1140 Euston - Wolverhampton* | *Nuneaton - Birmingham NS* | *Drag, 86236, This working unconfirmed* |
| 17-May-81 | 56069 | 1500 Wolverhampton - Euston | Birmingham NS - Nuneaton | Drag |
| 24-May-81 | 56048 | 1200 Wolverhampton - Euston | Birmingham NS - Nuneaton | Drag, 87002 |
| | 56056 | 0800 Wolverhampton - Euston | Barnsley - Nuneaton | Drag, 86248 |
| | 56056 | 1100 Wolverhampton - Euston | Birmingham NS - Nuneaton | Drag duty, 86315 |
| | 56056 | 1140 London - Wolverhampton | Nuneaton - Birmingham NS | Drag, 86213? |
| 2-Jun-81 | 56038 | 1205? Cardiff Central - Portsmouth | Cardiff Central - Bristol TM | Named *Western Mail* at Cardiff Central |
| 7-Jun-81 | 56006 | 1100 Wolverhampton - Euston | Birmingham NS - Nuneaton | Drag |
| | 56006 | 1040 Euston - Wolverhampton | Nuneaton - Birmingham NS | Drag |
| 14-Jun-81 | 56054 | 1500 Wolverhampton - Euston | Birmingham NS - Daw Mill | Drag, 56054 failed at Daw Mill |
| 14-Jul-81 | 56079 | ? ? - Paddington | Didcot Parkway - Paddington | 47484 failed |
| 23-Sep-81 | 56019 | 1135 Poole - Newcastle (Via Leeds) | ? - ? | reported at Burton |
| 30-Oct-81 | 56004 | 1150 Paddington - Birmingham NS | Leamington Spa - Birmingham NS | 47508 failed |
| 3-Jan-82 | 56067 | 1000 Wolverhampton - Euston | Birmingham NS - Nuneaton | Drag |
| | 56067 | 0940 Euston - Wolverhampton | Nuneaton- Birmingham NS | Drag |
| 14-Mar-82 | 56042 | 1342? ? - Euston | Birmingham NS? - Nuneaton? | OHL problems, drag 86204 |
| 21-Mar-82 | 56042 | 1000 Wolverhampton - Euston | Wolverhampton - Nuneaton | Drag |
| | 56042 | 1240 Euston - Wolverhampton | Nuneaton - Wolverhampton | Drag |
| | 56100 | 1055 Wembley Central - Wolverhampton | Nuneaton - Wolverhampton | Drag |
| | 56100 | 1140 Euston - Wolverhampton | Birmingham NS ? - Wolverhampton | Drag |
| | 56100 | 1400 Wolverhampton - Euston | Wolverhampton - Birmingham NS ? | Drag |
| 28-Mar-82 | 56083 | 1300 Wolverhampton - Euston | Birmingham NS? - Nuneaton | Drag |
| | 56083 | 1240 Euston - Wolverhampton | Nuneaton - Birmingham NS? | Drag |
| | 56101 | 1000 Wolverhampton - Euston | Wolverhampton - Birmingham NS ? | Drag, 86230 |
| 18-Apr-82 | 56050 | 1100 Wolverhampton - Euston | Birmingham NS - Coventry | Drag |
| 21-Apr-82 | 56047 | 0638 Poole - Birmingham NS | Whitmarsh - Birmingham NS | 47146 failed |
| 25-Apr-82 | 56047 | 0900 Birmingham NS - Liverpool Lime St | Birmingham NS - ? | |
| 8-May-82 | 56013 | 1135? Poole - Newcastle | Leamington Spa - Birmingham NS | 37177 failed |
| 23-May-82 | 56057 | 0900 Wolverhampton - Euston | Birmingham NS - Nuneaton | Drag |
| 20-Jun-82 | 56055 | 1000 Wolverhampton - Euston | Birmingham NS - Nuneaton | Drag |
| | 56055 | 0940 Euston - Wolverhampton | Nuneaton - Birmingham NS | Drag |
| | 56072 | 1140 Euston - Wolverhampton | Nuneaton - Birmingham NS | Drag |
| | 56072 | 1500 Wolverhampton - Euston | Birmingham NS - Nuneaton | Drag |
| 7-Aug-82 | 56003 | "Grid Iron Grice" | Redditch - Walsall - London Bridge | DAA railtour |
| | 56014 | "Grid Iron Grice" | London Bridge - Bedford | |
| | 56049 | "Grid Iron Grice" | Toton Centre - Redditch | |
| 29-Aug-82 | 56060 | 1000 Wolverhampton - Euston | Birmingham NS - Nuneaton | Drag, 86209 |
| | 56060 | 0940 Euston - Wolverhampton | Nuneaton - Birmingham NS | Drag, 86235 |
| 2-Sep-82 | 56002 | 1500 Sheffield - St Pancras | Sheffield - St Pancras | |
| | 56002 | 1924 St Pancras - Sheffield | St Pancras - Sheffield | |
| 25-Sep-82 | 56064 | 1355 Euston - Manchester Piccadilly | ? - ? | reported seen at Stoke-on-Trent |
| 7-Nov-82 | 56085 | 1200 Wolverhampton - Euston | Birmingham NS - Nuneaton | Drag |
| | 56085 | 1140 Euston - Wolverhampton | Nuneaton - Birmingham NS | Drag |
| 20-Nov-82 | 56103 | "Trans Pennine" | Tinsley Yd - Sheffield | LCGB railtour |
| 21-Nov-82 | 56036 | 1200 Wolverhampton - Euston | Wolverhampton - Coventry | Drag |
| | 56036 | 1140 Euston - Wolverhampton | Coventry - Wolverhampton | Drag |
| | 56036 | 1500 Wolverhampton - Euston | Wolverhampton - Coventry | Drag |
| 1-Dec-82 | 56100 | ? ?-? | ? - Birmingham NS ? | 47513 failed |
| 9-Jan-83 | 56065 | 0800 Wolverhampton - Euston | Wolverhampton - Nuneaton | Drag |
| | 56065 | 0940 Euston - Wolverhampton | Nuneaton - Wolverhampton | Drag |
| | 56065 | 1A20 1400 Wolverhampton - Euston | Wolverhampton- Nuneaton | Drag |
| | 56065 | 1J32 1340 Euston - Shrewsbury | Nuneaton - Wolverhampton | Drag |
| 31-Jan-83 | 56050 | 0835 Birmingham NS - Paddington | Leamington Spa - ? | 50018 failed |
| 25-Feb-83 | 56072 | 1741 Paddington - Manchester Piccadilly | Leamington Spa - Birmingham NS | 47454 failed |

| Date | Grid | Train Details | Grid Worked Train From / To | Notes |
|---|---|---|---|---|
| 16-Apr-83 | 56067 | 1925 Scarborough - Liverpool LS | Earlestown - Earlestown W Jn? - ? | 45106 failed, initially assisted at rear |
| 5-Jun-83 | 56059 | "Coalville Collier" | Wigston North Jn - Stapleford & Sandiacre<br>Toton Meadow Sdgs - Stapleford & Sandiacre | F&W railtour |
|  | 56066 | 1200 Wolverhampton - Euston | Birmingham NS - Rugby | Drag |
|  | 56066 | 1200 Euston - Wolverhampton | Rugby - Birmingham NS | Drag |
| 12-Jun-83 | 56052 | 1000 Euston - Wolverhampton | Nuneaton - Wolverhampton | Drag |
|  | 56052 | 1500 Wolverhampton - Euston | Wolverhampton - Nuneaton | Drag |
| 19-Jun-83 | 56083 | 1000 Wolverhampton - Euston | Birmingham NS - Nuneaton | Drag |
|  | 56083 | 1100 Euston - Wolverhampton | Nuneaton - Birmingham NS | Drag |
| 26-Jun-83 | 56059 | 1000 Wolverhampton - Euston | Wolverhampton - Nuneaton | Drag |
|  | 56059 | 1100 Euston - Wolverhampton | Nuneaton - Birmingham NS? | Drag, 86229 |
|  | 56062 | 1000 Euston - Wolverhampton | Nuneaton - Wolverhampton | Drag |
|  | 56062 | 1500 Wolverhampton - Euston | Wolverhampton - Nuneaton | Drag |
|  | 56071 | 1200 Wolverhampton - Euston | Birmingham NS - Nuneaton | Drag, 87013 |
|  | 56071 | 1200 Euston - Wolverhampton | Nuneaton - Birmingham NS | Drag, 86250 |
|  | 56102 | 0800 Wolverhampton - Euston | Birmingham NS - Nuneaton | Drag, 87032 |
| 3-Jul-83 | 56098 | 1200 Wolverhampton - Euston | Nuneaton - Birmingham NS | Drag, poss worked other drags on this day |
|  | 56098 | 1200 Euston - Birmingham NS? | Birmingham NS - Nuneaton | Drag, poss worked other drags on this day |
| 24-Jul-83 | 56055 | ?   Wolverhampton - Euston | Birmingham NS - Nuneaton | Drag, poss worked other drags on this day |
|  | 56055 | 1700 Wolverhampton - Euston | Birmingham NS - Nuneaton | Drag, poss worked other drags on this day |
|  | 56071 | 1000 Euston - Wolverhampton | Nuneaton - Birmingham NS | Drag |
| 28-Jul-83 | 56033 | 0740 Penzance - Liverpool LS | ? - Birmingham NS | 50050 failed |
|  | 56033 | 1047 Glasgow Central - Plymouth | Birmingham NS - Bristol TM | 50050 failed |
| 30-Jul-83 | 56053 | 0825 Manchester Picc. - Cardiff Central | Birmingham NS - Cardiff Central |  |
| 31-Jul-83 | 56033 | "White Rose Rambler" | Bristol TM - Ilkeston Grnd Frame<br>Toton Centre - Bristol TM | F&W railtour |
|  | 56122 | "White Rose Rambler" | Doncaster - Scarborough - Doncaster |  |
|  | 56062 | 1000 Wolverhampton - Euston | Birmingham NS - Rugby | Drag |
|  | 56062 | 1100 Euston - Wolverhampton | Nuneaton? - Birmingham NS | Drag |
| 14-Aug-83 | 56002 | 1000 Wolverhampton - Euston | Birmingham NS - Nuneaton | Drag |
|  | 56002 | 1100 Euston - Wolverhampton | Nuneaton - Birmingham NS | Drag |
| 19-Aug-83 | 56120 | 1950 King's Cross - Bradford | ? - Leeds? |  |
| 20-Aug-83 | 56036 | "South Wales Venturer" | Westbury - Cardiff Central | DAA railtour |
|  | 56045 | "South Wales Venturer" | Cardiff Cent. - Margam Abbey Works East Jn |  |
|  | 56052 | "South Wales Venturer" | Margam Abbey Works East Jn - Llanelli - Cardiff Central |  |
| 21-Aug-83 | 56007 | Nuneaton drags |  | exact trains worked not known |
|  | 56070 | 0800 Wolverhampton - Euston | Wolverhampton - Nuneaton | Drag |
|  | 56072 | 0900 Wolverhampton - Euston | Birmingham NS - Nuneaton | Drag |
|  | 56072 | 1200 Wolverhampton - Euston | Birmingham NS - Nuneaton | Drag, 86206 |
|  | 56072 | 1200 Euston - Wolverhampton | Nuneaton - Birmingham NS | Drag, 87002 |
| 28-Aug-83 | 56071 | Nuneaton drags |  | exact trains worked not known |
| 16-Sep-83 | 56031/32 | ?  Westbury - Merehead Quarry | Westbury - Merehead Quarry | British Rail "V.I.P. special", in multiple |
| 18-Sep-83 | 56029 | 1200 Wolverhampton - Euston | Wolverhampton - Nuneaton | Drag |
|  | 56029 | 1200 Euston - Wolverhampton | Nuneaton - Wolverhampton | Drag |
| 21-Oct-83 | 56032 | 1821 Paddington - Bristol TM | Paddington - Bristol TM |  |
| 26-Mar-84 | 56122 | 0820 Leeds - Birmingham NS | ? - ? | 45114 failed |
| 1-Apr-84 | 56113 | 2355 Glasgow Central - BTM (31/3) | Rugeley TV - Cannock | with 47563, 56113 banked train |
| 14-Apr-84 | 56131 | ?   ? - Holyhead | Crewe - Holyhead - Crewe | On test, 47xxx providing ETH only |
| 17-Apr-84 | 56053 | ?   Euston - Wolverhampton | Tring - Wolverhampton | 85035 failed |
| 19-Apr-84 | 56131 | 0755 Coventry - Holyhead | Crewe - Holyhead | On test, 47437 providing ETH only |
|  | 56131 | 1246 Holyhead - Euston | Holyhead - Crewe | On test, 47437 providing ETH only |
| 22-Apr-84 | 56053 | 0745 Birmingham NS - Scarborough | Birmingham NS - Crewe? | BR 'Adex' charter |
|  | 56074 | 0900 Wolverhampton - Euston | Birmingham NS - Nuneaton | Drag |
|  | 56074 | 1200 Wolverhampton - Euston | Birmingham NS - Nuneaton | Drag |
| 2-Jun-84 | 56031 | "Midland Executive" | Coventry - Reading - Derby? | railtour |
| 26-Jun-84 | 56007 | 2050 Aberdeen - King's Cross (25/6) | Doncaster - King's Cross | 47595 low on fuel |
| 13-Jul-84 | 56057 | 0940 Poole - Newcastle | Nr Clay Cross Tunnel South - Chesterfield | 45135 failed |
| 15-Jul-84 | 56037 | "South Yorkshireman" | Cardiff Central - Bristol TM - Cardiff Central | Severnside Railtours |
| 20-Jul-84 | 56133 | ?   ? - Holyhead (0935 ex Crewe) | Crewe - Holyhead | On test, 47451 providing ETH only |
| 28-Jul-84 | 56011 | "Plant Invader" | Brent Curve Jn - Toton Centre | Railway Enthusiasts Society Ltd railtour |
|  |  | Derby - Brent Curve Jn |  |  |
| 12-Aug-84 | 56044 | "Paxman Collier 1" | Bristol TM - Birmingham NS & return | F&W Railtours |
|  | 56068 | "Paxman Collier 1" | Nottingham - Toton Centre<br>Stapleford & Sandiacre - Toton Meadow Sdgs |  |
| 23-Aug-84 | 56102 | 0727 Nottingham - Glasgow Central | Chesterfield - Sheffield | 47436 failed |
| 15-Sep-84 | 56069 | 1740 St Pancras - Derby | St Pancras - Derby | HST failed |
| 16-Sep-84 | 56020 | "Midland Macedoine" | Derby - St Pancras | Hertfordshire Rail Tours |
|  | 56107 | "Midland Macedoine" | St Pancras - Derby |  |
|  | 56105 | 1500 Wolverhampton - Euston | Wolverhampton - Nuneaton | Drag |
| 21-Sep-84 | 56038 | 1747 Paddington - Plymouth | Paddington - Westbury? | No 47s/ 50s available |
| 23-Sep-84 | 56105 | 0857 Wolverhampton - Euston | Wolverhampton - Nuneaton | Drag |
|  | 56105 | 1200 Wolverhampton - Euston | Wolverhampton - Nuneaton | Drag |
|  | 56105 | 1200 Euston - Wolverhampton | Nuneaton - Wolverhampton | Drag |
|  | 56107 | 0757 Wolverhampton - Euston | Wolverhampton - Nuneaton | Drag |
|  | 56107 | 0957? Wolverhampton - Euston | Wolverhampton - Nuneaton | Drag |
|  | 56107 | 1100 Euston - Wolverhampton | Nuneaton - Wolverhampton | Drag |
|  | 56107 | 1500 Wolverhampton - Euston | Wolverhampton - Nuneaton | Drag |
| 30-Sep-84 | 56079 | 1200 Wolverhampton - Euston | Wolverhampton - Nuneaton | Drag |
|  | 56079 | 1200 Euston - Wolverhampton | Nuneaton - Birmingham NS? | Drag |
| 2-Oct-84 | 56016 | 1635 St Pancras - Nottingham | Leicester? - Nottingham | 47468 failed |
| 11-Oct-84 | 56066 | 1020 Inverness - Euston | Coventry? - Paddington | Diverted to Paddington, accident at Wembley |
| 12-Oct-84 | 56066 | 1428 Wolverhampton - Paddington | Wolverhampton - Paddington | Diverted to Paddington, accident at Wembley |
|  | 56066 | 1855 Paddington - Wolverhampton | Paddington - Wolverhampton? | Started at Paddington, accident at Wembley |
|  | 56107 | ?   ? - ? | ? - Paddington | Diverted to Paddington, accident at Wembley |
| 13-Oct-84 | 56088 | 0622 Wolverhampton - Paddington | Wolverhampton - Paddington | Diverted to Paddington, accident at Wembley |
|  | 56088 | 1050  Paddington - Wolverhampton | Paddington - Wolverhampton | Started at Paddington, accident at Wembley |
|  | 56088 | 1427 Wolverhampton - Paddington | Wolverhampton - Paddington | Diverted to Paddington, accident at Wembley |
|  | 56088 | 1120 Paddington - Wolverhampton | Paddington - Wolverhampton | Started at Paddington, accident at Wembley |
| 15-Nov-84 | 56135 | ?   ? - Holyhead | Crewe - Holyhead & return | On test, 47465 providing ETH only |
| 9-Dec-84 | 56060 | 2040 Paddington - Birmingham New St | Paddington - Birmingham New St | Started at St Pancras, OHL problems on WCML |
| 23-Dec-84 | 56097 | 1200 Euston - Wolverhampton | Nuneaton - Wolverhampton | Drag |
| 6-Jan-85 | 56118 | 0857 Wolverhampton - Euston | Birmingham NS - Nuneaton | Drag, 86252 |
|  | 56118 | 1000 Euston - Wolverhampton | Nuneaton - Birmingham NS | Drag, 87009 |
| 9-Feb-85 | 56115 | 1620 Liverpool LS - Newcastle | Ouston Jn - Newcastle | 47523 failed |

*115*

| Date | Grid | Train Details | Grid Worked Train From / To | Notes |
|---|---|---|---|---|
| 15-Feb-85 | 56091 | 1545 Euston - Carlisle | ? - ? | noted at Warrington, drag 87035 |
|  | 56091 | 1827 Blackpool - Euston | ? - ? | noted at Warrington, drag 86212 |
| 3-Mar-85 | 56116 | 1200 Wolverhampton - Euston | Birmingham NS - Nuneaton | Drag |
|  | 56116 | 1200 Euston - Wolverhampton | Nuneaton - Birmingham NS | Drag |
|  | 56116 | 1500 Wolverhampton - Euston | Birmingham NS - Nuneaton | Drag |
| 9-Mar-85 | 56088 | 1230 Birmingham NS - Peterborough | ? - Nuneaton | 31413 failed, assisted at rear |
| 24-Mar-85 | 56087 | 2325 Euston - Wolverhampton (23/3) | Nuneaton - Birmingham NS | Drag, 86425 |
|  | 56090 | 0857 Wolverhampton - Euston | Birmingham NS - Nuneaton | Drag |
| 31-Mar-85 | 56078 | 1200 Wolverhampton - Euston | Birmingham NS - Nuneaton | Drag, 86244 |
|  | 56078 | 1200 Euston - Wolverhampton | Nuneaton - Wolverhampton | Drag |
|  | 56078 | 1500 Wolverhampton - Euston | Wolverhampton - Nuneaton | Drag |
| 8-Jun-85 | 56070 | 1805 Liverpool LS - Newcastle | Stalybridge - Leeds ? / Newcastle ? | 47541 failed, though providing ETH |
| 28-Jun-85 | 56127 | 2145 Newcastle - King's Cross | Retford - Peterborough | HST failed |
| 30-Jun-85 | 56083 | 2335 Glasgow Central - Bristol TM (29/6) | Stafford - Birmingham NS | Drag, with 47571 providing ETH only |
| 28-Jul-85 | 56039/043 | "Darkle Dungeneer" | Westbury - Bristol TM | Pathfinder Railtours, in multiple |
|  | 56047/049 | "Darkle Dungeneer" | Bristol TM -Ashford - Westbury | In multiple |
| 18-Aug-85 | 56072 | 0827 Birmingham NS - Blackpool North | Wigan NW - Lostock Jn | Drag |
| 21-Sep-85 | 56084 | 1940 Euston - Wolverhampton | Nuneaton - Birmingham NS | Drag, 86207 |
| 4-Oct-85 | 56134 | 1043 Carlisle - Newcastle | Wylam - Newcastle | DMU failed |
| 13-Oct-85 | 56073 | 1200 Wolverhampton - Euston | Wolverhampton - Nuneaton | Drag, 87034 |
|  | 56073 | 1200 Euston - Wolverhampton | Nuneaton - Wolverhampton | Drag, 87014 |
|  | 56073 | 1500 Wolverhampton - Euston | Wolverhampton - Nuneaton | Drag, 87011 |
|  | 56082 | 2340 Glasgow Central - Bristol TM (12/10) | Stafford - Birmingham NS | Drag, with 47407 |
| 24-Oct-85 | 56071 | 1018 Birmingham NS - Euston | ? - ? | Drag, poss worked other drags on this day |
| 30-Oct-85 | 56056 | 1343 Swansea - Paddington | Patchway - Paddington | 43126 / 43165 failed |
| 13-Jan-86 | 56042 | 1105 Glasgow Central - Euston | Carlisle Goods Line - Carlisle Goods Line | Drag |
| 25-Mar-86 | 56034 | 0923 Penzance - Paddington | Westbury - Paddington | 47484 failed |
| 9-May-86 | 56023 | 1445 Leeds - King's Cross | Doncaster - King's Cross | HST failed |
|  | 56023 | 1850 King's Cross - Harrogate | King's Cross - Leeds | Assisted 43039 / 43109, terminated Leeds |
| 19-May-86 | 56098 | 1130 King's Cross - Dundee? | ? - ? | HST failed, reported at Doncaster |
| 15-Jun-86 | 56027 | 0903 Wolverhampton - Dover | Wolverhampton - Nuneaton | Drag |
|  | 56027 | 0900 Euston - Wolverhampton | Nuneaton - Birmingham NS | Drag, 86261 |
|  | 56027 | 1200 Wolverhampton - Euston | Birmingham NS - Nuneaton | Drag |
|  | 56027 | 1200 Euston - Shrewsbury | Nuneaton - Birmingham NS | Drag, 86316 |
|  | 56027 | 1500 Wolverhampton - Euston | Birmingham NS - Nuneaton | Drag |
| 22-Jun-86 | 56113 | 0856 Wolverhampton - Euston | Wolverhampton - Rugby | Drag, 86247 |
|  | 56113 | 0845 Manchester Piccadilly - Euston | Nuneaton - Rugby? | Drag |
|  | 56113 | 1000 Euston - Wolverhampton | Nuneaton - Birmingham NS | Drag, poss worked more drags on this day |
| 27-Jul-86 | 56012 | 0756 Wolverhampton - Euston | Birmingham NS - Nuneaton | Drag |
| 8-Aug-86 | 56042 | 1044? Fareham - York | Derby - York | BR charter, 47315 failed |
| 9-Aug-86 | 56066 | 0820 Newcastle - Llandudno | Chester - Llandudno | 45135 failed |
| 15-Aug-86 | 56057 | 0920 Euston - Holyhead | Crewe - Holyhead | On test, 47651 providing ETH only |
| 21-Aug-86 | 56067 | 0920 Euston - Holyhead | Crewe - Holyhead | On test, 47xxx providing ETH only |
| 29-Aug-86 | 56038 | 0920 Euston - Holyhead | Crewe - Holyhead | On test, 47540 providing ETH only |
| 10-Sep-86 | 56038 | 0920 Euston - Holyhead | Crewe - Holyhead | On test, 47415 providing ETH only |
| 13-Sep-86 | 56089 | 1740 Euston - Shrewsbury | Wolverhampton - Shrewsbury | 47641 failed |
| 14-Sep-86 | 56040 | 1015 Paddington - Weston SM | Paddington ? - Swindon |  |
| 2-Nov-86 | 56092 | 1620 Birmingham NS - Preston | Birmingham NS - Stafford | Drag 86242, OHL isolation overrun at ? |
|  | 56092 | 1421? Preston - Euston | Stafford - Birmingham NS | Drag 86231, OHL isolation overrun at ? |
| 20-Dec-86 | 56036 | ?   Paddington - Cardiff | Near Slough ? - ? | 47458 failed |
| 11-Jan-87 | 56019 | 1900 Nottingham - St Pancras | Nottingham - St Pancras |  |
|  | 56064 | 0005 St Pancras - Derby | Lenton Sth Jn - Derby |  |
| 12-Jan-87 | 56001 | 0100 Faversham? - London Victoria | Maidstone - London Victoria | EMU lost power/traction - ice & snow |
| 13-Jan-87 | 56001 | ?   London Victoria - ? | ? - ? | EMU lost power/traction - ice & snow |
|  | 56027/073 | 1705 Nottingham - St Pancras | Attenborough - Leicester | In multiple? |
| 14-Jan-87 | 56001 | ?   ? - London Victoria | ? - ? (seen at Rainham) | EMU lost power/traction - ice & snow |
|  | 56001 | 1600 London Victoria - Faversham | London Victoria - Faversham | EMU lost power/traction - ice & snow |
|  | 56021 | 0935 Lincoln - Birmingham NS | Beeston - Derby |  |
|  | 56062 | 1117 Charing Cross - Orpington | Charing Cross - Orpington | EMU lost power/traction - ice & snow |
|  | 56073 | ?   ? - ? | Kettering - Leeds |  |
| 15-Jan-87 | 56001 | ?   London Victoria - Rainham | London Victoria - Rainham | EMU lost power/traction - ice & snow |
|  | 56001 | ?   Rainham - London Victoria | Rainham - London Victoria | EMU lost power/traction - ice & snow |
|  | 56001 | 1734 London Victoria - Ashford | London Victoria - Ashford | EMU lost power/traction - ice & snow |
|  | 56001 | ?   Ashford - London Victoria | Ashford - London Victoria | EMU lost power/traction - ice & snow |
|  | 56062 | ?   ? - London Victoria | ? - London Victoria | EMU lost power/traction - ice & snow |
|  | 56062 | 1545 London Victoria - Rainham | London Victoria - Rainham | EMU lost power/traction - ice & snow |
| 16-Jan-87 | 56001 | 0903 London Victoria - Dover Priory? | London Victoria - Dover Priory? | EMU lost power/traction - ice & snow |
|  | 56001 | ?   London Victoria - Rainham | London Victoria - Rainham | EMU lost power/traction - ice & snow |
|  | 56001 | ?   Rainham - London Victoria | Rainham - London Victoria | EMU lost power/traction - ice & snow |
|  | 56001 | ?   London Victoria - Rainham | London Victoria - Rainham | EMU lost power/traction - ice & snow |
|  | 56062 | 1822 Faversham - London Victoria | Faversham - London Victoria | EMU lost power/traction - ice & snow |
| 17-Jan-87 | 56062 | 1024 London Victoria - Ramsgate | London Victoria - Ramsgate | EMU lost power/traction - ice & snow |
|  | 56062 | 1407 Ramsgate - London Victoria | Ramsgate - London Victoria | EMU lost power/traction - ice & snow |
|  | 56062 | 1824 London Victoria - Ramsgate | London Victoria - Ramsgate | EMU lost power/traction - ice & snow |
| 30-Jan-87 | 56024 | 0920 Euston - Holyhead | Crewe - ? | On test, 47xxx providing ETH only |
| 31-Jan-87 | 56023 | 1925 Euston - Liverpool LS | Rugby - Nuneaton | Drag |
|  | 56024 | 0920 Euston - Holyhead | Crewe - ? | On test, 47640 providing ETH only |
| 1-Feb-87 | 56077 | 1410 Newcastle - Poole | Clay Cross - Derby | In multiple with 58008 |
| 5-Feb-87 | 56061 | 0920 Euston - Holyhead | Crewe - ? | On test, 47598 providing ETH only |
| 11-Feb-87 | 56033 | 1720 Paddington - Milford Haven | Port Talbot - Swansea |  |
|  | 56061 | 0920 Euston - Holyhead | Crewe - Holyhead | On test, 47530 providing ETH only |
| 13-Feb-87 | 56046 | 0920 Euston - Holyhead | Crewe - Holyhead | On test, 47xxx providing ETH only |
| 15-Feb-87 | 56096 | 0920 Euston - Holyhead | Crewe - Holyhead | On test, 47615 providing ETH only |
| 20-Feb-87 | 56024 | 0920 Euston - Holyhead | Crewe - Holyhead | On test, 47434 providing ETH only |
| 25-Feb-87 | 56096 | 0920 Euston - Holyhead | Crewe - Holyhead | On test, 47615 providing ETH only |
| 10-Mar-87 | 56094 | 1333 Shrewsbury - Euston | Canley - Coventry |  |
| 12-Mar-87 | 56040 | 0930 Euston - Holyhead | Crewe - Holyhead | On test, 47xxx providing ETH only |
| 15-Mar-87 | 56062 | 1605 Sheffield - St Pancras | Sheffield - Leicester | Train terminated at Leicester |
|  | 56086 | 0822 Wolverhampton - Brighton | Birmingham NS - Nuneaton | Drag, 86425 |
|  | 56086 | 0903 Wolverhampton - Dover WD | Castle Bromwich - Nuneaton | 58009 failed whilst dragging 87018 |
|  | 56094 | 2310? Glasgow Central - Bristol TM (14/3) | Stafford - Birmingham NS | Drag, with 47547 providing ETH only |
| 17-Mar-87 | 56045 | 0920 Euston - Holyhead | Crewe - Holyhead | On test, 47530 providing ETH only |
| 24-Mar-87 | 56089 | 0920 Euston - Holyhead | Crewe - Holyhead | On test, 47xxx providing ETH only |
| 27-Mar-87 | 56069 | ?   ? - Euston | ? - St Pancras | Diverted to St Pancras |

| Date | Grid | Train Details | Grid Worked Train From / To | Notes |
|---|---|---|---|---|
| 29-Mar-87 | 56093 | 2310 Glasgow Central - Bristol TM (28/3) | Stafford - Birmingham NS | Drag, with 47540 providing ETH only |
|  | 56094 | 1300 Wolverhampton - Euston | Birmingham NS - Nuneaton | Drag, poss worked more drags on this day |
| 3-Apr-87 | 56024 | 0920 Euston - Holyhead | Crewe - Holyhead | On test, 47xxx providing ETH only |
| 6-Apr-87 | 56066 | 0632 Sheffield - Nottingham | Toton Centre - Nottingham |  |
| 12-Apr-87 | 56013 | 2350 Glasgow Central - Bristol TM (11/4) | Stafford - Birmingham NS | Drag, with 47503 providing ETH only |
| 15-Apr-87 | 56089 | 0920 Euston - Holyhead | Crewe - Holyhead | On test, 47615 providing ETH only |
| 21-Apr-87 | 56038 | 0812 Paignton - Paddington | Newbury - Paddington |  |
| 3-May-87 | 56033 | "Hastings Belle" | Bristol TM - London Victoria | Pathfinder Tours |
|  |  |  | Norwood Jn - Eastbourne |  |
|  |  |  | Hastings - London Bridge - Paddington |  |
|  | 56048 | "Hastings Belle" | Paddington - Bristol TM |  |
| 13-May-87 | 56090 | 0755 Coventry - Holyhead | Crewe - Holyhead | On test, 47xxx providing ETH only |
| 20-May-87 | 56090 | ? Euston - Holyhead | Crewe - Holyhead | On test, 47439 providing ETH only |
|  | 56090 | 1300 Holyhead - Euston | Holyhead - Crewe | On test, 47439 providing ETH only |
| 21-May-87 | 56090 | 1300 Holyhead - Euston | Holyhead - Crewe | On test, 47439 providing ETH only |
| 22-May-87 | 56090 | 0755 Coventry - Holyhead | Crewe - Holyhead | On test, 47xxx providing ETH only |
| 28-May-87 | 56090 | 1D43 0935 Euston - Holyhead | Crewe - Holyhead | On test, 47439 providing ETH only |
| 7-Jun-87 | 56081 | "Meldon Quarryman" | Birmingham NS - Westbury & return | Branch Line Society |
| 10-Jun-87 | 56044 | 0935 Euston - Holyhead | Crewe - Holyhead | On test, 47619 providing ETH only |
| 15-Jun-87 | 56046 | 1D33 0755 Coventry - Holyhead | Crewe - Holyhead | On test, 47xxx providing ETH only |
| 17-Jun-87 | 56044 | 1D43 0935 Euston - Holyhead | Crewe - Holyhead | On test, 47xxx providing ETH only |
| 18-Jun-87 | 56046 | 1D33 0755 Coventry - Holyhead | Crewe - Holyhead | On test, 47456 providing ETH only |
| 18-Jun-87 | 56046 | 1255 Holyhead - Euston | Holyhead - Crewe | On test, 47456 providing ETH only |
| 20-Jun-87 | 56124 | 1122? Sheffield - Liverpool LS | Irlam? / Sheffield? - Liverpool LS | 31462 failed |
| 26-Jun-87 | 56088 | 0935 Euston - Holyhead | Crewe - Holyhead | On test, 47632 providing ETH only |
| 1-Jul-87 | 56062 | 1710 Harwich PQ - Wolverhampton | Manton Jn - Wolverhampton |  |
| 3-Jul-87 | 56061 | 1420 Birmingham NS - Ipswich | Leicester - Peterborough | 31409 failed |
|  | 56088 | 0935 Euston - Holyhead | Crewe - Holyhead | On test, 47620 providing ETH only |
|  | 56125 | 1300 King's Cross - ? | Morpeth - Edinburgh Waverley | 43075 / 43159 failed, terminated at Edinburgh |
| 12-Jul-87 | 56080 | 1656? Wolverhampton - Euston | Birmingham NS - Nuneaton | Drag, 86227 |
| 23-Jul-87 | 56049 | 0935 Euston - Holyhead | Crewe - Holyhead | On test, 47616 providing ETH only |
| 26-Jul-87 | 56090 | ? ? - Holyhead  (1144 ex Crewe) | Crewe - Holyhead | On test, 47456 providing ETH only |
| 27-Jul-87 | 56049 | 0935 Euston - Holyhead | Crewe - Holyhead | On test, 47xxx providing ETH only |
| 28-Jul-87 | 56049 | 0935 Euston - Holyhead | Crewe - Holyhead | On test, 47xxx providing ETH only |
| 29-Jul-87 | 56049 | 0935 Euston - Holyhead | Crewe - Holyhead | On test, 47428 providing ETH only |
| 31-Jul-87 | 56090 | 0935 Euston - Holyhead | Crewe - Holyhead | On test, 47xxx providing ETH only |
| 9-Aug-87 | 56016 | 1311 Lancaster - Euston | Wolverhampton - Nuneaton | Drag |
| 13-Aug-87 | 56055 | 0720 Glasgow Central - Penzance | Bristol Parkway - Bristol TM |  |
| 18-Aug-87 | 56068 | 0755 Coventry - Holyhead | Crewe - Holyhead | On test, 47438 providing ETH only |
|  | 56068 | 1255 Holyhead - Euston | Holyhead - Crewe | On test, 47438 providing ETH only |
| 19-Aug-87 | 56059 | 1830 Birmingham NS - Norwich | Leicester - Peterborough | 31xxx failed |
| 21-Aug-87 | 56071 | 0845 Ayr - Euston | Rugby - Euston | 87006 failed |
| 22-Aug-87 | 56004 | "Northumbrian" | Newcastle - Ryhope Grange Jn - Morpeth | Pathfinder Tours |
|  | 56016 | "Northumbrian" | Birmingham NS - Carlisle & return |  |
| 26-Aug-87 | 56062 | 1640 Norwich - Birmingham NS | Manton Jn - Leicester | 31xxx failed |
| 1-Sep-87 | 56067 | 0935 Euston - Holyhead | Crewe - Chester | On test, 56067 failed at Chester |
| 2-Sep-87 | 56067 | 0935 Euston - Holyhead | Crewe - Bangor | On test, 56067 failed at Bangor |
| 3-Sep-87 | 56067 | 0935 Euston - Holyhead | Crewe ? - Holyhead | On test, 47520 providing ETH only |
| 5-Sep-87 | 56082 | 0955 Weymouth - Newcastle | Doncaster - Newcastle | 47567 failed |
| 15-Sep-87 | 56067 | 0935 Euston - Holyhead | Crewe - Holyhead | On test, 47xxx providing ETH only |
| 16-Sep-87 | 56014 | 0030 Manchester P - Euston | Rugby - Northampton |  |
| 24-Sep-87 | 56067 | 0935 Euston - Holyhead | Crewe - Holyhead | On test, 47xxx providing ETH only |
| 6-Oct-87 | 56090 | 1400 Euston - Glasgow Central | ? - Rugby | 87013 failed |
| 14-Oct-87 | 56061 | 0811 Exeter SD - London Waterloo | Whitchurch - Basingstoke | 50xxx failed, assisted at rear |
| 17-Oct-87 | 56097 | 1055 Oxford - Paddington | Reading - Paddington |  |
| 23-Oct-87 | 56076 | 0935 Euston - Holyhead | Crewe - Holyhead | On test, 47459 providing ETH only |
| 28-Oct-87 | 56033 | 0904 Canterbury ? - Liverpool LS | Canterbury ? - Mitre Bridge Jn |  |
| 3-Nov-87 | 56012 | 1355 Dover ? - Liverpool LS | Bescot - Stafford |  |
| 6-Nov-87 | 56011 | 0930 Euston - Holyhead | Crewe - Holyhead | On test, 47xxx providing ETH only |
| 11-Nov-87 | 56052 | 0930 Euston - Holyhead | Crewe - Holyhead | On test, 47xxx providing ETH only |
| 19-Nov-87 | 56108 | 0930 Euston - Holyhead | Crewe - Holyhead | On test, 47xxx providing ETH only |
| 22-Nov-87 | 56101 | 1715 York - King's Cross | Doncaster - King's Cross | 47588 failed, train started at Doncaster |
|  | 56133 | 2310 Glasgow Central - Bristol TM (21/11) | Stafford - Birmingham NS | Drag, with 47558 providing ETH only |
| 27-Nov-87 | 56101 | 1730 King's Cross - Newcastle | Grantham - ? | HST failed |
| 29-Nov-87 | 56110 | 2350 Glasgow Central - Bristol TM (28/11) | Stafford - Birmingham NS | Drag, with 47543 providing ETH only |
| 30-Nov-87 | 56100 | 2310 Glasgow Central - Bristol TM (29/11) | Stafford - Birmingham NS | Drag, with 47543 providing ETH only |
| 3-Dec-87 | 56107 | 0930 Euston - Holyhead | Crewe - Holyhead | On test, 47xxx providing ETH only |
| 6-Dec-87 | 56067 | 0835 Liverpool LS - Euston | Birmingham NS - Nuneaton | Drag |
|  | 56067 | 1140 Euston - Wolverhampton | Nuneaton - Birmingham NS | Drag, 87029 |
|  | 56067 | 1430 Wolverhampton - Euston | Birmingham NS - Nuneaton | Drag, 86419 |
| 8-Dec-87 | 56107 | 0930 Euston - Holyhead | Crewe - Holyhead | On test, 47xxx providing ETH only |
| 9-Dec-87 | 56052 | 0755 Coventry - Holyhead | Crewe - Chester | On test, 47xxx providing ETH only |
| 14-Dec-87 | 56089 | 1531 Shrewsbury - Euston | Coventry - Rugby | OHL problems, drag 86412 |
| 16-Dec-87 | 56052 | 0930 Euston - Holyhead | Crewe - Holyhead | On test, 47523 providing ETH only |
| 17-Dec-87 | 56100 | 0935 Euston - Holyhead | Crewe - Holyhead | On test, 47571 providing ETH only |
| 23-Dec-87 | 56015 | 1D33 0755 Coventry - Holyhead | Crewe - Holyhead | On test, 47450 providing ETH only |
|  | 56015 | 1255 Holyhead - Euston | Holyhead - Crewe | On test, 47450 providing ETH only |
| 29-Dec-87 | 56015 | 0755 Coventry - Holyhead | Crewe - Llandudno Jn | On test, 47xxx providing ETH only |
| 10-Jan-88 | 56006 | 0800 Wolverhampton - Euston | Birmingham NS - Nuneaton | Drag, 86423 |
|  | 56006 | 1000 Wolverhampton - Euston | Birmingham NS - Nuneaton | Drag |
|  | 56022 | 2310 Glasgow Central - Bristol TM (9/1) | Stafford - Birmingham NS | Drag, with 47520 providing ETH only |
| 11-Jan-88 | 56040 | 1510 London Waterloo - Exeter SD | Gillingham - Exeter SD | 50027 failed |
| 12-Jan-88 | 56036 | 0633 Poole Manchester Piccadilly | Reading - Birmingham NS |  |
| 15-Jan-88 | 56052 | 0930 Euston - Holyhead | Crewe - Holyhead | On test, 47xxx providing ETH only |
| 22-Jan-88 | 56106 | 1442? Cheltenham Spa - Paddington | Gloucester - Paddington | HST suffered loss of adhesion - leaf fall |
| 24-Jan-88 | 56026 | 2310 Glasgow Central - Bristol TM (23/1) | Stafford - Birmingham NS | Drag, with 47481 providing ETH only |
|  | 56026 | 1556 Wolverhampton - Euston | Birmingham NS - Coventry | Drag |
| 25-Jan-88 | 56069 | 0930 Euston - Holyhead | Crewe - Holyhead | On test, 47xxx providing ETH only |
| 29-Jan-88 | 56069 | 0755 Coventry - Holyhead | Crewe - Holyhead | On test, 47xxx providing ETH only |
| 2-Feb-88 | 56069 | 0755 Coventry - Holyhead | Crewe - Holyhead | On test, 47xxx providing ETH only |
| 21-Mar-88 | 56041 | 2010 London Waterloo - Exeter SD | Yeovil Pen Mill - Exeter SD | 50010 failed |
| 26-Mar-88 | 56004 | 0720 Harwich PQ - Manchester Piccadilly | Alfreton & Mansfield Parkway - Sheffield | 47472 failed |
| 8-Apr-88 | 56070 | 1530 Portsmouth Harbour - Waterloo | Liphook - Haslemere | 50047 failed, terminated at Haslemere |
| 15-Apr-88 | 56041 | 1725 Paddington - Westbury | Newbury - Westbury |  |

117

| Date | Grid | Train Details | Grid Worked Train From / To | Notes |
|---|---|---|---|---|
| 20-Apr-88 | 56122 | 1038 Poole - Newcastle | M.P. 66 3/4 (Near Durham) - Newcastle | 45141 failed |
| 23-Apr-88 | 56092 | 0806 Peterborough - Lincoln Central | Cherry Holt L.C. - Spalding | Dragged train back to Spalding |
| 3-May-88 | 56019 | 0930 Euston - Holyhead | Crewe - Holyhead | On test, 47435 providing ETH only |
| 6-May-88 | 56019 | 1238 Poole - Manchester Piccadilly | Banbury - Birmingham NS | |
| 8-May-88 | 56019 | 1311 Lancaster - Euston | Birmingham NS - Nuneaton | Drag |
| | 56108 | 1148 Southampton Cent. - Glasgow Cent. | Birmingham NS - Stafford | Drag |
| 12-May-88 | 56014 | 0930 Euston - Holyhead | Crewe - Holyhead | On test, 47453 providing ETH only |
| 15-May-88 | 56073 | 1515? Leeds - King's Cross | Doncaster - King's Cross | 47523 failed, train started at Doncaster |
| 24-May-88 | 56069 | 0950 Euston - Holyhead | Crewe - Holyhead | On test, 47xxx providing ETH only |
| 1-Jun-88 | 56033 | 0940 Plymouth - Portsmouth ? | Salisbury - Portsmouth ? | |
| | 56033 | 1530 Portsmouth ? - London Waterloo | Portsmouth ? - London Waterloo | |
| | 56033 | 1810 London Waterloo - Exeter SD | London Waterloo - Salisbury | |
| 23-Jun-88 | 56027 | 0950 Euston - Holyhead | Crewe - Holyhead | On test, 47526 providing ETH only |
| | 56027 | ?  Holyhead - ? | Holyhead - Crewe | On test, 47526 providing ETH only |
| 30-Jun-88 | 56106 | 0630 Plymouth - York | Aldwarke Jn - Doncaster | Train terminated at Doncaster |
| | 56126 | 0550 Newcastle - Hexham | Newcastle - Hexham | |
| | 56126 | 0647 Hexham - Newcastle | Hexham - Newcastle | |
| 13-Jul-88 | 56027 | 0950 Euston - Holyhead | Crewe - Holyhead | On test, 47xxx providing ETH only |
| 21-Jul-88 | 56126 | 1840 Darlington - Newcastle | Darlington - Newcastle | |
| 24-Jul-88 | 56022 | 1625 Manchester Piccadilly - Euston | Watford Jn - Euston | |
| 17-Aug-88 | 56004 | 1829 Skegness - Burton-on-Trent | Skegness - Derby | |
| 21-Aug-88 | 56028 | 0045 Holyhead - Euston | Rugby - Tring | |
| 30-Aug-88 | 56048 | 0950 Euston - Holyhead | Crewe - Holyhead | On test, 47xxx providing ETH only |
| 18-Sep-88 | 56101 | 0948 Wolverhampton - Euston | Birmingham NS - Nuneaton | Drag, 87007 |
| | 56101 | 0940 Euston - Shrewsbury | Nuneaton - Birmingham NS | Drag, 86437 |
| | 56101 | 1248 Wolverhampton - Euston | Birmingham NS - Nuneaton | Drag, 87013 |
| | 56101 | 1200 Euston - Birmingham NS? | Nuneaton - Birmingham NS | Drag |
| 24-Sep-88 | 56023 | "Test Valley Rambler" | Woking - Basingstoke | Woking 88 Committee tour, in multiple with 58014 |
| 7-Oct-88 | 56030 | 1340 Euston - Shrewsbury | Nuneaton - Birmingham NS | Drag |
| 16-Oct-88 | 56001 | 1605 Paddington - Taunton? / Plymouth? | M.P. 31 1/2 (Near Twyford) - Reading | 50042 failed, 56001 assisted at rear while on Brentford-Appleford 'Bins' |
| 3-Nov-88 | 56081 | 0030 Manchester Piccadilly - Euston | Rugby - Northampton | |
| 27-Nov-88 | 56017 | 1110 King's Cross - Leeds | Stoke Summit - Doncaster | Train terminated at Doncaster |
| 11-Dec-88 | 56060 | 1710 Brighton - Plymouth | Brighton - Preston Park | |
| 5-Jan-89 | 56004 | 1441 Birmingham NS - Paddington | Fenny Compton - Banbury | 50037 failed |
| 21-Jan-89 | 56042 | 1530 St Pancras - Sheffield | Leicester - Derby | HST failed, train terminated at Derby |
| 14-Feb-89 | 56074 | 2021 Hull - Sheffield | Rotherham Masborough - Sheffield | DMU failed |
| 23-Feb-89 | 56058 | 1330 Manchester Piccadilly - Euston | Nuneaton - St Pancras | Diverted to St Pancras, bomb scare on WCML |
| | 56058 | 1800 St Pancras - Carlisle | St Pancras - Nuneaton | Started St Pancras, bomb scare on WCML |
| | 56060 | 1430 Manchester Piccadilly - Euston | Nuneaton - St Pancras | Diverted to St Pancras, bomb scare on WCML |
| | 56060 | 1908 St Pancras - Blackpool North | St Pancras - Crewe | Started St Pancras, bomb scare on WCML |
| | 56063 | ?  ? - Euston | Nuneaton - St Pancras | Diverted to St Pancras, bomb scare on WCML |
| | 56063 | 2055 St Pancras - Carlisle | St Pancras - Crewe | Started St Pancras, bomb scare on WCML |
| 21-May-89 | 56017 | "InterCity Diesel Day" | Leicester - St Pancras & return | Hertfordshire Rail Tours |
| 29-May-89 | 56036 | 1728 Paddington - Bristol TM | Paddington - Bristol TM | No HSTs available |
| 12-Jun-89 | 56039 | 1618 Manchester Piccadilly - Plymouth | Yate - BTM | 47xxx failed |
| 17-Jun-89 | 56046 | 1302 Paddington - Paignton | Westbury - Exeter SD | 50023 failed |
| 25-Jun-89 | 56039 | "Westbury Open Day Specials" | Bristol - Westbury & return x 2 | Regional Railways charter |
| 20-Jul-89 | 56004 | 1824 Lancaster - Euston | Nuneaton - St Pancras | Diverted to St Pancras - Harrow derailment |
| 21-Jul-89 | 56004 | 0710? St Pancras - Manchester Picc. | St Pancras - Manchester Piccadilly | Started St Pancras - Harrow derailment |
| 30-Jul-89 | 56002 | 0910 Edinburgh Wav. - Manchester Picc. | Preston - Manchester Piccadilly | No 47s available |
| 4-Sep-89 | 56004 | 1710 Poole - Manchester Piccadilly | Leamington Spa - Birmingham NS | 47612 failed |
| 10-Sep-89 | 56050 | 1805 Brighton - Wolverhampton | Brighton - Redhill | 47808 failed |
| 13-Sep-89 | 56035 | 1610 Paddington - Penzance | Bedwyn - Plymouth | 43140 / 43160 failed |
| 14-Sep-89 | 56087 | 1442 York - Bristol TM | Wakefield ? - Sheffield | 47833 failed, train terminated at Sheffield |
| 30-Sep-89 | 56062 | "Cambridge Gala Specials" | Cambridge - Kings Lynn & return x 3 | With a pair of 31s |
| 2-Oct-89 | 56068 | 1410 King's Cross - Leeds | Doncaster - Leeds | 91008 failed |
| 5-Oct-89 | 56048 | 0918 Plymouth - Paddington | Westbury - Paddington | HST failed |
| 9-Oct-89 | 56036 | 1315 Cardiff Central - Liverpool LS | Hereford - Crewe | 37407 failed |
| 4-Nov-89 | 56104 | 0825 Leeds - Carlisle | Leeds - Carlisle | Settle & Carlisle pilots, 47503 providing ETH only |
| | 56104 | 1242 Carlisle - Leeds | Carlisle - Leeds | Settle & Carlisle pilots, 47503 providing ETH only |
| 11-Nov-89 | 56030 | 0825 Leeds - Carlisle | Leeds - Carlisle | Settle & Carlisle pilots, 47475 providing ETH only |
| | 56030 | 1242 Carlisle - Leeds | Carlisle - Leeds | Settle & Carlisle pilots, 47475 providing ETH only |
| 13-Nov-89 | 56026 | 0900 Poole - Newcastle | Banbury - Birmingham NS | 47537 failed |
| 18-Nov-89 | 56099 | 0825 Leeds - Carlisle | Leeds - Carlisle | Settle & Carlisle pilots, 47477 providing ETH only |
| | 56099 | 1242 Carlisle - Leeds | Carlisle - Leeds | Settle & Carlisle pilots, 47477 providing ETH only |
| 27-Feb-90 | 56013 | 2355 Paddington - Penzance (26/2) | Treverrin Tunnel - Par - Penzance | 47815 failed, assisted at rear to Par |
| 16-Mar-90 | 56035 | 1318 Salisbury - London Waterloo | Salisbury - London Waterloo | No 47s/50s available |
| | 56035 | 1640 London Waterloo - Salisbury | London Waterloo - Salisbury | No 47s/50s available |
| 17-Mar-90 | 56075 | 0825 Leeds - Carlisle | Leeds - Carlisle | Settle & Carlisle pilots, 47453 providing ETH only |
| | 56075 | 1242 Carlisle - Leeds | Carlisle - Leeds | Settle & Carlisle pilots, 47453 providing ETH only |
| 31-Mar-90 | 56041 | "Mendip Quarryman" | Westbury - Cranmore & return | Pathfinder Tours |
| 14-Apr-90 | 56040 | 0740 Paddington - Plymouth | Westbury - Plymouth | 50024 failed |
| 3-Jun-90 | 56070 | "Coalville & Calverton Caboodle" | Nottingham - Calverton Colliery | Hertfordshire Rail Tours |
| | 56078 | "Coalville & Calverton Caboodle" | Coalville - Nottingham | Hertfordshire Rail Tours |
| | | | Calverton Colliery - Leicester | |
| 1-Jul-90 | 56034 | "Gloucester Rail Day Specials" | Bristol TM - Birmingham NS & return x 2 | Pathfinder Tours |
| 15-Jul-90 | 56110 | 1705 St Pancras - Sheffield | Market Harborough - Derby | HST failed |
| 4-Aug-90 | 56060 | 1700 St Pancras - Sheffield | St Pancras - Sheffield | HST failed |
| 19-Aug-90 | 56032 | "Tees Maid" | Bristol TM - Doncaster & return | Pathfinder Tours |
| | 56123 | "Tees Maid" | Doncaster - Saltburn | |
| | | | Redcar Central - Boulby Mine | |
| | | | Darlington - Doncaster | |
| 29-Sep-90 | 56065 | "Cambridge Gala Specials" | Kings Lynn - Cambridge & return x 2 | With a pair of 31s |
| | | | Kings Lynn - Cambridge | With a pair of 31s |
| 10-Oct-90 | 56103 | 1409 Colchester - Birmingham NS | East Suffolk Jn - Ipswich | 156xxx failed, dragged back to Ipswich |
| 13-Oct-90 | 56077 | "Humber Navigator 2" | Potters Grange Jn Headshunt - Sheffield | Branch Line Society |
| 20-Oct-90 | 56035 | "Network North West Gala Day" | Manchester Victoria - Barrow & return | Organised by Network North West |
| | | | Manchester Victoria - Liverpool LS | |
| 13-Nov-90 | 56135 | 1200 Edinburgh Waverley - King's Cross | Acklington - Newcastle | |
| 2-Dec-90 | 56040 | 1455 London Waterloo - Exeter SD | Westbury - Exeter SD | 50048 failed |
| 8-Dec-90 | 56077 | ? Leeds ? - Doncaster ? | ? - Doncaster | Class 307 lost power/traction - ice & snow |
| | 56091 | Leeds-King's Cross | ? - ? | 91005, lost power/traction - ice & snow |
| 9-Dec-90 | 56049 | ?  Orpington - Beckenham Jn | Bickley Jn - Beckenham | EMU lost power/traction - ice & snow |

| Date | Grid | Train Details | Grid Worked Train From / To | Notes |
|---|---|---|---|---|
| 9-Dec-90 | 56060 | 0628 Faversham - London Victoria | Swanley? - London Victoria | EMU lost power/traction - ice & snow |
| 5-Jan-91 | 56086 | 1810 King's Cross - Bradford FS | Doncaster - Leeds | |
| 12-Jan-91 | 56041 | "Marches Line Gala Day" | Cardiff Central - Crewe | With 47972 providing ETH only |
| | | | Crewe - Newport | With 47972 providing ETH only |
| 8-Feb-91 | 56045 | 1253 London Victoria - Ramsgate | Longfield - Gillingham | EMU lost power/traction - ice & snow 47206, assisted at rear |
| 9-Feb-91 | 56032 | ?  ? - ? | London Bridge? / Cannon Street? - Dartford | EMU lost power/traction - ice & snow |
| | 56034 | ?  ? - ? | Bedwyn - Exeter SD | |
| | 56043 | ?  ? - ? | ? - ? | EMU lost power/traction - ice & snow |
| | 56046 | ?  St Pancras - ? | ? - ? | HST failed |
| 10-Feb-91 | 56001 | 2003 London Victoria - Faversham | London Victoria - Faversham | EMU lost power/traction - ice & snow |
| | 56001 | ?  Faversham - London Victoria | Faversham - London Victoria | EMU lost power/traction - ice & snow |
| | 56043 | ?  ? - ? | ? - ? | EMU lost power/traction - ice & snow |
| 11-Feb-91 | 56001 | 0030 London Victoria - Faversham | London Victoria - Faversham | EMU failed (ice), staff train for public use |
| | 56001 | ?  Faversham - London Victoria | Faversham - London Victoria | EMU failed (ice), staff train for public use |
| | 56056 | ?  Faversham - London Victoria | Faversham - London Victoria | EMU lost power/traction - ice & snow |
| 28-Mar-91 | 56026 | 1845 Glasgow Central - Stockport | Preston - Stockport | No 47s available |
| 6-Apr-91 | 56004 | "East Midlands Railtour" | Corby N Jn - BSC Corby | Institute of Mining Engineers charter |
| | | | Melton Mowbray W Jn - Melton Mowbray | |
| | | | Asfordby Colliery - Melton Mowbray | |
| | | | Nr site of Syston Stn - Loughborough | |
| | | | Gedling Colliery - Bennerley Opencast Mine | |
| | | | Trent DGL - Derby | |
| 14-Apr-91 | 56018 | 1400 Euston - Manchester Piccadilly | Stoke-on-Trent - Manchester Piccadilly | |
| 4-May-91 | 56033 | The Sussex Scot | Brighton- Reading | 47811 failed |
| 5-May-91 | 56053 | "Hereford Swansong" | Abergavenny - Hereford | Trainload Freight |
| 18-May-91 | 56002 | "Nottingham Forest Footex" | St Pancras - Nottingham | |
| 21-May-91 | 56050 | 1620 Paddington - Maidenhead | Paddington - Maidenhead | No 47s/ 50s available |
| | 56050 | 1735 Reading - Newbury | Reading - Newbury | No 47s/ 50s available |
| 26-May-91 | 56015 | "Coal Scuttler" | Denby Disposal Point - Coalville | Pathfinder Tours |
| | 56018 | "Coal Scuttler" | Preston - Derby - Denby Disposal Point | |
| | 56021 | "Coal Scuttler" | Nuneaton - Bristol TM | |
| | 56015 | "Coalville Swansong" | Knighton UDGL - Leicester | Hertfordshire Rail Tours |
| | 56018 | "Coalville Swansong" | Coalville - Knighton UDGL | |
| 5-Jul-91 | 56039 | 1418 Brighton - Manchester Piccadilly | Brighton - Birmingham NS | |
| 17-Jul-91 | 56015 | Liverpool LS - Paddington | Liverpool LS - Crewe | No 47/8s available |
| 4-Aug-91 | 56038 | "Gloucester Rail Day' | Gloucester - Nr Westerleigh Yd | Pathfinder Tours, with 37891 |
| 6-Aug-91 | 56006 | 1230 Liverpool St - Norwich | Stowmarket - Norwich | 86237 failed |
| 11-Aug-91 | 56009/028 | "Train Load Coal Motive Power Day" | Crewe - Llandudno & return | In multiple |
| | 56111/112 | "Train Load Coal Motive Power Day" | Crewe - Llandudno Jn - Derby | In multiple |
| 18-Aug-91 | 56022/025 | "The Strider" | Nuneaton - Paddington & return | Pathfinder Tours, in multiple |
| | 56034 | "Didcot Lupin" | Paddington - Didcot PS - Paddington | Hertfordshire Rail Tours |
| | 56055 | 1835 Paddington - Plymouth | Westbury - Plymouth | HST failed |
| 24-Aug-91 | 56059 | ?  Leeds - London Victoria VSOE | Luton - London Victoria | Sea Containers VSOE charter, 47818 failed |
| 1-Sep-91 | 56007 | "Worksop Open Day Specials" | Worksop - Elmton & Cresswell Jn | |
| | | | Chesterfield - Elmton & Cresswell Jn | |
| | | | Worksop - Doncaster | |
| | | | Worksop - Elmton & Cresswell Jn | |
| | | | Chesterfield - Elmton & Cresswell Jn | |
| | | | Worksop - Doncaster | |
| 3-Sep-91 | 56037 | 0918 Brighton - Glasgow Central | Brighton - Reading ? / Birmingham NS | 47841 failed |
| 14-Sep-91 | 56012 | "Cambridge Gala Specials" | Kings Lynn - Cambridge | With a pair of 31s |
| | | | Cambridge - Kings Lynn | With 60048 and a pair of 31s |
| | | | Kings Lynn - Cambridge | With a pair of 31s |
| | | | Cambridge - Kings Lynn | With a pair of 31s |
| | 56070 | 0707 Nottingham - St Pancras | Nottingham - St Pancras | No HSTs available |
| | 56110 | 0930 St Pancras - Nottingham | St Pancras - Nottingham | No HSTs available |
| | 56110 | 1137 Nottingham - St Pancras | Nottingham - St Pancras | No HSTs available |
| | 56110 | 1737 Nottingham - St Pancras | Nr Chiltern Green Village - St Pancras | 31408 failed substituting for an HST |
| 15-Sep-91 | 56016 | 0045 Liverpool LS - Stoke-on-Trent | Kidsgrove - Stoke-on-Trent | 47582 failed |
| | 56050/051 | "Tamar Tart" | Bristol TM - Plymouth | Pathfinder Tours, in multiple |
| | | | Plymouth Friary Depot - Laira Carriage Plat. | |
| | 56050/051 | "Plym Rose" | Exeter SD - Paddington | Hertfordshire Rail Tours, in multiple |
| 22-Sep-91 | 56037 | "Brighton Main Line Diesel Day Specials" | London Victoria - Brighton | BRC&W Type 3 Pres' Group |
| | 56057 | "Brighton Main Line Diesel Day Specials" | Brighton - London Victoria | BRC&W Type 3 Pres' Group |
| 13-Oct-91 | 56114 | "North Tyne" | Widdrington Colliery - Widdrington Exc. Sdgs | Institution of Mining Engineers |
| | | | NrLonghirst Level Crossing - Ashington Jn | |
| | | | Lynemouth Colliery - Alcan Branch Jn | |
| | | | Lynemouth Alcan - Blyth Alcan | |
| | | | Freemans Jn - Blyth Power Station | |
| | | | Newsham North Jn - Bates Staiths | |
| 14-Oct-91 | 56016 | 0710 Manchester Piccadilly - Euston | Macclesfield - Stafford | 87034 failed |
| 18-Oct-91 | 56034 | 1420 Brighton - Manchester Piccadilly | Balcombe - Reading | 47815 failed |
| 19-Nov-91 | 56024 | 2000 Manchester Piccadilly - Euston | Poynton - Stoke-on-Trent ? / Stafford ? | 87024 failed |
| 6-Dec-91 | 56020 | 1530 Manchester Piccadilly - Euston | Longport - Stafford | 87007 failed |
| 28-Dec-91 | 56055 | "Crompton Constructor" | Grain - Hoo Jn | Pathfinder Tours |
| | | | Sheerness-on-Sea - Dover WD | |
| 30-Dec-91 | 56117 | 1318 Carlisle - Leeds | Carlisle - Leeds | Settle & Carlisle pilots, 31418 providing ETH only |
| | 56134 | 0947 Leeds - Carlisle | Leeds - Carlisle | Settle & Carlisle pilots, 31418 providing ETH only |
| 31-Dec-91 | 56109 | 0947 Leeds - Carlisle | Leeds - Carlisle | Settle & Carlisle pilots, 47475 providing ETH only |
| 12-Jan-92 | 56119 | "Solent & Wessex Wanderer 2" | London Waterloo - Southampton Central | DC Tours, 33102 providing ETH only |
| | | | Southampton Central - Weymouth | with 33114 |
| | | | Weymouth - London Waterloo | with 33114 |
| 26-Jan-92 | 56019 | "Solent & Wessex Wanderer 4" | Eastleigh - Weymouth | 33114 providing ETH only |
| | | | Weymouth - Southampton | with 33114 |
| 9-Feb-92 | 56008/116 | "Southwark & Wandsworth Wanderette" | Waterloo - Virginia Water -Clapham Jn | DC Tours, in multiple |
| 22-Feb-92 | 56004 | "Meden-Maun" | Bilsthorpe Colliery - Rufford Colliery Jn | Pathfinder Tours |
| | | | Rufford Colliery - High Marnham PS | |
| | | | Bevercotes Colliery - Boughton Jn | |
| | | | Welbeck Colliery - Welbeck Colliery Jn | |
| 23-Feb-92 | 56020 | "Solent & Wessex Wanderer 7" | London Waterloo - Eastleigh | DC Tours, with 33116 |
| | | | Eastleigh - Basingstoke | with 20032 & 20007 |
| 27-Feb-92 | 56062 | 2054 Sheffield - St Pancras | Nr Chiltern Green Village - St Pancras | 43105/43122 failed |
| 1-Mar-92 | 56010 | "Thames & Weyside Wanderette" | London Waterloo - Woking - Clapham Jn | DC Tours |

| Date | Grid | Train Details | Grid Worked Train From / To | Notes |
|---|---|---|---|---|
| 27-Mar-92 | 56039 | 1850 Paddington - Plymouth | ? - Exeter SD | 47809 failed, terminated Exeter SD |
| 11-Apr-92 | 56080/095 | "Gainsborough Bridge 213 Special" | Cleethorpes - Sheffield | Regional Railways charter, in multiple |
| 16-Apr-92 | 56001 | 1747 Paddington - Westbury | Paddington - Westbury | No 47s/ 50s available |
|  | 56023 | 0640 Liverpool LS - Dover WD | St Mary Cray - Dover Priory | 47839 failed, terminated Dover Priory |
|  | 56023 | 1422 Dover WD - Liverpool LS | Dover Priory - Birmingham NS | 47839 failed, started Dover Priory |
| 18-Apr-92 | 56130 | "Blyth-Tyne Collier" | Crewe - Blyth Alcan |  |
|  |  |  | Nr Hirst Lane L.C. - Ryhope Grange Jn |  |
|  |  |  | Sunderland Sth Dock - Hartlepool PS |  |
|  |  |  | Hartlepool - Derby |  |
|  | 56120 | "Blyth-Tyne Collier" | Blyth Alcan - Nr Hirst Lane Level Crossing | Pathfinder Tours |
|  |  |  | Ryhope Grange Jn - Sunderland Sth Dock |  |
|  |  |  | Hartlepool Power Station - Hartlepool |  |
| 20-Apr-92 | 56001 | "Crewe Avoider" | Paddington - Hinksey Yd | Hertfordshire Rail Tours |
|  |  |  | Morris Cowley - Hinksey Yd |  |
| 22-Apr-92 | 56103 | 1405 Norwich - Liverpool St | Ipswich - Colchester | Drag 86218, OHL isolation nr Manningtree |
| 24-Apr-92 | 56041 | 1753 Paddington - Twyford | Paddington - Twyford | No 47s/ 50s available |
| 25-Apr-92 | 56106 | "Lancastrian 1" | Liverpool LS - Manchester Victoria | Pathfinder Tours |
| 26-Apr-92 | 56016 | 1330 Manchester Piccadilly - Euston | Stoke-on-Trent - Stafford | 87029 failed |
|  | 56091 | "Lancastrian 1" | Blackburn - Manchester Victoria | Pathfinder Tours |
| 2-May-92 | 56062 | "Aggregator" | Birmingham NS - Westbury & return | Pathfinder Tours |
|  | 56056 | "Aggregator" | Cranmore - Westbury Down Reception Sdg | Pathfinder Tours |
|  |  |  | Fairwood Jn - Clink Road Jn |  |
|  |  |  | Whatley Quarry - Westbury |  |
| 4-May-92 | 56011 | "North & West Enthusiasts Day" | Liverpool LS - Hereford & return | Regional Railways |
| 12-May-92 | 56010 | 1335 Birmingham NS - Manchester Picc | Stoke-on-Trent - ? | OHL problems at Prestbury |
|  | 56010 | 1500 Euston - Manchester Piccadilly | Stoke-on-Trent - Stockport | OHL problems at Prestbury |
|  | 56015 | 1200 Euston -Manchester Piccadilly | Macclesfield - Manchester Piccadilly | OHL problems at Prestbury |
| 30-May-92 | 56043 | "Brighton Rock" | Bognor Regis - Preston Park | A1A Charters |
| 6-Jun-92 | 56058 | "Denmark Grainette" | London Bridge - Denmark Hill - Victoria | Hertfordshire Rail Tours |
|  | 56063 | "Grain Train" | Euston - Ashford | Hertfordshire Rail Tours |
|  |  |  | Dover WD - Grain |  |
|  |  |  | Grain - Hoo Jn | with 60094, assisted at rear |
| 13-Jun-92 | 56009 | 1E31 Derby - Scarborough | Derby - Scarborough | 47822 failed |
|  | 56009 | 1013 Scarborough - Swansea | Scarborough - Derby | 47822 failed |
| 21-Jun-92 | 56033 | "Torbay & Dartmouth Railway Gala" | Paddington - Exeter SD & return | InterCity Great Western charter |
| 22-Jun-92 | 56055 | 0640 Liverpool LS - Dover WD | Nr Kensington Olympia - Dover Priory | 47836 failed |
| 27-Jun-92 | 56024 | "Dukeries Collier" | St Pancras - Thoresby Colliery Jn Sdgs | Hertfordshire Rail Tours |
|  |  |  | Thoresby Colliery - Thoresby Colliery Jn Sdgs |  |
|  |  |  | Thoresby Colliery Jn - High Marnham PS |  |
|  |  |  | Bevercotes Colliery - Boughton Jn |  |
|  |  |  | Bilsthorpe Colliery - Rufford Colliery Jn |  |
|  |  |  | Rufford Colliery - Welbeck Colliery Jn (Down) |  |
|  |  |  | Welbeck Colliery Jn (Up) - Welbeck Colliery |  |
|  |  |  | Welbeck Colliery Jn (Up) - Seymour Jn |  |
|  |  |  | Seymour Jn - Oxcroft Disposal Point | with 20059 & 20168, assisted at rear |
|  |  |  | Oxcroft Disposal Point - St Pancras |  |
| 28-Jun-92 | 56033 | 1655 Plymouth - Paddington | Westbury - Paddington | HST failed |
| 6-Sep-92 | 56003 | "Leicester Looper" | Derby - Leicester | Pathfinder Tours |
|  | 56003 | "Corby Circular" | Leicester - nr Kettering Station Jn |  |
|  | 56105 | "Corby Circular" | nr Kettering Station Jn - Leicester |  |
| 25-Sep-92 | 56057 | 0618 Birmingham NS - Stanstead Airport | Birmingham NS - Cambridge | No Sprinters available, terminated Cambridge |
|  | 56057 | 1116 Stanstead Airport - Birmingham NS | Cambridge - Birmingham NS | No Sprinters available, started Cambridge |
| 10-Oct-92 | 56069 | "Gaerwen Grid" | Crewe - Llandudno | Pathfinder Tours |
|  |  |  | Chester - Birmingham NS |  |
|  | 56097 | "Gaerwen Grid" | Llandudno - Holyhead - Chester |  |
| 15-Nov-92 | 56039 | "West of England Coalpower" | Salisbury - Exeter SD & return | DC Tours, with 33114 |
| 2-Jan-93 | 56007 | "Crompton Constructor 2" | Hither Green Yd - Angerstein Wharf | Pathfinder Tours |
|  |  |  | London Bridge - Haywards Heath |  |
|  |  |  | Ardingly - Haywards Heath |  |
| 10-Feb-93 | 56044 | 1V50 0648 Dundee - Penzance | Westerleigh Jn - Bristol Parkway | HST failed |
| 13-Feb-93 | 56128 | "Trent-Wreake" | Derby - Cotgrave Colliery | Pathfinder Tours |
|  |  |  | Netherfield Jn - Gedling Colliery |  |
|  |  |  | Calverton Colliery - Melton Jn |  |
|  |  |  | Edwalton - Melton Mowbray |  |
| 27-Mar-93 | 56126 | "Tyne-Tees Trekker" | Murton Colliery - Tyne Dock Bottom Sdgs | Pathfinder Tours |
|  |  |  | Tyne Dock Jn - Tyne Dock Coal Terminal |  |
|  |  |  | Jarrow Goods - Seal Sands Branch Jn |  |
|  | 56129 | "Tyne-Tees Trekker" | Newcastle - Murton Colliery |  |
|  |  |  | Tyne Dock Bottom Sdgs - Tyne Dock Jn |  |
|  |  |  | Tyne Dock Coal Terminal - Jarrow Goods |  |
|  |  |  | Seal Sands Branch Jn - Tees Yd |  |
| 24-Apr-93 | 56001 | "Scratcher" | London Waterloo - Salisbury | Pathfinder Tours |
|  | 56115 | "Scratcher" | Derby - Salisbury & return |  |
| 2-May-93 | 56103 | "Worcester Sorcerer" | Paddington - Worcester SH & return | Hertfordshire Rail Tours |
| 15-May-93 | 56031 | "Merry Wives" | Addiscombe - Windsor & Eton Riverside | A1A Charters |
|  | 56059 | "Cattle Grid" | Thorney Mill Yd - Brentford Goods | Hertfordshire Rail Tours |
|  |  |  | Southall Yd - Haywards Heath |  |
|  |  |  | Ardingly - Haywards Heath |  |
|  |  |  | Angerstein Wharf - St Pancras |  |
| 22-May-93 | 56027 | "Lancastrian 2" | Preston - Ormskirk | Pathfinder Tours |
|  | 56098 | "Lancastrian 2" | Morecambe - Heysham Sea Terminal |  |
|  |  |  | Morecambe - Blackburn |  |
|  |  |  | Blackburn - Preston |  |
| 23-May-93 | 56084/085 | "Lancastrian 2" | Preston - Wilmslow | Pathfinder Tours, in multiple |
| 29-May-93 | 56046 | "Mothball" | London Waterloo - Bletchley - Euston | Hertfordshire Rail Tours |
| 30-May-93 | 56064 | "Hereford & Shrewsbury Open day" | Hereford - Shrewsbury - Hereford | Regional Railways |
| 12-Jun-93 | 56074 | "Skirl Revisited" | Glasgow Central - Ayr | Pathfinder Tours |
| 13-Jun-93 | 56123 | "Skirl Revisited" | Stranraer Harbour - Ayr | Pathfinder Tours |
|  | 56128 | "Skirl Revisited" | Ayr - Stranraer Harbour |  |
| 19-Jun-93 | 56055 | "Hampshire & Sussex Explorer" | Redhill - Haywards Heath | Branch Line Society |
|  |  |  | Ardingly - Haywards Heath |  |
| 27-Jun-93 | 56134 | Edinburgh Waverley - Newcastle | Morpeth - Near Hepscott Level Crossing | Royal Train |
| 14-Jul-93 | 56077 | 1955 Fort William - Euston (13/7) | Edinburgh Waverley - Carlisle | OHL problems at Law Junc. |
|  |  | 2350 Euston - Glasgow Central (13/7) | Carlisle - Glasgow Central | OHL problems at Law Junc. |

| Date | Grid | Train Details | Grid Worked Train From / To | Notes |
|---|---|---|---|---|
| 14-Jul-93 | 56125 | 2120 Aberdeen - Euston (13/7) | Edinburgh Waverley - Carlisle | OHL problems at Law Junc. |
| | | 1S79 2203 Euston - Aberdeen (13/7) | Carlisle - Edinburgh Waverley | OHL problems at Law Junc |
| 17-Jul-93 | 56004 | "D.C. Green Flasher" | Derby - Eastleigh | Pathfinder Tours |
| | | | Southampton - Birmingham NS | |
| 28-Aug-93 | 56107 | "Canny Coalman" | Bates Staithes - Newsham North Jn | Pathfinder Tours |
| | | | Lynemouth Colliery - Alcan Branch Jn | |
| | | | Lynemouth Alcan - Ashington Jn | |
| | | | Nr Longhirst Level Crossing - Widdrington | |
| | | | Dean Road Exchange Sdgs - Newcastle | |
| | 56133 | "Canny Coalman" | Newcastle - Bates Staithes | Pathfinder Tours |
| | | | Newsham North Jn - Lynemouth Colliery | |
| | | | Alcan Branch Jn - Lynemouth Alcan | |
| | | | Ashington Jn - Nr Longhirst Level Crossing | |
| | | | Widdrington - Dean Road Exchange Sdgs | |
| 4-Sep-93 | 56007/011 | "Coal Scuttler 2" | Derby - Edinburgh Waverley | Pathfinder Tours, in multiple |
| | 56082/083 | "Coal Scuttler 2" | Edinburgh Waverley - Worksop | Pathfinder Tours, in multiple |
| 5-Sep-93 | 56082/083 | "Worksop Coalman" | Worksop - King's Cross | Hertfordshire Rail Tours, in multiple |
| | 56089/100 | "Worksop open day shuttles" | Sheffield - Cottam Power Station | Worksop Open Day Committee, in multiple |
| | | | Cottam Power Station - Sheffield | |
| | | | Sheffield - Cottam Power Station | |
| | | | Cottam Power Station - Sheffield | |
| 19-Sep-93 | 56048 | "Flying Dutchman" | Paddington - Newport - Paddington | Hertfordshire Rail Tours |
| 19-Sep-93 | 56113 | "Newport open day shuttles" | Machen Quarry - Newport | Newport Open Day Committee |
| | | | Nr Ebbw Vale South Gnd Frame - Newport | |
| 17-Oct-93 | 56104 | 1Z65 0720 Linlithgow - Aberdeen | Dunfermline Townhill Jn - Perth | SRPS, steam loco 60532 *Blue Peter* failed |
| 30-Oct-93 | 56096 | "Merseyman" | Eccles Headshunt - Weaste Jn | Pathfinder Tours |
| | | | Eccles Headshunt - Nr Ordsall Lane Jn | |
| | | | Chester - Nr Folly Lane Ground Frame | |
| | | | Runcorn Jn - Edge Hill | |
| | | | Seaforth Container Terminal - Edge Hill | |
| 11-Nov-93 | 56040 | 1712 Liverpool LS - Blackpool North | Just South of Leyland - Leyland | 31432 failed |
| 14-Nov-93 | 56092 | 1E26 1036 Derby - York | Langley Mill - Sheffield | 47839 failed |
| 11-Dec-93 | 56099 | "Cumbrian Grid" | Carlisle - Preston | Regional Railways, in tandem with 37422 |
| | 56132 | "Cumbrian Grid" | Preston - Carlisle | Regional Railways, in tandem with 37422 |
| 12-Dec-93 | 56047 | "Southern Mariner" | London Victoria - Woking | Pathfinder Tours |
| | 56054 | "Southern Mariner" | Bristol TM - Westbury | Pathfinder Tours, in tandem with 59002 |
| | | | Westbury - Romsey | In tandem with 59002, unlikely 56 was working |
| | | | Romsey - Eastleigh | In tandem with 59002 |
| | | | Salisbury - Bristol TM | |
| 3-Jan-94 | 56121 | "Pieman" | St Pancras - Leicester | Hertfordshire Rail Tours, in tandem with 47833 |
| | | | Melton Jn - Asfordby Colliery | |
| | | | Holwell Jn - Edwalton | |
| 15-Jan-94 | 56053 | "Scrummager 1" | Swansea - Tondu | Pathfinder Tours |
| 29-Jan-94 | 56009 | "Ivan-Hoe" | Denby D.P. - Drakelow C Power Station | Pathfinder Tours |
| | | | Coalfields Farm Colliery - Coalville | |
| | | | Bagworth Colliery Jn - Stud Farm Quarry | |
| | | | Knighton UDGL - Melton Jn | |
| | | | Asfordby Colliery - Melton Mowbray | |
| 8-Feb-94 | 56076 | 0705 Blackpool North - Manchester Vic | Just South of Preston - Preston | 37425 failed, dragged back to Preston |
| | | 0705 Blackpool North - Manchester Vic | Preston - Manchester Victoria | 37425 failed |
| 12-Feb-94 | 56118 | "Red Cabbage" | Redcar Mineral Term. - Seal Sands Branch Jn | Hertfordshire Rail Tours |
| | | | Billingham Jn - Nr Cliff House Signal Box | |
| | | | Hartlepool P.S. - Sunderland South Dock | |
| | | | Ryhope Grange Jn - Tyne Dock Bottom Sdgs | |
| 20-Feb-94 | 56033 | "Standedge Stomper" | Crewe - Didcot Parkway | |
| | 56073 | "Standedge Stomper" | Didcot Parkway - Birmingham NS | |
| 22-Feb-94 | 56038 | ? ? - Liverpool LS | Warrington - Crewe | Drag, 86255, OHL problems |
| 26-Feb-94 | 56009 | 1915 Euston - Carlisle | Rugby - Crewe | Drag, 90013 suffered broken window |
| 19-Mar-94 | 56124/128 | "Worksop Wanderer" | Ayr - Waterside | Worksop Open Day Committee, in multiple |
| 20-Mar-94 | 56131 | "Knaresborough Knave" | York - Leeds - Harrogate - York | Pathfinder Tours |
| 2-Apr-94 | 56106 | "Sector Swansong" | Nottingham - Derby | Pathfinder Tours |
| 25-Apr-94 | 56049 | 0645 Manchester Piccadilly - Euston | Rugby - Euston | 87014, failed with pantograph damage |
| 1-May-94 | 56125 | "Plym-Exe Cursioner" | Manchester Piccadilly - Westbury | Pathfinder Tours |
| | | | Bristol TM - Manchester Piccadilly | |
| 4-May-94 | 56010 | 1712 Liverpool LS - Blackpool North | Wigan Springs Branch Jn - Wigan NW | 31465 failed with low power |
| | 56029 | "Barchester Chronicles" | Preston - Stafford | A1A Charters |
| 22-May-94 | 56132 | "Worcester Open day shuttles" | Worcester SH - Birmingham NS | Worcester Open Day Committee |
| 30-May-94 | 56058 | 2325 Euston - Edinburgh Waverley (29/5) | Carstairs - Edinburgh Waverley | Signal problems at Haymarket |
| 31-May-94 | 56058 | 2350 Euston - Edinburgh Waverley (30/5) | Carstairs - Edinburgh Waverley | Signal problems at Haymarket |
| 1-Jun-94 | 56079 | 2350 Euston - Edinburgh Waverley (31/5) | Carstairs - Edinburgh Waverley | Signal problems at Haymarket |
| 2-Jun-94 | 56079 | 2350 Euston - Edinburgh Waverley (1/6) | Carstairs - Edinburgh Waverley | Signal problems at Haymarket |
| 3-Jun-94 | 56072 | 2350 Euston - Edinburgh Waverley (2/6) | Carstairs - Edinburgh Waverley | Signal problems at Haymarket |
| 4-Jun-94 | 56072 | 2350 Euston - Edinburgh Waverley (3/6) | Carstairs - Edinburgh Waverley | Signal problems at Haymarket |
| 5-Jun-94 | 56072 | 2210 Euston - Edinburgh Waverley (4/6) | Carstairs - Edinburgh Waverley | Signal problems at Haymarket |
| 6-Jun-94 | 56072 | 2325 Euston - Edinburgh Waverley (5/6) | Carstairs - Edinburgh Waverley | Signal problems at Haymarket |
| 7-Jun-94 | 56072 | 2350 Euston - Edinburgh Waverley (6/6) | Carstairs - Edinburgh Waverley | Signal problems at Haymarket |
| 11-Jun-94 | 56004 | "National Grid" | St Pancras - High Marnham Power Station | Hertfordshire Rail Tours |
| | | | Doncaster - Silverwood Jn | |
| | | | Silverwood Colliery - Silverwood Jn | |
| | | | Kilnhurst Central Jn - Nr Deepcar Grnd Frame | |
| | | | Woodburn Jn - Sheffield | |
| | 56133 | "National Grid" | High Marnham Power Station - Doncaster | |
| | | | Silverwood Jn - Silverwood Colliery | |
| | | | Silverwood Jn - Kilnhurst Central Jn | |
| | | | Nr Deepcar Grnd Frame - Woodburn Jn | |
| | | | Sheffield - St Pancras | |
| 9-Jul-94 | 56092 | "Trans-Pennine Freighter" | Crewe - Bradford Interchange | Hertfordshire Rail Tours |
| 10-Jul-94 | 56068/135 | "Donny Deviator" | Doncaster - Drax - Doncaster | Pathfinder Tours, in multiple |
| | 56077 | "Donny Deviator" | Silverwood Colliery - Doncaster | |
| 14-Jul-94 | 56022 | 1047 Birmingham Int- Glasgow Central | Clifton & Lowther - Carlisle | 86233 failed, pantograph brought OHL down |
| | | 1710 Edinburgh Wav. - Birmingham NS | Carlisle - Preston | Drag, OHL problems at Clifton & Lowther |
| | | 1830 Euston - Carlisle | Preston - Carlisle | Drag, OHL problems at Clifton & Lowther |
| 23-Jul-94 | 56088 | "Roxby Music" | King's Cross - Kellingley Colliery Branch Jn | Hertfordshire Rail Tours |
| | 56102 | "Roxby Music" | Kellingley Colliery Branch Jn - Knottingley | Hertfordshire Rail Tours |

| Grid | Train Details | | Grid Worked Train From / To | Notes |
|---|---|---|---|---|
| 23-Jul-94 | 56102 | "Roxby Music" | Knottingley - Royston Jn | |
| | | | Wakefield Kirk. West Jn - Scunthorpe Trent Jn | |
| | | | Scunthorpe Trent Jn - King's Cross | |
| 29-Jul-94 | 56114 | 1645 Cardiff Central - Manchester Ox Rd | Cardiff Central - Crewe | 37408 failed |
| 30-Jul-94 | 56124 | 2350 Euston - Edinburgh Waverley (29/7) | Carstairs - Edinburgh Waverley | Signal problems at Haymarket |
| 31-Jul-94 | 56123 | 1S07 1950 Euston - Fort William (30/7) | Carstairs - Edinburgh Waverley | Signal problems at Haymarket |
| 6-Aug-94 | 56104 | "Grampian Highlander" | Nr North end of Mossend - Rose Street Jn | Pathfinder Tours |
| 7-Aug-94 | 56101 | "Grampian Highlander" | Aberdeen - Edinburgh Waverley | Pathfinder Tours |
| 11-Aug-94 | 56037 | 0945 Euston - Wolverhampton | Coseley - Wolverhampton | 86240 failed, loss of power |
| 18-Aug-94 | 56022 | 1419 Wolverhampton - Euston | Rugby - Euston | 86103 failed |
| 21-Aug-94 | 56076 | "Crewe Cruiser" | Manchester Piccadilly - Crewe | Pathfinder Tours |
| | 56086/92 | "Crewe Cruiser" | Crewe - Bristol TM | In multiple |
| 3-Sep-94 | 56135 | "Magnificent 7" | York - Doncaster | A1A Charters |
| 10-Sep-94 | 56090 | "Blyth Spirit 3" | Newcastle - Morpeth | Hertfordshire Rail Tours |
| | | | Morpeth - Bedlington Jn - Blyth Alcan | |
| | | | Freemans Jn - Blyth Power Station | |
| | | | Nr Hirst Lane L.C. - Newsham North Jn | |
| | | | Bates Staithes - Jarrow Goods | |
| 17-Sep-94 | 56093 | "Lancastrian 3" | Manchester Piccadilly - Buxton | Pathfinder Tours |
| 18-Sep-94 | 56049 | "Lancastrian 3" | Preston - Bredbury Refuse Transfer Station | Pathfinder Tours |
| | 56056 | "Lancastrian 3" | Bredbury R.T.S. - Manchester Piccadilly | |
| | | | Rose Hill Marple - Avenue Sdgs | |
| 2-Oct-94 | 56087 | "Paragon Paradox" | Doncaster - Peterborough | Pathfinder Tours |
| 20-Nov-94 | 56114 | "Cheshire Chaser" | Newport - Coventry | Pathfinder Tours |
| 11-Dec-94 | 56052 | "Southern Serpent" | Eastleigh - Woking | Pathfinder Tours |
| | | | Basingstoke - Bristol TM | |
| 28-Jan-95 | 56036 | "Gladstone Bag" | Chester S Jn - Hooton Long Sdg | Pathfinder Tours |
| | 56036 | "Gladstone Bag" | Garston Church Road S.B. - Edge Hill Sdgs | |
| | | | Gladstone Dock - Liverpool LS | |
| 16-Feb-95 | 56133 | 1915 Euston - Wolverhampton | Wolverton? - Bletchley | Drag back to Bletchley, OHL problems |
| | | 2200 Euston - Manchester Piccadilly | Wolverton? - Bletchley | Drag back to Bletchley, OHL problems |
| 18-Feb-95 | 56039 | "Hymn 'n' Ham" | Sheffield - Barnetby | Pathfinder Tours, 47739 providing ETH only |
| | | | Cleethorpes - Marsh West Jn | |
| | | | Grimsby Brick Pit Sdgs - Great Coates No. 1 Jn | |
| | | | Immingham East Jn - Immingham Dock East | |
| | | | Humber Road Jn - Killingholme New Inn L.C. | |
| | | | Western Entrance L.C. - Immingham Dock West | |
| | | | Barnetby East Jn - Sheffield | 47739 providing ETH only |
| 26-Feb-95 | 56070 | "Capital Spinner" | Bletchley - Bowes Park Reversing Sdg | Pathfinder Tours |
| 15-Apr-95 | 56099 | 1234 Birmingham NS - Manchester Picc. | Sandwell & Dudley - Wolverhampton | 86255 failed, terminated at Wolverhampton |
| | | 1250 Euston - Manchester Piccadilly | Stone - Stoke-on-Trent | 87023 failed, assisted at rear while on ECS of the above train. |
| 6-May-95 | 56010 | "Cream T" | Newport - Kingswear | Transrail |
| | | | Kingswear - Newport | |
| | 56025/127 | "Cream T" | Newport - Crewe | In multiple |
| | | | Crewe - Crewe S Jn - Manchester Picc. | In multiple |
| | 56127 | "Cream T" | Manchester Piccadilly - Crewe | |
| | | | Crewe - Crewe Coal Yd Jn - Newport | |
| 8-May-95 | 56064 | "Grockle Grid" | Bristol TM - Plymouth | Pathfinder Tours |
| | | | Penzance - Bristol TM | |
| 20-May-95 | 56071 | "North Wales Coast Motive Power Day" | Crewe - Llandudno & return | Crewe Rail Events Committee |
| | | | Crewe - Chester & return | |
| 16-Jun-95 | 56127 | 1110 Euston - Liverpool LS | Warrington BQ - Liverpool LS | Drag, bridge strike at Runcorn |
| 1-Jul-95 | 56006 | "Cattal Grid" | York - Newcastle & return | Hertfordshire Rail Tours |
| 11-Jul-95 | 56092 | 1340 Glasgow Central - Euston | Near Rugeley? - Euston | 87023 failed, blown transformer |
| 30-Jul-95 | 56099 | 1135 Birmingham NS - Edinburgh Wav. | Penrith - Carlisle | 86214 failed, pantograph problems |
| 5-Aug-95 | 56072 | "Whisky Galore" | Edinburgh Wav - Carstairs - Edinburgh Wav | A1A Charters |
| 27-Aug-95 | 56049 | "Crewe Missile" | Euston - Crewe | Hertfordshire Rail Tours |
| | | | Crewe - Madeley Chord Jn | |
| | | | Silverdale Colliery - Madeley Chord Jn | |
| | | | Crewe - Euston | |
| 1-Sep-95 | 56104 | 1237 Edinburgh Waverley - Nth Berwick | Longniddry - Drem | 305502 failed, assisted at rear, terminated Drem |
| 2-Sep-95 | 56114 | "Crug & Glog Grid" | Paddington - Llandrindod Wells & rtn | Hertfordshire Rail Tours |
| | 56115 | "Newport Open Day Shuttles" | Nr Ebbw Vale Sth Grnd Frame - Newport x2 | Newport Open Day Committee |
| 16-Sep-95 | 56103 | 0925 Euston - Glasgow Central | Shieldmuir Jn - Glasgow Central | 87015 failed |
| 20-Sep-95 | 56114 | 0520 Carlisle - Euston | Hest Bank - Lancaster | 87025 failed, terminated at Lancaster |
| 10-Oct-95 | 56124 | 1S25 2130 Euston - Inverness (9/10) | Beattock Bank - ? | 87011 failed, slipped to a stand |
| 14-Oct-95 | 56067 | "Aire Freighter" | Sheffield - Hunslet East T.C. | Pathfinder Tours |
| | | | Neville Hill West Jn - Allerton Main Loading Pt | |
| | | | Knottingley - Doncaster Down Decoy Yd | |
| 17-Oct-95 | 56101 | 2114 Aberdeen - Edinburgh Wav (16/10) | South of Kirkcaldy? - Edinburgh Waverley | 47771 failed |
| 21-Oct-95 | 56040 | "Faulty Tower" | Tower Colliery - Cardiff Central | |
| | | | Cwmbargoed - Cardiff Central | |
| 18-Nov-95 | 56108 | "Boulby Prize" | Boulby Mine - Beam Mill Jn | Hertfordshire Rail Tours |
| 28-Nov-95 | 56111 | 1418 Paddington - Edinburgh Waverley | Beattock Bank - Edinburgh Waverley | 86205 failed |
| 3-Dec-95 | 56105 | ? ? - ? | ? - ? | noted at Redditch |
| 23-Dec-95 | 56103 | 0910 Edinburgh Waverley - Reading | Edinburgh Waverley - Carlisle | 86255 failed |
| 27-Dec-95 | 56039 | 1203 Newcastle - Plymouth | Croft Jn - Darlington | 43184/196 failed, terminated at Darlington |
| 28-Dec-95 | 56038 | 1440 Euston - Glasgow Central | Wigan North Western - Preston | 87003 failed with pantograph problems |
| 30-Dec-95 | 56101 | 2030 Inverness - Euston (29/12) | Edinburgh Waverley - Slateford | Drag, OHL problems at Haymarket |
| | | 2130 Euston - Inverness (29/12) | Slateford - Edinburgh Waverley | Drag, OHL problems at Haymarket |
| 11-Jan-96 | 56048 | 1505 Norwich - Liverpool St | Diss - Ipswich | OHL problems at Stowmarket |
| 21-Jan-96 | 56133 | 1212 Wolverhampton - Euston | ? - ? | AC loco hit a dog & came to a stand in a neutral section |
| 2-Mar-96 | 56133 | 1849 Wolverhampton - Euston | Monmore Green - Birmingham NS | 87009 failed |
| 21-Apr-96 | 56063 | 1605 Witham - Norwich | Ipswich - Diss | Drag, 86238 |
| 18-May-96 | 56045 | "Lost Horizon" | Harwich International - Felixstowe | A1A Charters |
| 25-May-96 | 56073 | "Paignton Decorator" | Paddington - Paignton & return | Hertfordshire Rail Tours |
| | 56073 | "Dartmoor Warbler" | Paignton - Okehampton & return | Hertfordshire Rail Tours |
| 13-Jul-96 | 56094 | "Yankee Doodle-Dandy" | Bradford Interchange - Doncaster | Pathfinder Tours |
| 14-Jul-96 | 56057 | 1437 Carlisle - Euston | Carlisle - Preston | 87007 failed with flat batteries |
| 3-Aug-96 | 56058 | "Road to the Isles" | Glasgow Central - Edinburgh Waverley | A1A Charters |
| 9-Aug-96 | 56128 | 1800 King's Cross - Glasgow Central | Motherwell - Glasgow Central | 91xxx failed |
| 18-Aug-96 | 56070 | 1208 Preston - Euston | Wigan NW - Warrington BQ | 90011 failed, terminated at Warrington BQ |

| Date | Grid | Train Details | Grid Worked Train From / To | Notes |
|---|---|---|---|---|
| 8-Sep-96 | 56061 | "Great Eastern Grid" | Ipswich - Felixstowe Creek Sdgs & rtn | Pathfinder Tours |
|  | 56113 | "Great Eastern Grid" | Bristol TM - Ipswich & return |  |
| 13-Oct-96 | 56070 | 1820 Bangor - Crewe | Holywell Jn - Crewe | 37xxx failed, assisted at rear |
| 26-Oct-96 | 56048 | "Settle & Carlisle Explorer" | Nr Heeley Loop/Dore - Derby | Pathfinder Tours, 47766 failed |
| 26-Oct-96 | 56081 | "Boulby Ghost" | Boulby Mine - York | NENTA charter |
| 11-Nov-96 | 56094 | 0545 Liverpool LS - Euston | Liverpool LS - Warrington BQ | Drag, OHL problems at Runcorn |
|  |  | 0645? Liverpool LS? - Euston? | Liverpool LS - Warrington BQ | Drag, OHL problems at Runcorn |
|  |  | 0745 Liverpool LS - Euston | Liverpool LS - Warrington BQ | Drag, OHL problems at Runcorn |
|  |  | 0805 Euston - Liverpool LS | Warrington BQ - Liverpool LS | Drag, OHL problems at Runcorn |
| 14-Dec-96 | 56032 | "Rooster Booster" | Bristol TM - Stratford Upon Avon | Pathfinder Tours |
|  |  |  | Birmingham NS - Bristol TM |  |
| 25-Jan-97 | 56081 | "Rock 'n' Robin" | Buxton Sdgs - Hindlow Briggs Sdgs |  |
|  |  |  | Buxton Sdgs - Bristol TM |  |
|  | 56105 | "Rock 'n' Robin" | Bristol TM - Buxton Sdgs |  |
|  |  |  | Hindlow Briggs Sdgs - BuxtonSdgs |  |
| 15-Feb-97 | 56066 | "Robin Reliant" | York - Scarborough | 33111 Charters |
| 1-Mar-97 | 56110 | "Maiden Voyager" | York - Newcastle & return | Mercia Charters |
| 15-Mar-97 | 56037 | "Spinning Gibbon" / "Rotating Monkey" | Cleethorpes - Nottingham | Pathfinder Tours |
| 31-Mar-97 | 56078 | "Scarborough Maid" | Scarborough - York | Pathfinder Tours |
| 5-Apr-97 | 56096 | "Garw Guru" | Newport - Aberthaw Reception Sdgs | Hertfordshire Rail Tours |
|  |  |  | Pontycymer - Gwaun-cae-Gurwen |  |
| 18-Apr-97 | 56094 | "V.S.O.E." | Chesterfield - Church Fenton | Sea Containers, 47733 failed with low oil |
| 19-Apr-97 | 56044 | "Welsh Wizard" | Alexandra Dock Jn Yd - Barry Dock No.2 | Pathfinder Tours |
|  |  |  | Cwmbargoed - Cardiff Central |  |
|  | 56118 | "Welsh Wizard" | Crewe - Newport |  |
|  | 56118 |  | Barry Dock No.2 - Cwmbargoed |  |
|  |  |  | Cardiff Central - Crewe |  |
| 27-Apr-97 | 56105 | 1550 Euston - Glasgow Central | 1/2 mile Nth of Milton Keynes - Milton Keynes | OHL problems, dragged back to Milton Keynes |
| 3-May-97 | 56075 | "Crewe Cut" | Liverpool LS - Stafford | Pathfinder Tours |
| 17-May-97 | 56063 | "Middlesborough Footex" | York - Middlesborough | 47726 failed, low power |
|  | 56114 | "Middlesborough Footex" | Bletchley South Jn - Rugby | 47726 failed |
| 1-Jul-97 | 56083 | 2130 Euston - Inverness (30/6) | Linlithgow - Bo'ness Jn Loop | 47769 failed, assisted at rear while on 6S62 Tees Yd - Aberdeen 'Enterprise' |
| 18-Jul-97 | 56123 | "Troon Golfex" | Thornhill - Carlisle | 47782 failed |
| 2-Aug-97 | 56065 | "Pembrokeshire Pageant" | Pembroke Dock - Whitland | Pathfinder Tours |
| 9-Aug-97 | 56079 | "Thirty-Nine Steps" | Braidhurst DGL - Glasgow Central | A1A Charters |
| 13-Aug-97 | 56027 | 1805 Norwich - Liverpool St | Diss - Ipswich | Drag, OHL problems at Diss |
|  | 56098 | 2330 Liverpool St - Norwich (12/8) | Colchester - Stowmarket | Drag, OHL problems at Ipswich |
|  | 56132 | 1643 York - Bristol TM | Aldwarke - Sheffield | 47831 failed |
| 16-Aug-97 | 56055 | "Spin Doctor" | Stratford Upon Avon - Reading | Hertfordshire Rail Tours |
| 6-Sep-97 | 56067 | "Inverness - Newcastle charter" | Alnmouth - Newcastle | North East Railtours, 47784 failed |
| 20-Sep-97 | 56006 | "Marching Cat" | Ipswich - Felixstowe | Pathfinder Tours |
|  | 56062 | "Marching Cat" | Wembley Up Goods - Ipswich |  |
| 13-Oct-97 | 56073 | 0910 Edinburgh Waverley - Reading | Birmingham NS - Reading | Motive power shortage no 47/8s |
|  |  | 1647 Reading - Liverpool LS | Reading - Birmingham NS | Motive power shortage no 47/8s |
|  |  | 2000 Brimingham NS - Derby | Birmingham NS - Derby | Motive power shortage no 47/8s |
| 1-Nov-97 | 56134 | "Nor'west Thunderbolt" | Liverpool LS - Warrington BQ | Pathfinder Tours |
| 10-Nov-97 | 56056 | 0920 Brighton - Edinburgh Waverley | Pangbourne - Didcot Parkway | 47818 failed |
| 13-Nov-97 | 56127 | 1143 York - Poole | ? - Birmingham NS | 47849 failed, assisted at rear to Leeds |
| 3-Dec-97 | 56083 | 1705 King's Cross - Leeds | 2 miles South of Grantham - Grantham | 91007 failed, assisted at rear while on 4D56 Biggleswade - Heck Plasmor block empties |
| 13-Dec-97 | 56035 | "Festive Fiend" | Coventry - London Victoria | Pathfinder Tours |
| 1-Jan-98 | 56119 | 1535 Euston - Glasgow Central | Lancaster - Tebay | Drag, 87019, OHL problems at Penrith |
| 2-Jan-98 | 56066 | 1230 Glasgow Central - Poole | North of Carstairs - Carstairs | 47624 failed, assisted at rear |
| 17-Jan-98 | 56109 | "East Coast Diversion" | York - Newcastle - York | Hertfordshire Rail Tours |
| 8-Mar-98 | 56022 | 1330 Glasgow Central - Euston | Wigan North Western - Crewe | 47727 failed |
| 21-Mar-98 | 56114 | "Rylstone Cowboy" | King's Cross - Skipton Station North Jn | Hertfordshire Rail Tours |
|  |  |  | Rylstone Quarry - Skipton Station North Jn |  |
|  |  |  | Skipton - King's Cross |  |
| 25-Mar-98 | 56078 | 1032 Swansea - Paddington | Port Talbot Parkway - Bridgend | 43139 failed, defective windscreen wiper |
| 30-Mar-98 | 56010 | 0450 Newcastle - King's Cross | North of Peterborough - Peterborough | Loco failure |
| 20-Apr-98 | 56060 | 1430 Manchester Piccadilly - Euston | Rugeley - Rugby | 86xxx failed |
| 25-Apr-98 | 56029 | "Barrow Docks Shuttles" | Barrow - Salthouse Jn | Pathfinder Tours |
|  |  |  | Barrow Ramsden Dock - Salthouse Jn |  |
|  |  |  | Barrow - Salthouse Jn |  |
|  |  |  | Barrow Ramsden Dock - Salthouse Jn |  |
|  | 56029 | "Barrow Buoy" | Barrow - Bristol TM | Pathfinder Tours |
|  | 56114 | "Barrow Buoy" | Bristol TM - Barrow | Pathfinder Tours |
|  | 56114 | "Barrow Docks Shuttles" | Salthouse Jn - Barrow Ramsden Dock |  |
|  |  |  | Salthouse Jn - Barrow |  |
|  |  |  | Salthouse Jn - Barrow Ramsden Dock |  |
|  |  |  | Salthouse Jn - Barrow |  |
| 2-May-98 | 56060 | "Chameleon Rose" | Nuneaton - Peterborough | Mercia Charters |
| 4-May-98 | 56018 | 1905 Euston - Liverpool LS | Ditton - Liverpool LS | Drag, OHL problems at Speke |
| 15-May-98 | 56004 | 0910 Edinburgh Waverley - Reading | Birmingham NS - Reading | Motive power shortage no 47/8s |
|  |  | 1647 Reading - Liverpool LS | Reading - Birmingham NS | Motive power shortage no 47/8s |
| 20-May-98 | 56035 | 0910 Edinburgh Waverley - Reading | Birmingham NS - Reading | Motive power shortage no 47/8s |
|  |  | 1647 Reading - Liverpool LS | Reading - Birmingham NS | Motive power shortage no 47/8s |
| 30-May-98 | 56033 | "Cheetham Fiddler" | Latchford Sdgs - Edge Hill Sdgs | Hertfordshire Rail Tours |
|  |  |  | Castleton DGL - Crewe |  |
|  | 56062 | "Cheetham Fiddler" | Stafford - Latchford Sdgs |  |
|  |  |  | Edge Hill Sdgs - Castleton DGL |  |
| 6-Jun-98 | 56047 | "Mersey Dee" | Liverpool LS - Bescot UDGL | Pathfinder Tours |
|  | 56047/095 | "Mersey Dee" | Bescot UDGL - Bristol TM | In multiple |
|  | 56048 | "Mersey Dee ECS" | Bristol TM - Exeter SD | ECS for the "Mersey Dee" ran as a pre-tour |
|  |  | "Mersey Dee" | Exeter SD - Liverpool LS |  |
| 13-Jun-98 | 56065 | "Birthday Bash" | Sheffield - Warrington BQ | Pathfinder Tours |
| 20-Jun-98 | 56019 | 0840 Glasgow Central - Paignton | Preston - Birmingham NS | 47814 failed |
|  |  | 0910 Edinburgh Waverley- Bournemouth | Birmingham NS - Bournemouth | Motive power shortage no 47/8s |
|  |  | 1814 Bournemouth - Manchester Picc. | Bournemouth - Birmingham NS | Motive power shortage no 47/8s |
| 29-Jun-98 | 56053 | 1418 Paddington - Glasgow Central | Paddington - Birmingham NS | Motive power shortage no 47/8s |
| 4-Jul-98 | 56011 | "Scottie" | Glasgow Central - Coltness | Pathfinder Tours |
|  | 56067 | "Scottie" | Coltness - Glasgow Central |  |
| 14-Jul-98 | 56118 | 0505 Edinburgh Waverley - Fort William | Edinburgh Waverley - Cowlairs Jn | 37409 failed |

| Date | Grid | Train Details | Grid Worked Train From / To | Notes |
|---|---|---|---|---|
| 16-Jul-98 | 56010 | 0755 Euston - Manchester Piccadilly | South of Stoke-on-Trent - Stoke-on-Trent | Assisted from rear while on a freight service |
| 20-Jul-98 | 56068 | "Lord of the Isles" | Connington South Jn - King's Cross | 86401 failed |
| 28-Jul-98 | 56057 | 2200 King's Cross - Newcastle | Newark North Gate - Doncaster | Drag, OHL problems at Doncaster |
| 5-Aug-98 | 56032 | 1418 Paddington - Glasgow Central | South of Banbury - Banbury | 47843 failed, assisted at rear |
| | | Banbury - Birmingham NS | | |
| 15-Aug-98 | 56018 | "North-East Excursioner" | Newcastle - Cardiff Central | Pathfinder Tours |
| | 56097 | "North-East Excursioner" | Cardiff Central - Newcastle | |
| 7-Sep-98 | 56055 | 1800 King's Cross - Glasgow Central | 1/4 mile North of Darlington - Darlington | 91021 failed, fractured coupling |
| 13-Sep-98 | 56010 | 0830 King's Cross - Glasgow Central | Cobbinshaw - Glasgow Central | 91006 failed |
| 18-Sep-98 | 56104 | 2115 Newcastle - Derby | Chesterfield - Derby | HST failed |
| 20-Sep-98 | 56078 | "Falmouth Packet" | Gloucester - Falmouth Docks | Pathfinder Tours |
| | | | Falmouth Docks - Penwithers Jn | |
| | | | Swindon - Gloucester | |
| 26-Sep-98 | 56072 | "Shapeshifter" | Swindon - Salisbury | Mercia Charters |
| 17-Oct-98 | 56108 | "Trawsfynydd Lament" | Llandudno Jn - Trawsfynydd | Hertfordshire Rai Tours |
| | | | Trawsfynydd - Blaenau Ffestiniog | With 47785, loss of adhesion, assisted at rear |
| | | | Llandudno Jn - Crewe | |
| | 56052 | "Mendip Rail Staff Charter" | Banbury - Castle Cary | Pathfinder Tours / Mendip Rail |
| 21-Oct-98 | 56089 | 0910 King's Cross - Leeds | ? - Peterborough | 91xxx failed |
| 30-Oct-98 | 56100 | "Blackpool Illuminations Merrymaker" | Blackpool North - Warrington Bank Quay | Hertfordshire Rail Tours |
| 7-Nov-98 | 56114 | "Cheshire Mole"/ "Magical Mystery Tour" | Wolverhampton UDG - Latchford Sdgs | Pathfinder Tours |
| | | | Madeley Chord Jn - Silverdale Colliery | |
| | | | Madeley Chord Jn - Chester | |
| 8-Nov-98 | 56086 | 1452 Plymouth - Newcastle | Gloucester - Birmingham NS | 43162 failed |
| 13-Nov-98 | 56118 | 0640 York - Bristol TM | Doncaster - Derby | 47845 failed, 47845 at rear, providing ETH Started at Doncaster |
| 9-Dec-98 | 56010 | 0639 Dundee - Penzance | Inverkeithing - Edinburgh Waverley | HST failed, started at Inverkeithing |
| | 56102 | 1016 Birmingham Int - Newcastle | Derby - Leeds | 43193/103 failed, terminated at Leeds |
| 10-Dec-98 | 56033 | 0922 Penzance-Edinburgh | assisted up Lickey bank | |
| 12-Dec-98 | 56116 | "Blade & Owl" | Stafford - Sheffield | Pathfinder Tours, in multiple with 58021 |
| 18-Dec-98 | 56089 | 0725 Leeds - St Pancras | Just South of Leeds - Leeds | HST failed, dragged back to Leeds & terminated |
| 9-Jan-99 | 56071 | "Merchant Capitalist" | Leamington Spa - Crewe | Pathfinder Tours |
| 16-Jan-99 | 56031 | "London Experience"/ "Kentish Container" | Crewe - London Victoria & return | Pathfinder Tours |
| 19-Jan-99 | 56126 | 1555 Plymouth - Manchester Piccadilly | Stoke Works Jn - Bromsgrove | 47xxx failed |
| 16-Feb-99 | 56112 | 0444 Manchester Piccadilly - Euston | Alderley Edge - Crewe | Drag, OHL problems |
| 24-Feb-99 | 56010 | 0515 Birmingham NS - Holyhead | Galton Jn - Wolverhampton | 37418 failed, assisted at rear while on steel train |
| 23-Mar-99 | 56107 | 0610 Bristol TM - Manchester Piccadilly | Cheltenham Spa - Birmingham NS | 47702 failed, terminated at Birmingham NS |
| 30-Mar-99 | 56010 | 0450 Newcastle - King's Cross | New England? - Peterborough | 91003 failed |
| 3-May-99 | 56050 | "Carlisle - Harlow charter" | Carlisle - Doncaster | Railtourer, 47778 providing ETH only |
| 8-May-99 | 56074 | "Kent Coastman" | Bristol TM - Canterbury West & return | Pathfinder Tours |
| 19-Jun-99 | 56098 | "Spinning Spectre" | Toton Centre - Worksop | Pathfinder Tours |
| 29-Jun-99 | 56025 | "V.S.O.E." | Kirkby Stephen - York | Sea Containers, 47763 providing ETH only |
| 3-Jul-99 | 56089 | "Captain Cook Explorer" | York - Battersby | NENTA charter |
| | | | Whitby - Battersby | |
| 31-Jul-99 | 56059 | "Spinning Haggis" | Dundee - Glasgow Central | Pathfinder Tours |
| 9-Jul-99 | 56134 | 2130 Euston - Inverness | Perth-Inverness | 47780 failed |
| 29-Aug-99 | 56120 | "Edinburgh Tattoo" | Carlisle - Settle - Peterborough | Hertfordshire Rail Tours, drag 86426 |
| 11-Sep-99 | 56102 | "Blyth Spirit" | Blyth Alcan - Marcheys House Jn | Hertfordshire Rail Tours |
| | | | Furnaceway Sdgs - Newcastle | |
| | 56103 | "Rotating Cleric" | Blackpool South - York | Pathfinder Tours |
| 21-Sep-99 | 56038 | 0821 Paignton - Newcastle | Thirsk? / Northallerton? - Newcastle | 47711 failed |
| 23-Sep-99 | 56010 | 1016 Birmingham Int - Newcastle | Derby - Newcastle | Motive power shortage, no HSTs, started Derby |
| | | 1502 Newcastle - Plymouth | Newcastle - Birmingham NS | Motive power shortage, no HSTs |
| 4-Oct-99 | 56072 | "Perth - Edinburgh Waverley charter" | ? - ? | |
| 20-Nov-99 | 56091 | "Crompton Collier" | Derby - Calverton Colliery | Pathfinder Tours |
| | | | Gedling Colliery - Bentinck Colliery | |
| 18-Dec-99 | 56090 | "Scratching Santa" | Oxley DGL - Dee Marsh Reception Sdgs | Pathfinder Tours |
| | | | Wrexham General - Latchford Sdgs | |
| 30-Dec-99 | 56114 | "Time Lord" | Cleethorpes - Barnetby | Hertfordshire Rail Tours |
| 6-Feb-00 | 56091 | 1338 Newcastle - Exeter | Croft Jn - York | 47874 failed, terminated at York |
| 26-Feb-00 | 56089 | "Weaving Weasel" | Sheffield - Oxford UDPL | Pathfinder Tours |
| 11-Mar-00 | 56103 | "London Excursion"/ "Medway Medicaster" | Crewe - London Victoria & return | Pathfinder Tours |
| 1-Apr-00 | 56115 | "Practical Joker" | Carlisle - Crewe | Mercia Charters |
| 12-Apr-00 | 56037 | 1300 Glasgow - Kings Cross | Corby Glen - Peterborough | 91010 failed, terminated at Peterborough |
| 22-Apr-00 | 56027 | "York Excursion"/ "Cleveland Crusader" | Darlington - Seal Sands Branch Jn | Pathfinder Tours |
| 6-May-00 | 56062 | "East Anglian Express" | Ely - Norwich | Chester Model Railway Club, 47761 failed |
| | 56131 | "Oil Leake" | Birmingham NS - Burton -on-Trent | Pathfinder Tours |
| | | | Lichfield TV - Wigston South Jn | |
| | | | Hotchley Hill - Leicester | |
| | | | Brownhills - Lichfield TV Jn | |
| | | | Birmingham NS - Reading | replaced 58016 which failed with brake fault |
| 20-May-00 | 56112 | "Cheshire Phoenix" | Chester - Warrington BQ | Pathfinder Tours |
| 8-Jul-00 | 56103 | "Skirling Postie" | Doncaster Royal Mail Terminal - Crewe | Pathfinder Tours |
| 19-Aug-00 | 56046 | "Edinburgh Tattoo" | Carlisle - Settle - Doncaster Decoy Yd | Hertfordshire Rail Tours, drag 90026 |
| 20-Aug-00 | 56120 | 1500 Bristol TM - York | Nr Peckfield Crossover - Leeds | Line blocked - accident at Level crossing |
| 31-Aug-00 | 56065 | 0537 Lancaster - Euston | Wigan NW - Crewe | Drag 90146  WCML blocked due to fatality |
| 23-Sep-00 | 56120 | "Calder Revolver" | Bradford Interchange - Preston | Pathfinder Tours |
| | | | Preston - Crewe | In tandem with 92036 |
| 9-Nov-00 | 56095 | 0640 Carlisle - Crewe | Carlisle - Preston | 90012 failed, terminated at Preston |
| 2-Dec-00 | 56058 | "Grassington Excursion" | Cardiff Central - Skipton Station North Jn | Pathfinder Tours |
| | | | Rylstone Quarry - Skipton Station North Jn | |
| | 56127 | "Grassington Excursion" | Skipton Station North Jn - Rylstone Quarry | |
| | | | Skipton Station North Jn - Cardiff Central | |
| 16-Dec-00 | 56033 | "Siberian Hamster" | Bescot UDGL - Worksop Up Reception | Pathfinder Tours |
| | 56046 | "Siberian Hamster" | Thorne Jn - Derby UG | |
| 19-Dec-00 | 56120 | 1830 Edinburgh - Doncaster | Nr Lucker Level Crossing - Newcastle | 91006 failed, pantograph problems |
| 6-Jan-01 | 56007 | "Power Porter" | Crewe - Manchester Piccadilly & rtn | Pathfinder Tours |
| 27-Jan-01 | 56111 | "Manchester Excursion" | Cardiff Central - Stockport | Pathfinder Tours |
| | 56111 | "Mancunian Marauder" | Stockport - Bredbury Stone Terminal | Pathfinder Tours |
| | | | Eccles Loop - Weaste Jn | |
| | | | Eccles Loop - Manchester Victoria | |
| | 56111 | "Manchester Excursion" | Manchester Victoria - Cardiff Central | Pathfinder Tours |
| 1-Feb-01 | 56115 | 1210 Bristol TM - Newcastle | Doncaster - Newcastle | 47847 failed, low coolant |
| | | 1840 Newcastle - Bristol TM | Newcastle - York | 47847 failed, low coolant, terminated at York |